Valuing Nature with Travel Cost Models

NEW HORIZONS IN ENVIRONMENTAL ECONOMICS

General Editors: Wallace E. Oates, *Professor of Economics, University of Maryland, USA* and Henk Folmer, *Professor of Economics, Wageningen Agricultural University, The Netherlands and Professor of Environmental Economics, Tilburg University, The Netherlands*

This important series is designed to make a significant contribution to the development of the principles and practices of environmental economics. It includes both theoretical and empirical work. International in scope, it addresses issues of current and future concern in both East and West and in developed and developing countries.

The main purpose of the series is to create a forum for the publication of high quality work and to show how economic analysis can make a contribution to understanding and resolving the environmental problems confronting the world in the twenty-first century.

Recent titles in the series include:

The Political Economy of Environmental Taxes
Nicolas Wallart

Trade and the Environment
Selected Essays of Alistair M. Ulph
Alistair M. Ulph

Water Management in the 21st Century
The Allocation Imperative
Terence Richard Lee

Institutions, Transaction Costs and Environmental Policy
Institutional Reform for Water Resources
Ray Challen

Valuing Nature with Travel Cost Models
A Manual
Frank A. Ward and Diana Beal

The Political Economy of Environmental Protectionism
Achim Körber

Trade Liberalisation, Economic Growth and the Environment
Matthew A. Cole

The International Yearbook of Environmental and Resource Economics
2000/2001
A Survey of Current Issues
Edited by Tom Tietenberg and Henk Folmer

Economic Growth and Environmental Policy
A Theoretical Approach
Frank Hettich

Principles of Environmental and Resource Economics
A Guide for Students and Decision-Makers
Second Edition
Edited by Henk Folmer and H. Landis Gabel

Valuing Nature with Travel Cost Models

A Manual

Frank A. Ward
Professor of Resource Economics,
New Mexico State University, USA

Diana Beal
Senior Lecturer in Finance,
University of Southern Queensland, Australia

NEW HORIZONS IN ENVIRONMENTAL ECONOMICS

Edward Elgar
Cheltenham, UK • Northampton, MA, USA

Published by
Edward Elgar Publishing Limited
Glensanda House
Montpellier Parade
Cheltenham
Glos GL50 1UA
UK

Edward Elgar Publishing, Inc.
136 West Street
Suite 202
Northampton
Massachusetts 01060
USA

A catalogue record for this book
is available from the British Library

Library of Congress Cataloguing in Publication Data

Ward, Frank A.
  Valuing nature with travel cost models: a manual / Frank A. Ward, Diana Beal.
    (New horizons in environmental economics)
  Includes bibliographical references and index.
  1. Natural resources—Management. 2. Economic policy—Decision making.
  3. Travel costs. I. Beal, Diana J. II. Title. III. Series.

HC21.W37   2000
333.7'07'23—dc21   99–053049

ISBN 1 84064 078 2

Printed and bound in Great Britain by Bookcraft (Bath) Ltd.

Contents

research and policy issues. Its popularity may also be because the group likes to meet in warm resort areas in the dead of winter.

My partnership with Diana in writing this book has produced many rewards. It was entirely her idea. She also is a gifted communicator, who brings structure, clarity and grace to ideas needing expression.

DIANA BEAL

Brisbane on the east coast of Queensland, Australia, was the city of my youth. We were lucky to live in one of the leafy suburbs. Our land backed onto a freshwater creek where we spent our spare time canoeing during floods and sliding down the banks on palm fronds until the seats came out of our pants.

I went straight from school to the University of Queensland (UQ) to study economics. After graduation, I was employed by the then Bureau of Agricultural Economics in Canberra and later by the Queensland Dept. of Primary Industries.

Working with agriculture every day but in a theoretical way sparked my interest in farming. My mother had a rural background so we decided to go into a partnership on a farm. We selected the Darling Downs as the best place, as it is an area with rich basaltic soil, reasonable rainfall and a pleasant climate. We bought our farm and grew lucerne and other hay crops and raised beef cattle.

After about 15 years of farming, when the farm development work had been completed, I saw an advertisement for an economics tutor at the local university (USQ). I got the job. It was soon obvious to me that university life was easier than farming and better paid. So, I decided I should upgrade my qualifications. The big problem was whether I had the confidence to start a new career.

I'd always been interested in the interaction of economics and natural resources, and the evidence left on the landscape of past economic activity. Just as Frank recounts in his story, I was amazed there was such a discipline and something really interesting gained academic credit. So I completed a Master of Philosophy by thesis, and loved doing it.

Once the Masters was complete, I thought I ought to do a PhD with more economics. So I entered UQ's PhD program and completed my thesis on a pricing policy for national parks to retain biodiversity. The examiners included Wiktor Adamowicz and Dick Walsh, names very familiar to TCM builders.

During the PhD research I studied, used and was intrigued by TCM. I thought a full length book treatment would be useful. Edward Elgar favored the idea, but suggested a more practised hand than mine would be an advantage, especially regarding multi-site models, of which I believe none have yet been built in Australia. So a fruitful partnership with Frank, for which I am most grateful, was created. He brings wide experience and sound knowledge of multi-site models.

Introduction

This chapter deals with why we need a book on travel costs methodology (TCM) models, what they achieve and the plan of the book.

WHY DO WE NEED A BOOK ON TCM MODELS?

Humankind relies on natural resources for continued existence, in common with other living species. Natural resources have historically supplied food, clothing, shelter, the means to care for our persons and both the environment and tools needed for various forms of relaxation and spiritual rejuvenation. Over millennia, people settled in all the continents except Antarctica and developed their various ethnic characteristics and cultures. One characteristic common to all was their reliance on nature to survive and flourish; another was their profound impacts on their local flora and fauna. They changed the relative abundance of various species.

In more modern times, the great European migrations placed Europeans with their cultures in new lands. Instead of adapting their cultural practises to new environments, by and large they tried to adapt the environments to their cultures. One result has been the considerable depletion of natural resources. More than sixty per cent of US timber reserves, for example, were cut in the nineteenth century. Another result has been the generally unanticipated change in populations of untargeted species. A third effect has been a huge increase in human standards of living over the last two hundred years accompanied by large scale transformation of natural resources into useful tools and products that have made our lives easier and longer.

All human cultures use and value environmental resources both in their natural state and for conversion into commodities such as irrigation water, power, minerals and farmland (Krutilla, 1967). Some of these conversions into commodities have caused considerable environmental damage. For example, an oil spill of *Exxon Valdez* proportions has substantial consequences in both the short and longer term – oil-fouled beaches, the suffering and loss of wildlife, the loss of fish stocks and fishers' livelihoods. Still, elaborately converted petroleum produces immense human benefit for transportation, space heating and materials. An important question faced by governments thus centers around the appropriate mix of policies to provide a balance in uses of environments in their natural state versus commodity production. Information on the economic values of preservation versus development of natural environments provides policy makers with essential information in making more informed decisions.

Environmental debates have raged around the world generally since the early 1970s. These have involved issues regarding the appropriate use of natural environments at all levels. A local concern, for example, may be the pollution of a creek running through a city with industrial waste such as oil or paint thinner from a motor vehicle repair shop. By the time that creek reaches the sea, the concern may be regional and additional groups such as fishers may be involved. If the creek empties into the sea near a world natural heritage treasure such as the Great Barrier Reef, the issue may become national or global.

The political process often suffers from the problem that little is done about an environmental issue until it becomes acute. Nevertheless, concern about environmental degradation has reached the world political stage. In 1992, the Rio Earth Summit was held, and a further International Conference on Greenhouse Gas Emissions Trading was held at Kyoto in Japan in 1997. Proponents for change at these forums have argued that considerable policy changes must be made in order to improve environmental quality. Opponents worry about the high cost of reducing environmental damages.

Arguments on environmental policy questions usually revolve around potential benefits and costs to both current and future generations. In drafting and considering legislation, governments often wish to know if benefits to be enjoyed by current and future generations will outweigh the costs of procuring those benefits. Sometimes these decisions are easy to make, but usually they are not. For example, if nearly everyone wants to set aside a certain patch of land as habitat for an endangered species and the land has no particular or valuable alternative use, there is no problem in making a decision. We simply set the land aside. If many people want the land for the species and the rest simply don't care, we can reserve the land uncontentiously. Those who prefer the project are better off and those who are indifferent are neither better nor worse off. Difficulty in choice occurs when many people approve of a project but many also disapprove.

Nearly all public environmental policy decisions have effects that cause some people to gain while others lose. Policymakers and voters want to know if a new decision will yield greater benefits than it will cost. Because economic impacts are a major factor in influencing public policy outcomes, economic analysis should be done objectively and fairly. This is especially true when outcomes of the analyses do not suit the interests of those who stand to lose something. The economic analysis tool of choice for environmental policy analysis is benefit-cost analysis (BCA).

BCA is an economic tool for comparing the desirable and undesirable impacts of proposed policies (Arrow et al., 1996). In particular, it is a method for ranking the economic performance of natural resource projects, policies and programs in which impacts are measured in non-technical terms and estimated by scientific methods (McAllister, 1980). It is a process of comparing all the gains and losses resulting from some action in common units. BCA organizes information in a way to promote the conduct of rational policy analysis. Rational policy analysis considers all the relevant alternatives, identifies and evaluates all the known consequences which would follow from the adoption of each alternative, and selects that alternative and its associated consequences which would be preferable in terms of society's most valued ends (Sander, 1983). A complete BCA compares alternative actions to determine which option provides society with the most economically beneficial use of its resources (Loomis, 1993). BCA helps make better management decisions by using a time-tested economic framework for organising economic data.

In environmental and natural resources, there are plenty of ways governments can make bad decisions. Management by tradition is a widely-applied method for making poor decisions. Resource agencies pursue activities, such as stocking x pounds of trout at a y sized lake or selling z board feet of timber from a national forest, simply because that's what they've done for years. Without information on benefits and costs, resource agencies often have no choice but to manage by tradition.

Fear of change also promotes bad decisions. Machiavelli warned there is nothing more difficult to do, more perilous to conduct or more uncertain of its success, than taking the lead in the introduction of a new order of things, because the innovator faces as enemies all who have done well under the old conditions. While change is resisted by virtually everybody, BCA nevertheless gives a quantitative basis for deciding which changes are worthwhile and which ones should be rejected.

Poor decisions are also promoted by the desire or necessity of government resource agencies to appease special interests. In the western US, for example, many policies have been enacted to please special interests (Gardner, 1997). The US Congress subsidizes federal timber, water, recreation, minerals and forage because powerful special interests benefit economically.

Finally, poor decisions are promoted when public resource managers' personal biases are allowed to influence decisions instead of sound economic analyses based on economic principles and carried out consistently. In the realm of natural resource management, local bureaucrats violate the national interest when they are permitted to decide the mix of grazing and recreation on public lands based on personal biases or political connections. The decision should be made through the consistent and objective application of time-tested economic principles. These principles should be set up at the national level and applied to resources and resource issues at the local level.

In principle, the benefit of any natural resource management decision is measured by what resource users are willing to pay for it. Costs are benefits displaced by the decision. These are two pivotal concepts which underlie much of what is in this book. These concepts apply to both market goods and non-market goods.

For the case of market goods, suppose the US Secretary of the Interior proposes limiting logging in the southwest to produce more critical habitat for the Mexican spotted owl. The benefits lost (costs) from such a policy are timber. Timber is sold in markets. The total cost of the policy is thus the sum of prices times quantities of timber precluded by the decision.

The same concepts apply to decisions affecting non-market goods. Imagine that the US Congress is considering passing a law that requires shipbuilders to build double-hulled oil tankers, in order to reduce future environmental damages from oil spills. The benefit is the value of fish not killed, beaches not fouled by spilled oil, marine wildlife not killed, and ecosystems not damaged. For these non-market goods, prices typically must be estimated by some indirect method.

The TCM is one of the few techniques available for estimating values of environmental policy decisions, decisions which we define as any public or private action that has some influence on human benefits received from the environment in current or future generations. There is currently no book-length treatment of TCM. There are brief accounts of the method in most environmental and natural resource economics textbooks, but these are typically too sketchy to be of much use to the professional resource manager who needs a TCM to provide information on environmental policy decisions. Conversely, articles dealing with TCM in the published economics journal literature usually presume intimacy with the method and knowledge of advanced microeconomics and econometrics. Hence, we have assigned ourselves the task of filling the void in the literature and providing an accessible manual on the methodology so that resource managers may start to use TCM as a part of their decision-making processes.

WHAT DO TCM MODELS ACHIEVE?

Many people believe that communities should invest in natural resource facilities and possibly even take natural environments out of commodity production to promote outdoor recreation, because these investments provide important human benefits, such as better health, a place to develop and improve skills and a place to relax and have a good time. However, getting and keeping these facilities and natural environments call for both the money and the natural resources of suitable quality and amount, whilst these resources typically have values in other uses that are also important to people. For example, in places like the dry western US and Australia, streams, lakes and reservoirs are used for fishing, boating and other outdoor recreation, but the water is also used for drinking, crop irrigation and power production.

People who make the decisions that allocate resources to outdoor recreation are well aware that these alternative uses produce important benefits that are valued in organized markets. Hence, analyses of price data collected in these markets, such as the price of water that cities charge customers in a water bill, provide estimates of benefits accruing to people who would rather use the resources for something outside recreation and the environment. Moreover these estimates may be presented with a fair degree of confidence in their accuracy. Conversely, recreation and environmental managers are called upon to defend their outdoor recreation and environmental programs in the face of little or no data that indicate what those benefits are worth. TCM is one method for estimating recreational values, so that these values can be compared with competing values consistently.

Apart from recreational and environmental policy applications, TCM models have been used to estimate user benefits of a very wide range of unpriced goods and services, based on users' travel patterns. There are rarely established markets for enjoying such benefits as breathing crisp clean air, sight-seeing, watching whales sporting in the seas or, in some cases, benefits from gaining valuable information. An example of this final instance is the value of additional information derived by livestock producers who go physically to watch a livestock sale, rather than relying on radio broadcasts or published data of the results. TCM models have been used with success to value that additional information.

Despite its wider applicability, TCM has been mostly used to support environmental policy decisions, such as investments in nature-based recreational infrastructure, on-site recreational enhancement decisions and various proposed environmental regulations. Examples of applications include benefits arising from fish stocking programs, mammal breeding programs for recreational hunters, enhanced hiking trails and facilities, better picnicking facilities at lakes and dams and improved camp grounds in national parks and forest reserves. It has also been used to estimate the environmental cost of private decisions, such as schemes to drain fishing lakes in droughts to provide water for crops and private coal-fired power plant developments near national parks. A study has been under way in the US for some time, in which TCM estimates of on-site recreation benefits in natural areas are being used to evaluate proposed national policies that would regulate air pollution more stringently.

TCM has had five decades of development since the germ of the concept was first suggested by Harold Hotelling in 1947. TCM is a method for estimating economic benefits of a recreation site based on observed travel patterns of people who visit that site. Analysts who estimate these benefits using TCM apply the principle that people who live closer to a site overcome less travel distance and are subject to lower travel time barriers than more distant visitors, and therefore receive more benefit due to the site's presence.

Numerous issues have been examined and canvassed in the academic literature, and some hundreds of estimations have been made. US economists have probably produced the largest volume of TCM analyses. Theoretical development of the method has been promoted by pressure brought to bear by many US legislative and judicial bodies' requiring environmental benefit or opportunity cost estimates before environmentally-damaging developments can be approved. Legislative and judicial process in many other countries appears to be not so far advanced, possibly because of a greater need for and value of material services provided by natural environments. However, there have still been some important contributions to the literature with studies reported from the UK, continental Europe, Canada, Australia, New Zealand and Asia.

Several reviews of TCM have been published, for example, Ward and Loomis (1986), Durden and Shogren (1988), and Smith (1989; 1990; 1993). They have generally concluded that the methodology is robust and produces an acceptable estimate of benefits accruing to users of natural resources for nature-based recreation. Additionally, they all provide some insight into how TCM can be used to evaluate policies, programs and plans that damage or improve that recreation.

THE PLAN OF THIS BOOK

The intent of this book is to present a self-contained treatment of TCM along with a wide range of applications to natural resource and environmental policy questions, for readers who have little formal background in economic theory or statistics. It should be of great professional and personal interest to policy analysts, biologists, foresters, hydrologists and others who need to formulate, implement or evaluate proposed environmental policies, projects, or programs. This manual has been written to pass onto you the insights gained over the last half-century on the development and use of this important methodology.

To this end, Chapter 1 discusses some of the environmental and natural resource decisions which TCM models can support. The chapter starts with a brief review of the economic framework for benefit-cost analysis, shows the kinds of decisions which need recreation benefits data, touches on outdoor recreation program planning and considers more fully the evaluation of management actions. Chapter 2 gives a brief history and overview of TCM. TCM models are concerned with the estimation of demand; thus, an understanding of the theory of demand is essential if the methodology is to be used successfully. Chapter 3 takes you through the necessary demand theory without burdening you with unnecessary theoretical sophistication. Some of the concepts underlying demand theory are discussed, followed by some of the mechanics of demand estimation. The theory and measurement of benefits are then examined in Chapter 4. The crux of the use of TCM lies in the estimation of consumer surplus, compensating variation or equivalent variation, depending on the circumstances of each case. This chapter gives a comprehensive account of these measurements.

Chapter 5 continues the examination of the various forms of TCM models and discusses their applicability to differing situations. Principles for the design of models are examined. Chapter 6 considers some important aspects of the administration of surveys – identifying the population, selecting a sample, developing and testing a questionnaire, planning survey procedures and finally considering response rates. An important question considered is what response rate is sufficient to give reliable data.

No matter how much thought is given in the survey planning stage to the definition of variables, survey respondents manage to introduce new situations which analysts had not previously considered. Hence, it is important to develop protocols (rules) to deal with the many variations in the reported data. These can be developed in the planning stage and later as the data are recorded. Similarly, respondents may encounter difficulties in providing information and it is important to give guidance on the questionnaire. These issues are discussed in Chapter 7.

One variant of TCM is the zonal TCM (ZTCM) model. Chapter 7 also briefly considers the definition and identification of zones. Should they be concentric or based on existing administrative units such as countries, states, or counties, or city blocks? ZTCM models pose several requirements for structuring, gathering and analysing data, but they present important advantages for being able to analyse an impressive range of policy questions.

Chapter 8 introduces data management and analysis. PCs, spreadsheets and data base management programs have taken much of the drudgery out of survey-based research in recent years. This chapter presents helpful hints for designing a questionnaire and organising the data storage and retrieval system to make data input and output flow easily and efficiently. Anyone who has organized, planned for and conducted a TCM for policy analysis is well aware of the costs incurred by poor foresight in planning. This lack of forethought causes the majority of time to be spent on struggling with the data flow, diverting precious resources and time away from model estimation and policy analysis. It has been our experience that TCM studies are often under-budgeted and conducted under the umbrella of another job or program. Many well-intentioned efforts to estimate a TCM were shelved for a lack of good planning. The chapter also considers several issues surrounding regression analysis. As with demand theory in Chapter 3, regression analysis is viewed as an instrument for estimating TCMs and not as an end in itself. So you are taken through only the aspects of regression you need to know to understand what is being achieved with the TCM models. After a brief introduction, the chapter examines the interpretation of regression coefficients for policy analysis. It then mentions suitable regression software. The selection of an algebraic functional form is shown to be critical to the usefulness of a regression model used for policy analysis. This chapter also discusses the various test statistics which are available to evaluate the estimated model.

As a reader, your needs will differ depending on the policy issues you face, your budget, available time and other circumstances. Lest you think that all the problems and issues surrounding TCM are resolved, Chapter 9 introduces some of the many unresolved and emerging issues. These are principally the issues of what travel costs should be counted, the value of time both during travel and on site, multi-purpose or multiple destination trips and varying lengths of visits. The chapter also points you towards the most significant journals that publish TCM papers. TCM continues to undergo development by economists and other policy analysts who have interests in public and private decisions that affect the environment, natural resources and recreation. Whilst managers at a recreation site who face compelling day-to-day pressures may believe themselves less interested in academic debates, they still may wish to stay abreast of the various issues both in TCM itself and in emerging policies for which TCM can effectively support decisions. For example, in the realm of US water policy, the Bureau of Reclamation and Army Corps of Engineers have invested considerable money and staff in recent years on studies that measure the value of water-based recreation. These values influence how their reservoirs and associated streamflows are operated in an environment of legally-mandated multiple use benefits maximisation. Similarly the US Forest Service and Bureau of Land Management are both mandated by 1970s legislation to manage public forests and rangelands to account for all uses and benefits of these lands.

A little crystal ball work is included in the Conclusion, together with a few numbers on the worth of outdoor nature-based recreation which have come from review papers. The book ends with an annotated bibliography, listing many of the papers that have dealt with TCM. The papers are coded to guide readers through the list. The book concludes with one of the most important features of any useful manual, an index.

We have tried to write this manual for natural resource site managers, policy analysts and others who face responsibilities in planning, programming, budgeting and project operations. Accordingly, we hope we have described sufficient material to allow you to use TCM in your own analyses. We hope you find the book intellectually stimulating in its own right as well as useful for analysis that underpins the formulation, implementation and evaluation of decisions affecting recreation and the environment. Additionally, we hope this book will give you insight into the current professional debates and that you can follow up in the journals any aspects which particularly intrigue you.

We thank the many economic researchers who have been at the cutting edge of developments in TCM for the last twenty years. They include Wiktor Adamowicz, John Bergstrom, Rich Bishop, Nancy Bockstael, Bill Brown, Oscar Burt, Charles Cicchetti, Marion Clawson, Ken Cordell, Michael Hanemann, Daniel Hellerstein, Catherine Kling, Jack Knetsch, John Loomis, Ted McConnell, Bill Martin, John McKean, Rob Mendelsohn, Alan Randall, Douglass Shaw, Kerry Smith, Ivar Strand, John Stoll, Dick Walsh and Elizabeth Wilman to name only a few, without whose work this book would not have been possible. None of our errors are the fault of any of these people.

REFERENCES

Arrow, K.J., M.L. Cropper, G.C. Eads, R.W. Hahn, L.B. Lave, R.G. Noll, P.R. Portney, M. Russell, R. Schmalensee, V.K. Smith and R.N. Stavins (1996), 'Is There A Role for Benefit-Cost Analysis in Environmental, Health and Safety Regulation?', *Science*, **272**, 221-2.

Durden, G. and J.F. Shogren (1988), 'Valuing Non-Market Recreation Goods: An Evaluative Survey of the Literature on the Travel Cost and Contingent Valuation Methods', *Review of Regional Studies*, **18** (3), 1-15.

Gardner, B.D. (1997), 'Some Implications of Federal Grazing, Timber, Irrigation and Recreation Subsidies', *Choices*, **12** (3), 9-14.

Krutilla, J.V. (1967), 'Conservation Reconsidered', *American Economic Review*, **57** (4), 777-86.

Loomis, J.B. (1993), *Integrated Public Lands Management*, New York: Columbia University Press.

McAllister, D.M. (1980), *Evaluation in Environmental Planning*, Cambridge: MIT Press.

Sander, W. (1983), 'Federal Water Resources Policy and Decision-Making', *American Journal of Economics and Sociology*, **42** (1), 1-12.

Smith, V.K. (1989), 'Taking Stock of Progress with Travel Cost Recreation Demand Models: Theory and Implementation', *Marine Resource Economics*, **6** (4), 279-310.

Smith, V.K. (1990), 'What Have We Learned since Hotelling's Letter: A Meta-Analysis', *Economic Letters*, **32** (3), 267-72.

Smith V.K. (1993), 'Nonmarket Valuation of Environmental Resources: An Interpretative Appraisal', *Land Economics,* **69** (1), 1-26.

Ward, F.A. and J.B Loomis (1986), 'The Travel Cost Demand Model as an Environmental Policy Assessment Tool: A Review of Literature', *Western Journal of Agricultural Economics,* **11** (2), 164-78.

1. Support for Environmental Policy Decisions

This chapter illustrates the range of environmental and natural resource questions for which information on economic values of outdoor recreation can assist in making better decisions. By showing the range of questions policymakers face, we also demonstrate the importance of finding good data and assembling useful models to produce that information. We draw our examples principally from US experience, because environmental policy and legislation appear to be most advanced in that country.

The first section describes the economic framework of benefit-cost analysis, which is a highly structured and well-developed method for organizing information that supports the formulation of policy. The next section shows the kinds of environmental and natural resource policy decisions for which values of outdoor recreation are needed. These decisions are made by both the public and private sectors.

The third section describes how recreation value information can help parks and recreation administrators who practise 'benefits-based-management' to formulate, implement and evaluate their programs better. The fourth section shows how recreation demand analysis can be used for forecasting demand for recreation and recreation facilities. The final section concludes with a discussion of the challenges placed on methods that attempt to estimate economic values of outdoor recreation, if those methods are to produce the kind of information that environmental and natural resource policy analysts need most.

THE ECONOMIC FRAMEWORK

The design of institutions or mechanisms for resource allocation that meets society's objectives has confronted individuals and governments since the beginning of time. What may be the most important contribution of Adam Smith's *Wealth of Nations* was to show why and how markets are a powerful and efficient institution to solve this problem. In the 1940s, Lange (1942) and Lerner (1944) explored ways of organizing resources that would result in the maximum possible attainment of society's objectives, while still being accomplished through decentralized decision-making that uses economic and technical information at the local level.

People who formulate or implement policies that affect environmental and natural resources are also interested in comparing the likely effects of alternative options for allocating these resources. We take it as given that policies should produce the greatest possible total human benefits summed over current and future generations and that they should also produce a fair distribution of those benefits.   Many economic studies dealing with environmental and natural resource policy have found that one way to assure that total human benefits are maximized is to design institutions or frameworks that confront people with the real cost that their actions impose on other people. These institutions can operate in an environment of free markets, government regulations or some combination of both. Institutions that confront people with the real cost of their actions promote the maximization of total benefits. For example, individual water users implement only those actions for which their own expected benefits exceed their expected costs. However, when water users' decisions are made in environments that confront them with the real social cost of their actions, they will implement only those actions for which society's total benefits exceed total costs. The challenge for people who set up or carry out environmental and natural resource policies is to design institutions, such as better laws, more effective regulations, improved markets and the like, so that all individuals who come under the influence of those institutions indeed face the real cost of their actions.

Most modern textbooks on natural resource economics conclude that there are several characteristics of good resource allocation mechanisms which would effectively require all people to face the real cost of their actions. The typical approach is to view it as a problem in property rights. As long as property rights are completely specified, exclusive, transferable and enforceable, then all market prices reflect opportunity costs. Moreover the market system is an efficient institution for maximizing total human benefits. Good examples are to be found in Tietenberg (1996) or Howe, Schurmeier and Shaw (1986).

The concept of confronting all resource users with the real cost of their actions as a way to promote widest beneficial use of resources (economic efficiency) has been well-established for years. This concept has been widely applied to the case of setting up property rights with the above four features to make markets work better. Good examples of their application to contemporary issues are the cases of transferable water rights and discharge permits for pollution. However, where policymakers wish to design more effective non-market institutions, such as environmental laws and policies, a major difficulty in their implementation lies in measuring social benefits and social costs of individuals' actions. The problem stems from the lack of information which is nevertheless necessary.

Benefit-cost analysis (BCA) is an economic method of analysis for comparing the desirable and undesirable impacts of proposed environmental and natural resource policies (Arrow et al., 1996). It is a method for ranking the economic performance of natural resource projects, policies and programs in which impacts are measured in non-technical terms and estimated by scientific methods. It is a process of comparing in common units all the gains and losses resulting from an action.

Foundations of BCA

Welfare economics is a study of the contribution economics can make to policy evaluation using concepts of measurable social welfare. BCA is the most extensively developed method of policy analysis grounded in welfare economics. The objective of BCA is to assist governments in enacting laws, implementing policies and evaluating plans for improving the public welfare.

While public welfare has long been an aim of public policy, possibly the first attempt to define formally society's aggregate welfare occurred in the writing of the utilitarian philosopher, Bentham (1780). He stated that the impact on 'aggregate welfare' should be the basis for evaluating the effectiveness of government policy. Bentham's aggregate welfare is the intellectual foundation of modern BCA.

The US government gave formal statutory authority to Bentham's philosophy when it enacted the *Flood Control Act of 1936*. It was an attempt to stop huge amounts of taxpayers' revenue from being spent wastefully in an economic depression. Congress stated that federal money could not be spent on flood control projects unless 'the benefits to whomsoever they may accrue' exceeded the costs. However, methods of economic analysis had not advanced nearly far enough by that time to provide reliable methods for estimating these benefits and costs.

One piece of the puzzle was developed by three economists who developed the Potential Pareto Improvement (PPI) criterion. This criterion is used to evaluate two competing states: *with* compared to *without* the proposal. Based on Bentham's utilitarian philosophy, the economic state with the proposal is socially superior to the economic state without it if those who gain with the proposal could compensate those who lose. This does not mean that the winners must compensate the losers. If total gains are high enough so that hypothetical compensation would make nobody worse off and at least one person is better off, then the proposed plan is better according to the PPI criterion. The PPI criterion was developed in three pieces in separate papers by Kaldor (1939), Hicks (1939) and Skitovsky (1941).

As a practical matter of public policy, if institutions for making those payments cannot be erected to complement the proposed plan, politicians in some democratic nations typically vote against the plan. So an important challenge for economists and policy analysts remains to devise institutions so that the benefits of proposed plans can be distributed to produce mostly winners.

The last remaining development was the need to define 'utility gains or utility losses' in money terms that could be algebraically added across affected individuals. These utility changes needed to be expressed in money terms, because interpersonal comparisons of satisfaction gains and losses are difficult to implement. This important advance was developed by Hicks (1956) who defined the 'compensating variation' (CV) and 'equivalent variation' (EV) as indicators of welfare change. He defined the CV (EV) as the change in money income that compensates for (is equivalent to) the change in real income (satisfaction) brought about by the proposed plan.

This three-piece package provides the completely assembled engine of welfare economics that is currently used for benefit-cost evaluations of proposed public plans. With it, analysts aim to estimate the total change in benefits summed over all individuals affected positively or negatively by the proposed plan.

An individual's benefit from a policy action is typically measured as the maximum amount by which the individual's income could be reduced to offset the welfare gain due to the policy. Cost to an individual is, of course, the increase in income which would compensate for a welfare loss due to a policy. This can be measured as an individual's CV, operationalized as the willingness to pay in the case of a welfare gain or a willingness to accept compensation when the policy produces a loss. It can also be measured as an EV, operationalized as the willingness to accept payment that produces an equivalent gain in lieu of the policy (or a willingness to pay that produces an equivalent loss as the policy). For a small price, quantity or quality changes in either market goods or unpriced goods, the CV usually produces very similar benefits and costs as the EV. For large changes, such as may occur when an endangered species becomes extinct, the two welfare measures can be quite different.

Function of BCA

A complete BCA compares alternative actions to determine which one provides society with the most economically beneficial use of its resources (Loomis, 1993). As stated above, BCA has been used widely in the US to decide whether any federal water project should be started. It has also been used to decide which should be introduced if funds are limited.

BCA uses a simple decision rule. If, for some action, the sum of its benefits exceeds the sum of the costs by a larger amount than from any other action with the same aim, the proposed action should be adopted. Otherwise it should not. This assumes that all individuals are treated equally, so that an incremental unit (e.g. dollar) of benefit accruing to a rich person is valued the same as a dollar of cost lost by a poor person. An advantage of BCA is that money as a unit of measurement for ratings is easily understood by everyone and does not require technical specialists to interpret it.

For the concept of revenue to the private firm, BCA substitutes the idea of benefit to society. For the notion of cost of the private firm, the BCA analyst substitutes the concept of opportunity cost or the value of benefits foregone when resources are displaced from other economic activities to support the resource management proposal in question. For the profit of the firm, BCA substitutes the concept of excess benefit over cost.

BCA values all natural resource policy proposals with a common denominator. Consider the huge range of services produced by natural resource decisions: electric power, water quantity, water quality, critical habitat for endangered species, timber, forage for livestock and wildlife, recreation, fish, minerals and others. By expressing all these outputs in the same units, all natural resource policy proposals can be compared.

Because public and private resources to formulate or comply with regulations are constrained, BCA helps clarify trade-offs resulting from various policy decisions or public investments. In principle, it addresses the question of where to stop regulating the environment or developing natural resources. The point of where to stop is defined by the equi-marginal rule, which mandates that expenditure on all proposed projects should continue until the ratios of marginal benefits to marginal costs for all proposals are equal.

USE OF TCM IN ENVIRONMENTAL AND NATURAL RESOURCE POLICY

This section discusses the kinds of environmental policy questions for which information on recreation benefits can make a contribution. Economic values of outdoor recreation can play a part in establishing more economically productive environmental policies. Many policy areas are considered and they include:

- reservoir management
- water supply
- natural disasters
- hydro dam relicensing
- wildlife
- energy

- natural resource damage
- clean air
- clean water
- rangelands
- forests
- outdoor recreation facilities.

Reservoir Management

Since 1902 under the auspices of the *Reclamation Act*, the federal government has dammed hundreds of rivers in the western US, a blessing for farmers who needed the water for irrigation. However, many of these reservoirs have become first class areas to fish, boat and picnic. Many people have discovered that the 1700 lakes the government built since the turn of the century for hydroelectric power, irrigation farming and flood control are good for recreation.

Supported by a national love for water sports in the US, the Bureau of Reclamation reservoirs alone draw nearly 100 million visitors per year. These reservoirs account for more than half of the lake fishing in the western US. The government would like to draw even more visitors, but many of the facilities at these lakes are 30-40 years old and need costly repairs.

Recreation is one source of economic survival of many rural western towns. Rural areas in many parts of northern California, Oregon and Washington once supported timber industries, but were hit by federal timber harvest restrictions in the 1980s. Tourism at federal reservoirs has picked up some of the economic slack. Recreation at the biggest 490 federal reservoirs produces an estimated $44 billion and more than 600,000 jobs per year (Hughes, 1998). Water-based recreation is a major draw at the largest federal reservoirs, including Lake Mead, Lake Oahe, Lake Powell, Shasta Lake and Elephant Butte Lake.

The question of what water levels to maintain at these multi-purpose reservoirs continues to grow in importance, especially in the summer when values of recreation and irrigation are at their peak. Boaters are unhappy when the government draws down water levels in the spring for flood control and in the summer for irrigation and use by endangered species and salmon.

The Congressionally-appointed National Recreation Lakes Study Commission is studying the national recreation policies of the federal agencies that manage these lakes. These agencies include the US Army Corps of Engineers, Bureau of Reclamation where endangered species are involved, the US Fish and Wildlife Service, US Forest Service, Bureau of Land Management and the Environmental Protection Agency where environmental issues are important. All these agencies have different missions, separate enabling legislation, unlike beliefs and contrary ways of coping with natural resource conflicts.

The commission wants to ascertain if new federal policies can increase recreational opportunities while maintaining the original intentions behind the lakes. Important policy questions include the type and intensity of improvements, who will pay for recreational improvements and who will do the work. Studies based on models that estimate the benefits of various management actions or policy changes are objective means to help decisionmakers answer these questions.

Water Supply

Potential losses of outdoor recreation benefits associated with water expansion plans are a major factor influencing water planning in the southwestern US. Many large cities in this area suffer from water problems. These problems typically come from at least one of four sources: the cities are growing rapidly because high, dry, mild climates are attractive places in which to live; there are institutional rigidities that discourage market transfers of water from agriculture to the cities; these cities typically fail to price their water at its replacement cost; and replacement cost, particularly the environmental cost, is considerable.

For example, one reason that Denver, Colorado, turned to conservation pricing of water in the early 1990s was that the proposed Two Forks Dam would have destroyed a renowned trout fishery and recreational area and would have threatened endangered whooping cranes and other species. The projected cost of losing the trout fishery was an important factor in the decision by EPA in March 1989 to reject the dam's permit. Similarly, Los Angeles turned to marginal cost pricing of water because of scarcity brought on by a serious drought and the high costs of that drought on recreation and the environment (Ward, Roach and Henderson, 1996).

Coping with Natural Disasters

Coping with natural disasters such as drought, floods and pests continues to attract the attention of politicians and natural resource planners. In the late 1970s, the pine beetle, spruce budworm, gypsy moth and other insects caused extensive damage to forests throughout the US, particularly in the northwest, northeast and south. Nations around the world face similar problems of how much they can afford to pay for the protection of forests from insect pests and other hazards such as wildfire (Vaux, Gardner and Mills, 1984), drought (Ward et al., 1998) and acid rain (Crocker, 1985).

Hydro Dam Relicensing

The US Federal Energy Regulatory Commission (FERC) administers a program of licensing non-federal hydroelectric power plants. FERC licenses incorporate conditions affecting the owners' operation of the plants; typical conditions include instream flow requirements and other fishery protection measures. When a license expires, the project owner can start the relicensing process with the hope of obtaining permission to operate for another 25-50 years.

The relicensing process gives environmental groups the opportunity to seek instream flows more compatible with outdoor recreation and the needs of endangered species. Although use of water for hydropower generation does not consume water through evaporation, hydro generation does impose costs in terms of other values lost. Changes in the amount and timing of water used for power generation affects other uses downstream.

A FERC case was recently settled in central Nebraska. The hydro facilities at Lake McConnaughy on the Platte River produced significant habitat for endangered piping plovers and least terns and influenced outdoor recreation benefits at several multi-purpose reservoirs on the Platte. Recreation and environmental values were important factors in deciding the conditions under which FERC relicensed operation of the dam.

Wildlife

To cope with the problem of disappearing species in the US, the *Endangered Species Act (ESA) of 1973* was passed. This Act and its amendments assign to the US Fish and Wildlife Service (USFWS) the responsibility to list US plant and animals species that are threatened or endangered. USFWS also designates critical habitat for listed species. Designation can alter outdoor recreation opportunities and other economic activity in critical habitat areas, either positively or negatively. The ESA requires the USFWS to assess the economic impacts of all proposed critical habitat designations. Thus, economic analysis is essential to the process.

Setting aside critical habitat for endangered species typically involves a change in the allocation of several natural resources, such as land, water, fish, forests or rangelands. Limiting or prohibiting timber harvest to provide habitat for spotted owls, for example, may produce a benefit in forest-based recreation. Where streamflows are managed to reflect the natural hydrograph to protect endangered species, river and reservoir-based recreation may be altered. Where streamflows for a fish or wildlife species come from releases at popular upstream reservoirs, there may be a large negative impact on existing outdoor recreation.

Szentandrasi et al. (1995) attempted to value conservation reserve program land previously used in agriculture with potential use as wildlife habitat. One possible source of effective species protection is on land that is used primarily for agriculture. The profitability and utility of these lands as wildlife habitat can be influenced by public policies and programs. The conservation reserve program (CRP), the most extensive land retirement program in the US, is a good example of such a program. Information on the benefits of wildlife habitat possibly derived from recreation demand models could provide important information to the policy debate.

In an interesting study from Sweden, Gren (1996) compared the values of nitrogen abatement produced by investing in several substitute measures: investing in wetlands, building sewage treatment plants and developing agriculture. Findings showed that incremental values of wetlands investment to current and future generations exceeds the other two. This is because the economic capacity to produce the latter two will grow in quantity and fall in cost, while wetlands will increase in scarcity. According to the author, results for Gotland suggest that the value of programs that invest in wetlands preservation may considerably exceed the value of sewage treatment plants or added agricultural development. One of the values of wetlands is as wildlife habitat and is likely to be strongly supported by waterfowl hunters and other outdoor recreationists.

Many seacoast areas of the world face important policy conflicts between commercial and sport fishing. Bishop and Samples (1980) developed a theoretical model to explain policies that account in a balanced way for these two values. Easley (1992) also examined several ways to improve our understanding of allocation of fishery harvests between commercial and sport harvesters. Recreation demand models have the potential to give important information on economic values of sport fishing to policymakers who need to balance the two values in setting up regulations that govern these fisheries.

Energy

In industrialized countries, energy is of prime importance to national military and economic security. To illustrate the point, recall that the US, Britain and their allies fought the Gulf War in 1991 largely to guarantee widespread access to energy.

Energy development imposes high costs. Since the late 1970s, there has been considerable interest in estimating the monetary cost of the environmental effects of various electricity generating technologies so that environmental costs can be incorporated more effectively into public and private energy policy. These environmental cost studies have attracted the attention of a variety of legislators and regulators. Consequently, laws in more than half of the US require utilities to consider environmental costs in some way when they choose among electricity supply options. Many other states are considering such measures. Several federal statutes also mandate that utilities or agencies estimate environmental costs.

Credible and reliable information about environmental costs will be a critical component of future state and federal policies. Good information could also allow quantification of the potential benefits associated with electricity technologies that have lower environmental impact (e.g., solar, hydro and wind energy) and technologies or regulations that reduce energy use (e.g., energy efficient buildings). These costs are particularly important because many of these alternative technologies currently cost more initially in market prices than do environment-damaging technologies, so they will be bypassed in favor of more traditional technologies unless their environmental benefits are factored into the analysis.

There is no clear consensus on quantitative estimates of environmental costs of electricity, or even on methods of analysis for estimating those costs. The methods of these studies, and the estimates themselves, vary widely. The differing methods and results have produced a contentious debate over appropriate measurement methodology among analysts and policymakers who wish to use the results of environmental cost studies to make decisions.

Valuation is the process of taking an environmental impact (e.g., acres of damaged forest or miles of lost trout streams) and estimating a monetary value for that impact. TCM is one accepted method for performing environmental valuations. While analysts and others disagree strongly about the proper method of estimating environmental costs, most people agree that, when applied properly, TCMs provide good estimates of what recreationists would be willing to pay for the environmental improvement or what they would be willing to pay to avoid environmental damage.

Natural Resource Damage Assessments

Following Three-Mile Island and other environmental disasters of the 1960s and 1970s, the *Comprehensive Environmental Response, Compensation and Liability Act (CERCLA) of 1980* was passed. It imposes financial liability for damages on people responsible for the release of chemical and other hazardous wastes. This Act established the legal right of natural resource trustees, who include local governments, state governments, the federal government and Indian tribes, to collect damages from firms or individuals.

In January 1996, the National Oceanic and Atmospheric Administration

(NOAA) published its final regulations concerning natural resource damage assessments conducted under the *Oil Pollution Act (OPA) of 1990*. NOAA's regulations are for use by authorized federal, state, Indian tribe and foreign trustees to determine appropriate actions to restore natural resources or calculate damages to those resources injured by a discharge of oil into navigable waters and areas around the United States. These regulations took effect in February 1996.

Congress saw NOAA's goal would be achieved by returning natural resources and services to baseline conditions and compensating for any interim losses of natural resources and services through the restoration, rehabilitation, replacement or acquisition of equivalent natural resources or services.

The regulations provide a framework for the trustees to conduct natural resource damage assessments that achieve restoration under OPA. The assessments performed by trustees receive the legal status of a rebuttable presumption. A rebuttable presumption is important because it means that responsible parties bear the burden of demonstrating that the damages estimated by trustees are inappropriate. So a considerable amount of attention therefore is expected to focus on the method of economic analysis used to estimate the damages. In order to collect damages in court, trustees must present evidence of the existence of economic damages. The federal government has established guidelines for methods of analysis that have legal standing. These guidelines include TCM.

Because there is considerable controversy surrounding the use of contingent valuation methodology (CVM) in these damage assessments, the NOAA commissioned a blue ribbon panel of expert economists including two Nobel Prize winners to make recommendations as to the best way CVM could be applied to assess the monetary value of these damages. According to this panel, criteria for an acceptable CVM are quite demanding and have been met by very few, if any, CVM studies.

Clean Air

Since the 1950s in many large US cities, air pollution has been a problem of growing political and economic importance. The *Clean Air Act of 1970* (CAA) and later amendments put strong regulatory controls on air emissions of many sectors of the economy. Achieving air pollution control objectives set up by Congress in the 1990 amendments will require an estimated $25-50 billion each year to be spent by both public and private sectors. Before the 1990 amendments, there were fewer than 20 regulated pollutants. The CAA currently regulates more than 380 pollutants at considerable cost to industry. While most of these costs will be passed to final consumers, some industries will suffer more than others.

In October 1997, the EPA released a report that concluded that the public health protection and environmental benefits of the CAA indicate estimates of total benefits over the period between 1970 and 1990 exceeded total costs by more than a ratio of 42 to 1. Nevertheless, many of these estimated benefits were subject to considerable uncertainty and the authors emphasized the importance of developing more reliable methods for valuing air quality improvements, particularly where ecosystems and related recreation were affected. Any future developments in methods for estimating recreation benefits stand to make an important contribution to clean air policies.

Clean Water

Responding to the problem of widespread polluted, dead and dying waters in the US, Congress passed the *Clean Water Act of 1972* (CWA) and thus redefined the country's approach to water pollution control. The Act set up a role for the federal government as main enforcer of US water quality programs.

Using two principles to manage water pollution, the Act set up a federal construction grant program to help cities build sewage treatment plants. It also required all direct industrial and municipal dischargers to treat their wastewater to best available technological standards before releasing it into waterways. The main goal of the CWA is to improve and maintain the quality of US waters. Additionally, it called for the restoration and maintenance of beneficial uses, including drinking, fishing, swimming and propagation of aquatic life. The CWA has curtailed the release of pollutants which affect the quality of US rivers. One notable example has been the spending of more than $100 billion by 1984 for the control of conventional pollutants, particularly oxygen-demanding wastes from municipal and industrial point sources (Smith, Alexander and Wolman, 1987; EPA, 1984).

The Act has been amended several times since 1972 and was significantly revised in 1987. At that time the emphasis shifted to control of toxic industrial pollutants and non-point sources of pollution, especially farm and urban runoff. This kind of pollution has increased over the years, even as stricter controls have succeeded in reducing water quality problems stemming from point sources, such as industrial discharges and municipal sewage treatment plants. The 1987 amendments also changed financial responsibility for construction of treatment plants from the federal loan program to state and local government loan funds. States were also given considerably more authority to control non-point sources and discharges of toxic pollutants.

A major difficulty in assessing the effects of pollution control programs versus the impact of other factors on national water quality has been the difficulty in obtaining reliable information on water quality trends in the nation's rivers. A related problem is the difficulty of finding reliable economic data on the value of the reduction of water pollution, even if the physical evidence could be found.

Freeman (1985) estimated that nearly half of the total benefits for controlling water pollution in the US could be attributed to improvements in water-based recreation opportunities. Conflicts between mining companies dumping toxic wastes into blue ribbon trout streams and sport fishers are classic examples. The New Mexico Department of Game and Fish has not stocked trout in several northern New Mexico streams for many years because these streams are biologically dead due to their close proximity to toxic mining operations. Recreation and environmental benefits resulting from cleaning up those streams, particularly where good trout fishing is already scarce, stands to bring considerable economic benefit.

Cooper (1995) addressed a similar problem when he used TCM to examine the relationship between agricultural practises and recreation benefits by linking recreation benefits with agricultural activities in the California Central Valley. He examined effects of contaminated irrigation run-off on waterfowl hunting and compared the value of water in recreational uses versus agricultural uses. Knowledge of these impacts provides important information in the formulation of more economically balanced policies.

Rangelands

The federal government administers more than 300 million acres of lands in the western US. The US Forest Service and Bureau of Land Management operate under a multiple use mandate, in which economic values of all uses must be balanced in setting up management plans. The *US Federal Lands Policy and Management Act of 1976* requires the Bureau of Land Management (BLM) to account for all uses of the lands in setting up management plans, presumably through competent economic analysis. While livestock grazing is a dominant use on most of this land, recent years have seen growing conflicts between livestock and outdoor recreation. The eleven western US states account for about 20 per cent of the US beef cattle and a higher proportion of its wildlife habitat.

Decisions about alternative uses of natural resources are being made constantly on public and private US rangelands. Two important competing uses of western rangelands are non-priced outdoor recreation and commercially produced livestock. Wildlife and livestock are two important competitors for grasses produced on these rangelands. This competition for forage occurs both on federally administered lands and on private ranches where forage supports publicly-owned wildlife.

One of the most important and emotional policy questions surrounds the pricing and allocation of livestock grazing permits on BLM and Forest Service lands. An implicit methodological question is how should prices and values derived for recreational hunting on the public lands be compared to the prices and values estimated for livestock uses of the same forage. Two important studies have been conducted that examined the elk–cattle tradeoffs, both in Arizona (Martin, Tinney and Gum, 1978; Cory and Martin, 1985). For different reasons, policy decisions on the pricing and quantity of state-supplied elk hunting licenses are especially important where elk compete with cattle on private ranch lands. Commercial economic choices face ranchers who must decide how much forage to allocate to cattle or elk which are hunted by fee-paying visitors.

The 1978 study showed that hunting values could be directly compared to cattle values and thus provide important information to decisionmakers. The value of all hunting in Arizona was compared to the value of all range beef cattle production in the same land area. The value of hunting was defined as what hunters would pay for the hunting experience rather than be deprived of it. The value of cattle produced by the same land was defined as the sum of rancher income and consumer surplus produced by lower final beef prices resulting from Arizona beef cattle production. The authors were careful to define 'value' for the two competitors in equivalent ways; they found the value of beef production to be over five times as large as that for hunting. This was an important study in searching for a production possibilities frontier between cattle ranching and hunting on a given land base, for it is this kind of study that is needed to resolve economic conflicts in a theoretically correct manner.

The 1985 study focused on the competition for grass by elk and cattle, but raised a more sophisticated economic question. The policy question of interest was changing the size of a wildlife herd and how it should be compared to the value of altering various activities, such as the size of a cattle herd. They recognized that knowing the total consumers' surplus generated by all hunting activity or the average consumers' surplus per trip gives no information that may be used to estimate the optimum numbers of cattle and game to be produced on a given range. Where cattle and game compete for the same forage resource, the economically optimum combination of cattle and game numbers is the desired decision. It is important to realize that the decision is much more complicated than merely eliminating one group or the other.

To make the optimum decision, the manager must know the value of the marginal game animal, the value of the marginal ox and the production possibilities tradeoff curve. Without being able to measure the economic value of the added recreation produced by additional wildlife when grass is freed up by a decision to reduce cattle numbers, the recreation value estimate has little value to managers who must make decisions. One very important issue facing recreation researchers is an ability to relate the size of wildlife herds and hunting success. A related issue is the relationship between hunting success and total recreation benefits of that added success. Neither of these two issues have been given much attention by economists and for that reason recreation values have had less influence on rangeland conflict resolution than could be the case.

Forests

Forests of the world produce many products, including timber, wildlife habitat, livestock grazing, water and recreation. Conflicts and tradeoffs between logging, wildlife habitat and outdoor recreation are several generations old on federal forest lands. One example of a recent forest management conflict between recreation and timber centers around a coalition of sportsmen and environmentalists who asked a federal court in September 1998 to halt logging in all 151 national forests on economic grounds.

The Tucson-based Southwest Center for Biological Diversity, a coalition of environmental groups, filed a lawsuit in the US District Court in San Francisco and sought an injunction against any logging in national forests. This coalition wants the US Forest Service to acknowledge that logging produces limited economic benefits. The Center claims that forest service reports indicate that hiking, rafting and fishing are more economically productive. According to them, the Forest Service issued a draft plan for the period 1995–2000 that showed that recreational activities in national forests, such as hiking, rafting and fishing, contributed 32 times as much income and jobs as the timber industry (*Albuquerque Journal*, 1998).

Whether or not these recreation benefits data are objective and correct remains to be seen, but this suit and similar cases certainly raise the question of the sign and size of economic values produced by various forms of recreation in national forests. It also raises questions about how those recreation values should be calculated and correlated with proposed policy actions, so balanced forest management policies can be formulated. Studies that correlate the demand for and benefits of outdoor recreation with numerous forest policy variables such as timber harvest levels, pest control expenditures and endangered species critical habitat plans could shed valuable information on economic impacts of proposed management plans. It could also help formulate more balanced plans.

Outdoor Recreation Facilities

A wide range of interrelated decisions faces managers of outdoor recreation facilities. Decisions include the basic questions of site acquisition and policy: which sites to buy, which to develop, what price to charge, which sites to improve or restore from decline and which to sell. In addition, there are questions pertaining to how each site should be configured to produce maximum public benefit with available resources. Examples include: how many trees should be planted, how many picnic tables, camping facilities and signs should be installed, how much should be spent on hiking trails, where trails should be built and at what point should fish hatcheries be built, rather than continuing to buy from outside sources?

More generally, the site quality question is 'what is the benefit-maximizing plan for altering programs and program elements to meet changes in public values?' None of these questions is easy to answer, but recreation demand models offer one method for planning for and organizing data on visitor use to be able to answer these questions.

APPLICATION TO OUTDOOR RECREATION PROGRAMS

Outdoor recreation programs compete with other programs for funds, labor and, where there are competing uses of natural resources, water, timber and other resources. For years, park and recreation managers established performance objectives related to opportunity- and facilities-based management. That is, recreation programs were set up to provide opportunities for recreation, such as a good fishing experience. Facilities to support recreation activities, such as concrete boat ramps, trash cans and hiking trails, were built. The problem with these aims is that they fail to distinguish between the process of management and its outputs. In recent years benefits-based management has been developed and embraced by many as a new way of formulating and evaluating outdoor recreation programs.

Benefits-Based Management (BBM)

All land and water management programs aim to provide benefits for people (Wagar, 1966). This basic principle applies to recreation, timber, power production or any other use of land or water. Nevertheless, recreation programs have always confronted special difficulties. As emphasized by Allen, Stevens and Harwell (1996), continued scarcity of public money and the public's perception of a lack of payoff of many recreational programs continue to create a climate where recreation and park managers are asked to account directly to the paying public in the face of flat or falling public tax revenues.

Recreation programs emphasize desired outcomes to respond to this skepticism and to establish better programs. Programs should address social problems facing communities and their citizens, not simply providing leisure recreation for the public (Borrie, B. 1998, pers. comm., 10 September). Because of the growing need for design, implementation and evaluation of program outputs, the BBM approach takes a fundamentally different view of management compared to opportunity- and facilities-based management. Two important points rate a mention.

First, BBM shifts the evaluation of recreation programs from a supply-based view, where programs are evaluated by miles of trails installed and feet of concrete boat ramps built, to benefits produced by the program. That is, instead of focusing on what managers want to provide, BBM emphasizes what people who use the program need and want. The challenge for the recreation manager is first to identify the needs and then to provide recreation opportunities that best meet those needs. The accountability does not just stop at providing opportunities, however. If managers can think in terms of the outcomes of their programs and facilities instead of just promoting use of well-established programs and facilities, then they have a better opportunity to document, judge and improve the value of their projects.

Secondly, it is politically more astute to move standards for evaluating recreation programs away from just fun and games, particularly where recreation programs are expensive and compete with more basic human needs, such as food and shelter. If managers measure success simply by the number of people participating, as at a fishing reservoir, with no indication of how valuable the experience is, then managers are unable to document the program's social worth.

Recreation planners may need to examine the values of outdoor recreation programs in terms of their impact on health, longevity and productivity. These will no doubt present difficult challenges in establishing dollar values of program outputs, particularly since costs are measured in money, but these programs will ultimately be held accountable.

BBM has attracted greatest interest from larger parks and recreation operations. These are the ones who most need to judge the worth of their programs by the outcomes for the community. BBM has also allowed some managers to break with traditions and initiate new programs and facilities aimed at under-served people in the community. Equally, it has the opportunity to give them a clearer sense of when to close down out-of-date programs. BBM works best where the needs and communities to be served are clearly identifiable.

One of the biggest barriers is the resistance of people within organizations who have run the same old programs and facilities year after year. These people measure their success by the fact that their programs are always full or close to capacity. Often they resent being asked to justify the social worth of their programs, or even give consideration as to whom they are serving.

A second barrier is the difficulty in measurement. Not only is there difficulty in identifying the outcomes but there is a lack of established scales, methodologies or analyses to draw upon. Even when identified, there is a difficulty of comparing the costs with benefits in any objective way. For example, how many reformed youth should society receive for $100,000 invested in youth programs? The difficulty of translating indicators of recreation program successes into operational recreation demand models such as discussed by this book will no doubt be a challenge. Nevertheless, properly estimated and interpreted demand models provide the basis for evaluating recreation programs and thus potentially have an important role in establishing objectives and implementing them.

APPLICATION TO FORECASTING

There are many factors beyond the direct control of project managers and environmental policy makers that nevertheless affect the demand for recreational facilities. Several demographic factors that characterize the population in a market area will influence recreational visitation. Examples include the distribution of age, ethnicity, income and education. Being able to use the relationship between demographic factors in an area and the demand for facilities enables forecasts to be made for future demands. While environmental and natural resource policy makers cannot directly influence the evolution of demographic factors, they can still enact laws or modify facilities to accompany these changes. In fact, one of the arguments that support democratic government and free markets is that these institutions respond better than their competitors to changes in people's wishes.

Economically efficient management decisions would accompany changes in future recreation demands in such a way as to produce the highest possible NPV of benefits. For example, in the realm of water policy, while income changes in a region are beyond the control of water resource managers, suppose rising regional income over time increases the demand for boats and reduces the demand for day-trip picnic outings. Where this occurs, increases in NPV can occur if water managers invest in more boat launch lanes and less in picnic tables. Similarly where per capita demands have been estimated for outdoor recreation, independent estimates of total population can be used to obtain estimates for future demand for facilities. That is, estimated total demand for some future year equals forecast per capita demand multiplied by forecast total population. Information provided by a recreation demand and benefits model could enable managers to make better decisions based on those forecasts in response to changing demographic or population patterns.

CONCLUSION: THE CHALLENGES

Presumably decisionmakers want enough information and authority to take actions that maximize the objectives of themselves or their clienteles. Outdoor recreation planners may wish to find the mix of programs, program elements and facilities that provides the greatest benefits. Multiple use natural resource management agencies presumably wish to implement plans that produce the greatest possible public benefit for their available resources.

Where recreation programs can be characterized by quantitative measures of inputs, where they produce a measurable output (e.g. visitor days) and where changes in the output can be linked reliably to measured changes in inputs, optimization models offer a powerful tool for managers. Managers who pursue an optimization approach would pose the question: what mix of program elements maximizes total recreation benefits from my limited resources?

A good example of this problem is faced by sport fishery managers who must produce fish and implement defensible fish stocking schedules. This represents a classical problem of public resource allocation in three related ways. First, it is difficult to formulate stocking schedules that allocate fish efficiently and equitably among competing demands at all sites, where the schedules are based on objectively-measurable benefits produced to the fishing public. Second, there rarely exists a single efficient and fair mechanism to coordinate stocking schedules among several managers within an agency who operate competitively to secure the quantities of fish they believe are necessary to satisfy their fishing public. Finally, few mechanisms that permit managers to make quick and easy adjustments to a steady stream of unexpected changes in fish market conditions are widely applied. These three problems are pervasive challenges to fishery managers who confront tight budgets, scarce water, limited hatchery supply of fish and changing demands by the fishing public (Cowley et al., 1998).

Changes to fish stocking programs can encounter administrative and political resistance if the changes are not founded in good science with clear objectives. As will be shown later in this book, TCMs offer one mechanism to link program inputs like numbers of fish stocked to program outputs like visitor days. For this reason, estimated recreation demand models are a potentially important first step for managers who wish to experiment with program optimization models.

BCA makes the explicit value judgement that if society aims to make the most beneficial uses of all its resources, then it should compare the values of what its individual members receive from any proposed environmental or natural resource policy action with the values of what its members give up by taking resources from other uses. Because benefits are valued in terms of their impacts on individuals' well-being, this book uses the terms 'economic value' and 'welfare change' and 'benefit' to mean the same thing.

In light of this discussion, what is needed is a monetary measure of an individual's gain in welfare brought about by an environmental or natural resource policy action. The policy action affects the decisions and behavior of environmental polluters or natural resource supplies. This behavior in turn affects the price, quantity or quality of the pollutant or natural resource. Thus, we need to conduct balanced and objective benefit cost analyses of these policies. The ability, limitations and required assumptions necessary for recreation demand models to adapt to these rather stringent requirements is examined in the remainder of this book.

REFERENCES

Allen, L.R., B. Stevens and R. Harwell (1996), 'Benefits-Based Management Activity Planning Model for Youth in At-Risk Environments', *Journal of Parks and Recreation Administration*, **14** (3), 10-19.

Arrow, K.J., M.L. Cropper, G.C. Eads, R.W. Hahn, L.B. Lave, R.G. Noll, P.R. Portney, M. Russell, R. Schmalensee, V.K. Smith and R.N. Stavins (1996), 'Is There A Role for Benefit-Cost Analysis in Environmental, Health and Safety Regulation?', *Science*, **272**, 221-2.

Albuquerque Journal (1998). 'National Forest Logging Ban Sought: Timber Sales Lose Money, Groups Say', September 11.

Benthem, J. (1780), *Principles of Morals and Legislation*, London: Oxford University Press (reprinted in 1823).

Bishop, R.C. and K.C. Samples (1980), 'Sport and Commercial Fishing Conflicts: A Theoretical Analysis', *Journal of Environmental Economics and Management*, **7** (3), 220-33.

Cooper, J.C. (1995), 'Using the Travel Cost Method to Link Waterfowl Hunting to Agricultural Activities', *Cahiers d'Economie et Sociologie Rurales,* **1** (36), 6-26.

Cory, D. and W.E. Martin (1985), 'Valuing Wildlife for Efficient Multiple Use: Elk Versus Cattle', *Western Journal of Agricultural Economics*, **10** (2), 282-93.

Cowley, D., F.A. Ward, M. Hatch and S. Hilty (1998), 'Development of a Procedure for Optimizing the Allocation of Hatchery Produced Trout', unpublished manuscript prepared for New Mexico Department of Game and Fish, August.

Crocker, T.D. (1985), 'On the Value of the Condition of a Forest Stock', *Land Economics,* **61**, 244-54.

Easley, J.E. (1992), 'Selected Issues in Modeling Allocation of Fishery Harvests',

Marine Resource Economics, **7** (2), 41-56.

EPA (US Environmental Protection Agency) (1984), *The Cost of Clean Air and Water,* Report to Congress 1984 (EPA 230/05-84-008), Washington: EPA.

Freeman, A.M III (1985), 'Methods for Assessing the Benefits of Environmental Programs', in A.V. Kneese and J.L. Sweeney (eds), *Handbook of Natural Resource and Energy Economics,* Volume I, New York: North-Holland.

Gren, I.M. (1995), 'The Value of Investing in Wetlands for Nitrogen Abatement', *European Review of Agricultural Economics,* **22** (2),157-72.

Hicks, J.R. (1939), 'The Foundation of Welfare Economics', *Economic Journal,* **49**, 696-712.

Hicks, J.R. (1956), *A Revision of Demand Theory,* Oxford: Oxford University Press.

Howe, C.W., D.R. Schurmeier and W.D. Shaw (1986), 'Innovative Approaches to Water Allocation: The Potential for Water Markets', *Water Resources Research,* **22** (4): 439-45.

Hughes, J. (1998), 'Federal Reservoirs Strain in New Role', *Albuquerque Journal,* September 9.

Kaldor, N. (1939), 'Welfare Propositions of Economics and Interpersonal Comparisons of Utility', *Economic Journal,* **49**, 549-52.

Lange, O. (1942), 'The Foundations of Welfare Economics', *Econometrica,* **10**, 215-28.

Lerner, A.P. (1944), *The Economics of Control: Principles of Welfare Economics,* New York: Macmillan.

Loomis, J.B. (1993), *Integrated Public Lands Management,* New York: Columbia University Press.

Martin, W.E., J.C. Tinney and R.L. Gum (1978), 'A Welfare Economic Analysis of the Potential Competition Between Hunting and Cattle Ranching', *Western Journal of Agricultural Economics,* **3** (2), 87-97.

Skitovsky, T. (1941), 'A Note on Welfare Propositions in Economics', *Review of Economic Studies,* **9**, 77-88.

Smith, R.A., R.B. Alexander and M.G. Wolman (1987), 'Water-Quality Trends in the Nation's Rivers', *Science,* **235**, 1607-15.

Szentandrasi, S., S. Polasky, R. Berrens and J. Leonard (1995), 'Conserving Biological Diversity and the Conservation Reserve Program', *Growth and Change,* **26,** 383-404.

Tietenberg, T. (1996), *Environmental and Natural Resource Economics,* New York: Harper Collins.

Vaux, H.J., P.D. Gardner and T.J. Mills (1984), *Methods for Assessing the Impact of Fire on Forest Recreation,* Pacific Southwest Range and Forest Experiment Station, General Technical Report PSW-79, Berkeley: US Forest Service.

Wagar, J.A. (1966), 'Quality in Outdoor Recreation', *Trends in Parks and Recreation,* **3** (3), 9-12.

Ward, F.A., M. Fraiser, J.F. Booker, R. Lacewell, J. Ellis and R.A. Young (1998), 'An Economic Hydrologic Modeling Approach for Assessing Alternative Institutional Innovations for Coping with Drought on an Interstate River', presented at American Agricultural Economics Association Meetings, Salt Lake City.

Ward, F.A., B.A. Roach and J. Henderson. (1996), 'The Economic Value of Water in Recreation: Evidence from the California Drought', *Water Resources Research,* **33** (5), 1075-82.

2. History and Scope of TCM

In this chapter we give a concise history of the origin of TCM and its early development. We then examine briefly the most significant advances over the last three decades or so, which will give you an appreciation of its scope. We then summarize what TCM does well, as you saw in Chapter 1 and what it cannot do. You might like to scan this chapter initially and come back and read it more thoroughly after you become familiar with the methodology. A more comprehensive examination of some of these issues is presented later in the book at appropriate points.

HISTORY OF TCM

The history of TCM is examined in this section in terms of the original proposal and execution, followed by a concise examination of later developments.

Original Suggestion and Execution

TCM has developed from a suggestion made by Harold Hotelling in 1947 in a release on the economics of recreation in US national parks by the National Park Service. The Service wanted to know how economic principles could be used to demonstrate economic values produced by national parks in the hope that parks could be shown to produce benefits exceeding costs to taxpayers. The Park Service contacted a number of prominent economists of the day to find out what could be done to value the parks. Among the many responses they received, only the one by Hotelling was based on solid economic principles. In retrospect this should have been little surprise, since Hotelling had already written what were then classic papers on mineral economics and on marginal cost pricing.

Hotelling suggested measuring differential travel rates according to travel distances that visitors overcame in reaching a park. Exploiting the empirical relationship between increased travel distances and associated declining visitation rates should permit one to estimate a true demand relationship. If estimated empirically, this demand schedule could be used to compute the total benefits produced to park visitors, which were equal to any entry fees they paid plus their remaining unpriced benefits, called consumer surplus

(Hotelling, 1949). It can be said that virtually all research on TCMs in the last 50 years has attempted to elaborate on Hotelling's original suggestion, either theoretically or empirically.

Early developers of the methodology had a clear view of their goal, based on the underlying theory of consumer choice. It was generally believed then and is still believed that development of a method to measure economic values of outdoor recreation and outdoor recreation policies should be based on underlying preferences of visitors and the economic constraints that govern their choices. Any methodology not based on actual visitor preferences and the economic constraints they confront usually generates nonsense numbers, which bear little relationship to the real worth of the resource in terms of what the resource users would be prepared to pay for it. Economics is fundamentally concerned with making resource allocation decisions where the outcome of the decision produces something for consumers and for which the worth of the decision can be expressed in monetary terms to people.

Building on the belief that the basis for valuation in human society is the benefit derived by people, further assumptions were made. These included: that values are based on benefits produced by using the good; and that goods for which there are currently no markets (non-market goods) may also give users a benefit and thus have value in the economic sense. The immediate problem was how to estimate the benefit or welfare derived from the non-market use of nature-based sites for recreation.

Demand functions for the natural and other resources needed to support these recreational goods, if they could be estimated, would give a measure of users' benefits and thus provide a basis for comparing them with the cost of their supply. A related driving force was the knowledge that unmeasured benefits are commonly ignored by both policy makers and managers, when compared with proposals that produce monetary benefits valued in commercial markets, such as agricultural or mineral outputs. The common result was that areas with significant recreational use and benefit tended to undergo development that displaced the recreational potential in favor of commercial uses (Krutilla, 1967).

Clawson (1959), Knetsch (1963) and later Clawson and Knetsch (1966) were instrumental in further development of TCM. Exploiting an assumption of predictability, that is, that the average of a large group of recreational users will react to costs as will another group of users and assuming recreationists would react to an entry fee in the same way as an increase in travel costs, Clawson and Knetsch (1966) showed how a zonal methodology (ZTCM) could be used to derive a demand curve for a site. Essentially, if a group of people with a travel cost of $5 reacted to that cost by visiting a site at the rate of 200 per 1000 population and if another group with $10 of travel cost visited at the rate of 100 per 1000 population, then it could be assumed that the rate of visits of the first group would drop to 100 per 1000, if an additional charge of $5 for entry to the site were imposed. By sequentially adding additional charges to travel costs, they were able to construct a demand curve for the resource itself, unaffected by the benefits arising from other recreational experiences which visitors enjoyed when visiting the site.

The derived demand curves estimated by Clawson and Knetsch appeared generally satisfactory. They exhibited a negative relationship between price and output, in accordance with demand theory. Elasticity (the responsiveness of the quantity demanded to small changes in price) values also appeared consistent with economic theory. The elasticity of the derived demand was generally less than the elasticity of demand for the whole recreational experience. The great economist, Alfred Marshall, described this derived demand phenomenon as early as 1890. Demand for components is generally less price sensitive than the demand for final products and the more essential the component, the more price inelastic is its demand.

Clawson and Knetsch, however, drew attention to a number of the practical problems that may arise from attempting empirical estimates. They were aware that demand for visits to sites was constrained by many factors apart from distance. Even distance could be further divided into separate constraints – money, time and travel – and money implied further determinants, travel costs and income. The importance of time depended on individuals' employment status and conditions. Further, travel could imply a cost or a benefit. Multi-site or multi-purpose visits posed another problem for cost allocation. Lack of adequate data was to be a persistent problem.

The need to incorporate the constraint of travel time led to the next major advance in the methodology. The zonal methodology suffers from two major limitations. First, it is difficult to account for the effects of travel time on individuals, because there is a high correlation between travel cost and travel time when individual experiences are averaged to estimate zonal values. To overcome multicollinearity in the regression analysis, travel time has to be omitted. Secondly, the aggregation and averaging process necessary to estimate zonal values usually is instrumental in making some demand determinants, particularly the socioeconomic variables, statistically non-significant. In effect, there is a loss of information efficiency.

Brown and Nawas (1973) and Gum and Martin (1974) developed a new form of TCM based on individual visitors, where the dependent variable, quantity consumed, is the number of trips taken per period by individuals or households (ITCM). This form is able to incorporate both travel time and travel cost and socioeconomic variables as demand shifters are often found to be statistically significant. However, there are still difficulties to be worked around. Firstly, visitors may typically take only one trip per period to some types of sites such as wilderness or big game hunting areas. This may be the result of legislation, cost or distance. Whatever the reason, the effect is that the dependent variable is often equal to one, no matter what values the independent variables take. This causes havoc with regression analysis. In addition, because only existing visitors are sampled, potential visitors are omitted from this framework and this causes an error of the estimated consumer surplus (Brown et al., 1983).

Solutions to these problems have been worked on by various economists interested in TCM. Some of these will be discussed later in this manual. In the meantime, we will examine some of the other issues which have intrigued developers of the methodology.

Developments since the 1960s

The three decades following the issue of Clawson and Knetsch's (1966) book have been characterized by the publication of empirical analyses and attempts to develop the methodology further. Walsh, Johnson and McKean (1992) conducted a survey of published and unpublished empirical studies in the US and found that 156 benefit estimates had been completed during the period 1968-88. During the same period, of course, there was additional activity among economists in other countries, although the volume of published material was small in relation to the output from the US. Moreover, there have been many more estimates and theoretical contributions made since 1988.

The purpose of the Walsh, Johnson and McKean study was to analyse empirical results to develop an understanding of the factors that are most important to predicting recreational use and benefit to the visitor. They were also concerned with attempting to identify additional variables which might have more explanatory power than those employed in past studies. Variables found to be significant at the 10 per cent level or greater were site quality; nature of site and the type of recreational experience it afforded, whether general or specialized; survey sample coverage, whether limited to in-state or not; travel time cost as a dummy variable; substitute price, also as a qualitative variable; and whether individual or zonal data were employed. Highly valued leisure activities such as big game hunting and anadromous fishing when included as independent variables were also found to be statistically significant predictors of visitor use and benefit.

In addition to the identification of statistically significant variables, this study confirmed theoretical expectations of the signs (the directions of the effects, whether positive or negative) of the coefficients relating to the explanatory variables. For example, site quality was found to have a positive effect on consumer welfare – the higher site quality was perceived to be by consumers, the higher the consumer benefit. Similarly, the use of individual data tended to increase the estimated value of consumer benefit in comparison with the use of zonal data. Conversely, the omission of the cost of travel time and the inclusion of the price of substitute sites or experiences tended to overstate the impacts of increased travel cost by itself and therefore depress estimated benefits.

Concurrently with the empirical estimate work, economists investigated theoretical issues with the aim of developing and refining the methodology. Clawson and Knetsch had foreshadowed many of these issues – the value of time, the separate effects of travel distance, travel time and on-site time, incorporation of multi-site or multi-purpose visits, the effect of substitutes and the effects of differences in socio-economic characteristics of populations. In addition, issues of concern included individual versus zonal models, which travel costs to include, length of visits, site quality, model specification and the effects of specification errors.

The value of time
The value of time is a complex issue, made more complex by the need to separate the valuation of travel time from on-site time.

The value of travel time   The value and cost of travel time have been issues vexing economists interested in the use of recreation or wilderness sites. Failure to account for the value of time will lead to under-estimation of consumer surpluses. The argument over the value of time stems from the notion in economics of opportunity cost. A person traveling to a recreation site bears the cost of not doing something else as well as the cash costs of the trip. The opportunity cost is thus the benefit or utility which could have been gained by doing the next best alternative activity in the time spent traveling to the recreation site. There are two fundamental concerns and a third troublesome issue to be considered.

The two fundamental concerns are the time pricing and time rationing issues. Regarding time pricing, is there a monetary opportunity cost in traveling to and from the site? In other words, have individual visitors given up an income earning opportunity to work for payment in order to travel for recreation? In a simple world characterized by the conventional labor supply model where there is a continuous trade-off between work and recreation, the opportunity cost of recreation is the monetary benefit (i.e. the individual's wages) and other benefits of work. However, in modern industrialized countries where many people work fixed hours and are provided with week-end and public holidays as well as paid recreation leave, this trade-off notion is often irrelevant, because such people take recreation at the appropriate times and there is no opportunity to work in those holiday times. On the other hand, the work-recreation trade-off may be applicable to self-employed people and for those who have opportunities to work in second and part-time employment. See Bockstael, Strand and Hanemann (1987) for discussion of a US situation and Beal (1995a) for an Australian case.

Apart from the situation where the opportunity cost involves time when income could be earned, there are many possible components of opportunity cost. Alternatives to recreation at a particular site may be voluntary work, participation in organized or self-managed sport, pottering around at home, doing manual crafts, reading, studying or indeed going to another site for recreation. The opportunity cost of going to the site in question is thus the foregone benefits of not doing one or more of those myriad other activities. The measurement and aggregation of those benefits would be fraught with difficulty for the researcher. On the other hand, if individuals maintain they have 'nothing else to do', the opportunity cost of the time spent on the visit is zero.

The second fundamental concern relates to time rationing. Distance as well as travel cost rations traveling so that, even if individuals do not give up opportunities to work, the opportunity cost of scarce time acts as a impediment to visiting more distant sites (Cesario and Knetsch, 1970). In addition, as noted above, estimates of consumer surpluses as measures of benefit produced by the natural resource are likely to be understated, if the expenditure of scarce time is not incorporated into analyses.

Cesario and Knetsch (1970) suggested that the cost of travel time should be estimated and added to the other travel costs. This solution would eliminate probable multicollinearity in regression analyses where travel cost and travel time are included as separate explanatory variables. They suggested the cost would be some proportion of the wage rate, but the choice would be arbitrary. Cesario (1976) summarized a number of studies of commuting and suggested travel time should be valued at one-third to one-half the wage rate. McConnell and Strand (1981) developed this theme further by suggesting that the cost would be some proportion (k) of each individual's wage rate and that the value of k could be determined by the usual estimation methods within regression analysis where travel time multiplied by the individual's income per hour is selected as the relevant variable. They estimated the value of k to be 0.6 of the wage rate.

Ward (1983) observed the ready disposition of visitors to trade travel time for cost and concluded the opportunity cost of travel was not necessarily related to an individual's wage rate. In a paper which discussed the difference between the concepts of 'value' and 'cost' with regard to leisure time, Shaw (1992) concurred that the opportunity cost of an individual's time is not necessarily related to the wage rate and that information on personal situations and preferences is necessary before appropriate assumptions can be made.

McKean, Johnson and Walsh (1995), building on Shaw's (1992) work, theorized that time rationing rather than time pricing may be more appropriate given labor market institutional considerations. They concluded increased survey information is necessary to apply an appropriate model to each individual. Casey, Vukina and Danielson (1995) agreed with this view.

The third issue concerns the point of how to accommodate cases where visitors gain utility or benefit from the travel itself. Walsh, Sanders and McKean (1990) raised the point that travel to and from a site may produce its own benefit that complements the trip destination, particularly where travel occurs through scenic or other desirable areas or where the trip is undertaken to get out of the same old behavior pattern. There would thus be the measurement of benefits as well as costs to deal with and an acceptable estimation of net travel cost would need to have the travel benefits deducted. As noted above in relation to the cash costs of travel, researchers are dealing with people's perceptions and only the individuals concerned can say whether traveling time associated with a particular destination results in net cost or net benefit beyond that of the end point itself.

The value of on-site time   Valuing on-site time has been another much discussed issue. McConnell argued the opportunity cost of on-site time should be included in the price variable, because failure to do so will bias downwards any estimated consumer surpluses. Cesario and Knetsch (1976) advocated exclusion. Wilman (1980) argued generally for exclusion, but developed a model incorporating inclusion in some circumstances. Smith, Desvousges and McGivney (1983) suggested the value of on-site time is relevant and related to the wage rate only indirectly through the income effect, if recreation time cannot be traded for work time. They found k to vary considerably between individuals. Ward (1984) proposed that on-site time be included as an endogenous demand determinant. Bockstael, Strand and Hanemann (1987) omitted on-site time from their model but showed the opportunity cost may be greater than the wage rate.

McConnell (1992) concluded that accounting for on-site time presents so difficult a problem that no systematic method had been developed, either conceptually or empirically. The valuation of on-site time has more relevance for estimates of the value of retaining natural areas in substantially unchanged condition than for estimation of demand equations for predictive purposes, because of the problem of the differential perception of costs by consumers. Time spent on-site provides visitors with benefits and it must be presumed in the absence of evidence to the contrary that the benefits are at least equal to the time cost and probably exceed it by a significant amount because visitors are willing to incur additional costs to travel.

Incorporating multi-site or multi-purpose trips
A further difficulty in the estimation of travel cost arises with those visitors for whom a visit to the target site is not the only purpose of the trip. Some visitors may spend time at a site and time during the same trip either camping or staying in accommodation elsewhere. In extreme cases, visitors may be traveling for some weeks or months and spend only one night at any individual site.

These multiple destination trips have received some consideration in the literature. The fixed costs of travel spread among a number of sites constitute joint costs. There is no single theoretically-acceptable method of allocating such costs. Thus, any method to allocate those joint costs to any single site must be arbitrary. Smith (1971) recommended that only the cost of traveling the marginal distance from a previous site be included but, as Ulph and Reynolds (1981) noted, this method can result in negative bias as a highly regarded site might be only a short distance from another stop-over site. Haspel and Johnson (1982) assigned part of total costs to each destination and then estimated separate site demand curves. Clough and Meister (1991) suggested adjustments to travel cost for multi-site visits may bias results and instead adjusted aggregate consumer surplus. Stoeckl (1993) in her study of Hinchinbrook Island in Queensland allocated costs according to the time spent on the island as a proportion of total time spent at sites nominated by visitors as being important to them on their trips.

Mendelsohn et al. (1992) reported a solution of combining a number of popular sites as a single joint site in order to overcome the multi-site problem. While this solution may be acceptable in some situations such as a group of lakes in close proximity where most of the lakes in the group are visited by recreationists in a single trip, it suffers from the problem of researcher-designated values, in that the researcher must define the group of sites. This solution does not advance the methodology for estimating demand for a single isolated site.

The problem that arises with most methods of cost allocation is that the allocation process reduces the apparent cost to the point where it undermines the basis of the methodology. TCM relies on the central tenet that demand falls to low levels when prices rise to high levels. Accordingly, a given site will be visited by few people from far distant origins because costs will be high. Yet, once that cost is split between a number of destinations, the allocated cost is much lower. In Stoeckl's (1993) study, for example, visitors to Hinchinbrook Island from Townsville, 100 km distant, paid an average of $389 per person in travel costs yet visitors from Tasmania, 2000 km distant, paid an average of $187 in travel costs, the incongruity being due to the cost allocation formula.

On the other hand, cost allocation might be justified on the basis that multi-site visitors did not value the site in question highly enough to spend their whole recreation time there. In contradiction, Sorg et al. (1985) found by use of contingent valuation methods that multiple-destination visitors interested in fishing actually placed a higher value on the particular site than single-destination visitors.

The effect of substitutes
Demand theory postulates that the demand for a good is related to the prices and qualities of substitutes as well as its own price and other factors. Some recreation researchers have attempted to incorporate the prices and qualities of substitute sites in their models. Ribaudo and Epp (1984) deleted substitute prices from their demand function for a given site on the basis of near-perfect collinearity of the substitute sites with the price of the given site. Had they kept the substitute site price variables in the regression equation, the near perfect correlation with the price of the given site would have made it impossible to disentangle statistically the separate effects of the given site from that of the substitutes.

Caulkins, Bishop and Bouwes (1985) found the omission of substitute prices biased the estimation of the slope of the demand curve and that the algebraic sign of the bias depended on the correlation between the own price and the prices of the substitutes. If the correlation between the prices is positive, then omitting the substitute prices biases the own price elasticity towards zero. This means that the price elasticity produced by the regression analysis will be closer to zero than an estimated price elasticity produced by an experiment of raising the site entry fee to all visitors. Conversely, if the travel costs at the various substitute sites are negatively correlated, the estimated own price coefficient will be overstated. The sign of the correlation among the travel costs depends on the spatial distribution of the visitor population relative to the location of the sites. Similarly, Rosenthal (1987) reported prices of substitutes were necessary for the estimation of demand curves, omission causing bias in the estimated consumer surplus. Kling (1989) found omission of the substitute price does *not* bias the estimate of a single price coefficient, if own and substitute prices are uncorrelated.

So the tradeoff we face as TCM researchers is typically to choose one of two paths. We can follow the theoretically correct path of keeping all prices in the model, but risk high correlation among the price variables, which produces poor standard errors and unstable estimated elasticities. Or we can follow what may seem to be the safer path of deleting the substitute site prices. Unfortunately, this produces biased but stable price elasticities.

Apart from these technical considerations related to the statistical estimation of the coefficients in the demand equation by regression analysis, there is the related issue of whether national parks encompassing unique ecosystems or outstanding natural features have any substitutes. Visitors with a keen interest in nature-based recreation and the more technical aspects of ecology may believe that each national park is unique and has no substitute. Conversely, for some people other forms of outdoor recreation, such as water-skiing at a local Corps of Engineers reservoir, or other forms of recreation in general, such as going to a movie, are substitutes for outdoor nature-based recreation in national parks.

Freeman (1993) approached the substitute site dilemma by suggesting researchers ask visitors which other single site is visited frequently and include only that site's price as the relevant substitute price. The difficulty with this approach is that many sites will be named and, while the substitute site for one visitor may be another national park, the substitute site for another person may be, for example, a theme park or watching a sporting event. Freeman (1993) asserted the next-best site yielding similar attributes (a national park in this case) is the appropriate alternative and warned that care must be taken to avoid violation of the property of Independence of Irrelevant Alternatives (IIR) which may occur when two or more different types of recreational resources are included in the choice set.

As an alternative to user-defined substitutes, researchers could hypothesize sites that constitute substitutes for the site to be valued, then test their hypothesis by using the regression model itself. Random utility models (RUMs) or discrete choice models usually focus on the choice of a site for recreation among a set of sites which are considered to be substitutes, such as a group of lakes for fishers. However, Vaske, Donnelly and Tweed (1983) found that their researcher-defined substitutes were not statistically related to user-defined substitutes. Stoeckl (1993) concluded that a model incorporating researcher-imposed values for substitutes may well be as inaccurate as one which ignores other goods. Peters, Adamowicz and Boxall (1995) investigated the effect on welfare estimates of individual users' specifying their own sets of substitute sites over the more usual researcher-designated choice set in a RUM analysis. They found the welfare measures were significantly different when individually specified sets are used and concluded that researcher-designated substitutes had little validity even within a closely defined region.

RUM analysis is suitable for use when the demand choice rests on the quality of substitute sites. It has been used extensively, for example, to value changes in specific characteristics of a site, such as water quality or fish catch rates (Bockstael, McConnell and Strand, 1991). More recently, a more advanced model has been developed which incorporates choice of site and frequency of visits (Yen and Adamowicz, 1994). RUM analyses do not produce conventional demand curves. The issue of how to define substitute sites to be theoretically consistent with choices actually facing visitors, while producing theoretically and statistically acceptable estimates of price elasticity is still a very important issue and will no doubt see considerable attention in economics journals in the years ahead.

The effect of demographic characteristics

Age, sex, family composition, race, income, education, occupation and other demographic characteristics of consumers can have a bearing on the pattern of visitation to an outdoor recreation site. Studies using ZTCM are forced to aggregate zonal data so that an average value of each demographic variable is used for each zone. Averages may differ little among zones so that the coefficients of the socio-economic variables may be found to be not statistically distinguishable from zero. However, some ZTCMs based on US counties have found that demographic factors, such as per capita income, ethnic diversity, education and age composition of the family, differ considerably among zones and that these differences have an important influence on outdoor recreation use patterns. That is, ethnic characteristics, per capita income and related factors that vary considerably from one county to the next are highly correlated with differential visitation rates from those counties to a given site.

Statistically non-significant variables are normally deleted from final equations used in demand estimation. Hence demand equations estimated by zonal methodology often contain no demographic variables. The effect on estimated consumer surplus depends on the relative signs and magnitudes of the dropped variables. This finding supports the more general principle that greater aggregation in defining sampling units for site visitors reduces the number of variables that will enter a regression equation with acceptable statistical significance. However, greater aggregation will typically produce an apparently more appropriate model which explains a greater percentage of variation in use.

Zonal, individual or hybrid TCM

As we have seen, there are two basic approaches to TCM, the zonal travel cost method and the individual travel cost method. ZTCM has lesser data requirements and adjusts automatically for frequency of participation by recreationists (Bergstrom and Cordell, 1991). That is, zones that are farther away from the site of interest will produce both fewer trips for given individuals and smaller frequencies of households taking trips.

The dependent variable in the ITCM is the number of trips per period made to a site by each individual. Practically, this approach works best when individuals take a highly variable number of trips in the period to the site. However, where recreation sites are greater than two or three hours' driving time distant from their homes, multiple visits by consumers to a given site are less common and probably a better variable is either the probability of participation or the rate of participation per capita (Walsh 1986, p.217). Brown et al. (1983) suggested a combination of the individual and per capita approaches where the number of trips by each user in a sample is scaled up to represent the zonal total use and then divided by the zonal population adjusted to user 'shares', that is, population of the zone divided by the number of users.

The most important issues raised by consideration of the ZTCM dependent variable are the loss of information by aggregation into zones, the definition of zones and the problem of zones with zero visitation. The zonal approach aggregates observations relating to individual consumers and thus each zone is represented by a single average travel cost or a single value for each of the other variables included in the analysis. The averaging process reduces the apparent variability across zones and thus the statistical tests of various aspects of the regression analysis may give the appearance of better coefficients and a better fit of the regression equation than would be the case with the use of individual observations (Walsh 1986, p.225).

Originally in the Clawson and Knetsch (1966) methodology, concentric zones were identified around the site so that the distances to the site from each zone were approximately the same. This was conducive to ease of calculation of travel costs. Later it was realized that definition of zones in terms of administrative units or regions had decided advantages in that population data could be obtained from official collections and were more accurate.

Theoretically, as distance increases, the price (cost) of visiting a park will increase and ultimately reach a point where there will be no demand. In terms of conventional demand theory, the curve cuts the price axis and demand is zero. Economists often refer to this upper end of the demand function as the 'choke' price. Others refer to this point as the outside boundary of the market area. When working with empirical data, especially small samples, however, there may be many zones with zero visitation rates, some near and some far from the recreation site. This consequence depends, in part, on sample size and on the way zones are defined. Nevertheless there may appear to be no unique choke price. Necessarily, in this case some of the further zones will have positive visitation rates at higher prices. Some researchers opt to omit zones with zero visitation rates to avoid having a range of observations along the cost axis with zero demand. An alternative solution is to change the basis of the definition of zones. The question of how to best deal with the 'zero visit problem' still raises very lively debate among practitioners and theoreticians and a definitive solution is yet to be seen.

Which travel costs?
TCM uses the cash costs directly incurred by visitors to travel to a given site to estimate a demand equation for that site. The question arises as to which cash costs should be included. Some researchers have investigated closely the costs of fuel, oil, tires, repairs and maintenance for vehicles to estimate appropriate travel costs. A demand curve is, however, a model of consumer behavior. If it is to be used to predict the quantity of a good which potential consumers will demand at various prices, then the relevant prices are those that potential consumers perceive as the prices. Consumers can only react to what they perceive to be the trip's cost when they are making the decision to undertake the journey. If, for example, two tires blow out during the trip and the replacements cost $300, they cannot then decide against taking the trip, because the actual cost has increased. While this cost is a relevant economic cost for an analyst working after the fact, it has no bearing on the visitor's decision made some time earlier to demand a visit. Recognizing this, Seller, Stoll and Chavas (1985) used only the cost of fuel among the range of

possible vehicle costs on the basis that these costs are most easily recognized by travelers as the relevant costs. However, they also included in their demand equation other variable costs such as accommodation and food costs additional to those that would have been incurred had the travelers stayed at home.

Beal (1995b) reported an investigation into which costs visitors to an Australian national park perceived as relevant to their trip decision. She found only a minority of respondents considered all relevant costs. Most considered fuel, food and accommodation costs; a minority took into consideration servicing, tire and other vehicle repairs and the cost of unforeseen incidentals. The differences in the perception of costs among consumers raises the issue whether consumers are able to respond to surveys in any meaningful way. Even if the survey questions are highly structured and allow users to report every class of cost incurred, consumers still may not have responded to the aggregate of these costs in their demand behavior. As Stoeckl (1993) noted, individuals may believe they are paying less than a researcher who estimates economic costs believes to be the case. Thus, any increase in park entry fees will be viewed by them as proportionately greater.

Where this occurs, the TCM-estimated demand curve will be less price elastic than the theoretically correct one. One possible approach for resolving this ambiguity and similar difficulties of estimating a TCM is to find a situation where policymakers are willing to experiment with a variety of entry fees at a single site in a fairly short period of time. Then a theoretically correct demand function could be estimated based on tracking how visitors respond to varying the entry fees. This elasticity could then be compared with TCMs estimated according to several definitions of travel cost, travel time, on site time and the like. Armed with a known price elasticity, one could observe which definition of price in the TCM estimated equation produced an estimated elasticity closest to the known correct one.

The effect of the visit length

Dealing with visits of different duration has proved difficult for researchers, because on-site time has implications for both the costs of the trip and the utility derived from each trip. It is reasonable to expect people traveling a long distance to a destination to stay longer than those traveling a shorter distance, to make up for the high cost of getting there. Exceptions to this expectation occur, however, especially in relation to parks used as stop-overs on long journeys. The visitation pattern of such parks may exhibit a negative relationship between distance traveled and length of stay.

Numerous researchers have investigated how decisions regarding recreation are made by consumers. Kealy and Bishop (1986) hypothesized that individuals choose the maximum number of recreation days per year and take these in a variable number of trips as suits their circumstances. Wilman (1987) reported a model where visitors minimize the cost of the total number of recreation days. Constant duration-of-stay demand curves could then be estimated. McConnell (1992) investigated the implications of alternative assumptions in the context of day visits – either time on-site being chosen for each trip, or on-site time being exogenous. Larsen (1993) hypothesized that individuals chose both total time at sites and the number of trips, thereby implicitly choosing the average on-site time; on-site time is therefore chosen simultaneously with length of stay.

One solution to the representation of stays of varying duration is to treat visits of different periods as separate products and estimate a separate demand curve for the most frequently observed duration. The separate curves could then be aggregated horizontally to estimate an aggregate demand curve for camping at the park.

Site quality and congestion in recreation areas

The quality of natural sites used for outdoor recreation varies widely. At one end of the spectrum, there are public parks in cities or well-used lakes, which are littered with the usual collection of consumer trash (deliberate degradation) and show severe environmental (unwitting) degradation. At the other end of the spectrum, there are wilderness areas, which are substantially undegraded on both counts. In between, there are sites with varying degrees of littering and ecological wear. In addition to the state of sites, a further aspect of quality is the degree of crowding or congestion, which has a bearing on the quality of experience enjoyed by visitors. Moreover, site quality can be thought of as a decision variable under the control of park managers who stock fish and build boat ramps, as well as factors chosen by regional and national political bodies, such as US state legislatures and Congress. For these agencies, a major question pertaining to site quality is what level of quality to establish, given that higher quality costs more, but it also produces greater benefits.

Congestion is a very special attribute of site quality that poses some very difficult analytical questions. Congestion is both an independent variable influencing use of the site while also being implicit in the dependent variable. It occurs at many publicly-managed outdoor recreation sites because the normal rationing mechanism of price does not operate effectively. In contrast, private recreation enterprises may increase fees at peak demand periods to manage demand. For example, green fees at golf courses or ski lift fees may vary throughout the week. Price is a rationing device which regulates the allocation or distribution of the goods among those who desire to consume or use them. However, where an entrance fee is minimal or zero, price fails to ration entry to those with the highest value use and congestion is a widespread problem.

Congestion is both a sociological and an ecological issue. The sociological aspects of congestion involve both physical density (numbers of visitors in a given area) and the perceptions and preferences or susceptibilities of visitors. In addition, the on-site use of natural areas by people for any purpose produces change. Ecologically, that change may be small or large and temporary or permanent.

A lively discussion developed in the economics literature over the effect of congestion on consumer surplus and how congestion should be incorporated into the TCM. Wetzel (1977) showed that TCMs that fail to account for congestion produce underestimated recreation benefits at sites affected by congestion. Commenting on Wetzel's work, McConnell (1980) found that demand curves should be estimated with congestion held constant and that proper measurement of consumer surplus depended on correct sampling and specification of the demand function.

Congestion of recreation areas has attracted a good deal of interest in disciplines apart from economics. Lime and Stankey (1971) compiled a bibliography of more than 200 references on the subject, covering both the ecological and sociological aspects. Numerous papers have been written since (see, for example, Kuss, Graefe and Vaske, 1990). As population continues to grow around the world, the issue of how to manage high densities of people at outdoor recreation sites, most of whom desire an escape from high densities elsewhere, will continue to be important.

Selection of the recreational demand model and specification error

Researchers using TCM have overwhelmingly favored ordinary least squares (OLS) regression analysis as their data analysis technique. Multivariate regression has been found to be appropriate in research using national household recreation surveys, while simpler two variable models have often been found to be more suitable for surveys involving users of particular sites (Walsh 1986, p.158).

The specified model of visitor behavior should be consistent with economic theory. This theory hypothesizes that visitors' decisions are governed by their preferences and are limited by their time and income constraints. Thus the algebraic form of the model should reflect what is believed to be the relationships between the variables of the system under study. In addition, the analyst should expect algebraic signs of the estimated coefficients to reflect the nature of the relationship indicated by theory.

A number of algebraic forms of a TCM demand model are consistent with demand theory. Equations for these forms are described in some detail in a later chapter. Linear relationships are the most commonly estimated and easiest to understand, manipulate, interpret and explain to managers and policymakers. Other forms such as quadratic, reciprocal, linear-log, log-linear and double log have also been reported. Luzar, Hotvedt and Gan (1992) used linear, log-linear and double log functional specifications and opted for the double log form in their study of deer hunting in Louisiana. Knapman and Stanley (1991) in their study of Kakadu National Park rejected the double log form and used a reciprocal model.

The double log or multiplicative form is commonly used, because it takes into account extreme values of visits or travel costs. In other words, it can accommodate, for example, those few visitors who value a site so highly that they would pay thousands of dollars for a visit. While this may seem attractive, this capability is seen by some researchers to be a fault (e.g. Knapman and Stanley, 1991), because the curve is asymptotic to both the price and output axes, so that there is no defined choke price nor a defined upper limit on output (Cheshire and Stabler, 1976). In this case if price elasticity is less than one in absolute terms, calculated consumer surplus is infinite unless the analyst places some upper limit on price.

A number of researchers have reported the effects of specification errors in recreation demand models (Wetzstein and McNeely, 1980; Ziemer, Musser and Hill, 1980; Adamowicz, Fletcher and Graham Tomasi, 1989). Bockstael and Strand (1987) related benefit estimates to sources of error in the demand specification. They were particularly interested in the effects of omitted variables, measurement error in the dependent variable and random behavior. They concluded that, if researchers assumed error resulted from omitted variables alone, they are likely to overestimate consumer surplus. On the other hand, if researchers attribute error to inaccurately measured numbers of trips, then consumer surplus is likely to be underestimated.

Smith (1988) and Bockstael et al. (1990) considered the implications of biases in sample selection. Smith found, in relation to local recreation sites, that sample selection effects from on-site surveys do not lead to important changes in the qualitative description in the determinants of site demand, nor would have any effects distorted any policy recommendations. Bockstael et al. (1990) explored methods of correcting for sample selection bias.

WHAT TCM CAN AND CANNOT DO

According to Smith (1993) TCM is one of the unambiguous successes in natural resource valuation methodology and occupies a major place in the applied research programs of environmental economists. This conclusion has been supported by Ward and Loomis (1986) and Bockstael, McConnell and Strand (1991). Its use has also been supported by the US and other public administrations for a wide variety of applications, as has been noted previously.

In justifying his view, Smith (1993) described evidence found in empirical studies that consistently point to four attractive features of TCM. First, estimates are generally consistent with what consumer demand theory tells us to expect, in that quantity demanded is negatively related to price, other things held constant.

Second, there is a broad consistency in the relative magnitudes of price and income elasticities. Different types of sites produce the differences in elasticities that would be intuitively expected. Demand for sites with numerous substitutes, for example, has been found to be more price sensitive than those with few alternatives. For example, the TCM-estimated demand for Corps of Engineers reservoirs in California's Central Valley were very price elastic, as would be expected given the high quality of substitute outdoor recreation in the nearby Sierra Nevada Mountains and Pacific Ocean. As expected, equivalent TCM-estimated demands for Corps reservoirs in the southeastern US, where there are fewer good quality outdoor recreation substitutes, were found to be much less price elastic (Ward, Roach and Henderson, 1996). This consistency of price and income elasticities produced by TCMs has major policy implications. The pronounced difference in price elasticities due to different substitute opportunities means that it is better economics to invest in maintaining recreation at Corps reservoirs in the southeast than in the California Central Valley. Even if improvements such as fish stocking or building boat ramps cost the same in both regions, it is better economics to put the improvements in areas where there are fewer good substitutes.

Thirdly, estimates of demand are sensitive to the assumptions and judgements made during the modeling process and thus exhibit strong connections to underlying preferences, motivations and behavior constraints. Finally, controlled experiments have endorsed the method's ability to characterize underlying consumer preferences. Kling's (1988) work comparing estimates of welfare changes resulting from changes in environmental quality provides a good example.

TCM has been used principally to value the benefits provided by nature-based recreation sites, rather than to estimate the value of changes in the quality of services. Attempts have been made in recent years to use the method to evaluate quality changes and this use will be discussed elsewhere in this book.

Limits of TCM

TCM is designed to capture recreational use values or benefits produced by a natural resource or natural resource policy. However, many environmental goods and sites such as national parks have considerable public good characteristics. Public goods are those goods which are non-excludable and non-rival in consumption. This means that, once they exist or are provided, no potential consumer can be prevented from enjoying the good, nor does one person's use preclude another person from enjoying the good. Indirect valuation methods such as TCM are incapable of capturing these benefits.

The volume of literature exploring just what constitutes the suite of non-use public good benefits has grown spectacularly in the last two to three decades. The many public good benefits may be divided into six broad categories:

- existence value – the value of the knowledge that a natural resource exists;
- option value – the value of retaining the option to use the resource in the future;
- quasi-option value – the value of the opportunity to obtain better information in the future by delaying a decision to use in a way that might lead to loss;
- bequest value – the value of knowledge that the resource has been retained for the benefit and use of future generations;
- stewardship value – the value of knowledge that the resource is managed as well as possible to preserve its values; and
- vicarious value – the value of indirect consumption of a resource through print and other media.

Contingent valuation (CV) methodology has been developed to deal with the estimation of non-use benefits. Cummings, Brookshire and Schulze (1986) and Mitchell and Carson (1989) gave comprehensive assessments of the use of CV methodology.

One of the areas of interest to state managers of natural resources is the extent of regional economic impact of various development decisions. So far in this chapter we have confined our discussion to issues related to the estimation of economic effects of the use of resources by individuals. Collectively, however, use by individuals has regional or whole-of-society effects and regional or state managers may wish to measure the current economic impacts or, alternatively, how some projected changes or developments will impact on the region.

TCM cannot perform the whole task of measuring the regional impacts. Nevertheless, TCM can be used as one of the building blocks in the analysis by providing estimates of use after the completion of various developments. Combined with estimates of average per capita expenditure, use data will give estimated total expenditures. From these data, many other estimates of economic variables can be computed – changes in output, increases in employment, changes in taxation collections and so on. Regional applications are discussed later in this book.

CONCLUSION

In this chapter, we have outlined the bases from which economists have developed the TCM for valuing the benefits gained by visitors to outdoor nature-based recreational sites. We have examined the development of the basic technique and have briefly discussed some of the theoretical issues which have concerned economists in the last three decades. We will revisit some of these issues later in this book. Finally in this chapter, we have recapitulated the role of TCM and noted what the technique cannot achieve.

REFERENCES

Adamowicz, W.L., G.L. Fletcher and T. Graham-Tomasi (1989), 'Functional Form and the Statistical Properties of Welfare Measures', *American Journal of Agricultural Economics*, **71**, 414-21.

Beal, D.J. (1995a), 'The Cost of Time in Travel Cost Analyses of Demand for Recreational Use of Natural Areas', *Australian Journal of Leisure and Recreation*, **5** (1), 9-13.

Beal, D.J. (1995b), 'Sources of Variation in Estimates of Cost Reported by Respondents in Travel Cost Surveys', *Australian Journal of Leisure and Recreation*, **5** (1), 3-8.

Bergstrom, J.C. and H.K. Cordell (1991), 'An Analysis of the Demand for and Value of Outdoor Recreation in the US', *Journal of Leisure Research*, **23** (1), 67-86.

Bockstael, N.E., K.E. McConnell and I. Strand (1991), 'Recreation' in J.B. Braden and C.D. Kolstad (eds), *Measuring the Demand for Environmental Quality*, Amsterdam: Elsevier.

Bockstael, N.E. and I.E. Strand (1987), 'The Effect of Common Sources of Regression Error on Benefit Estimates', *Land Economics*, **83**, 11-18.

Bockstael, N.E., I.E. Strand and W.M. Hanemann (1987), 'Time and the Recreational Demand Model', *American Journal of Agricultural Economics*, **69** (2), 293-302.

Bockstael, N.E., I.E. Strand, K.E McConnell and F. Arsanjani (1990), 'Sample Selection Bias in the Estimation of Recreation Demand Functions: An Application to Sportfishing', *Land Economics*, **66**: 40-49.

Brown, W.G. and F. Nawas (1973) 'Impact of Aggregation on the Estimation of Outdoor Recreation Demand Functions', *American Journal of Agricultural Economics*, **55**, 246-9.

Brown, W.G., C. Sorhus, B. Chou-Yang and J.A. Richards (1983) 'Using Individual Observations to Estimate Recreation Demand Functions: A Caution', *American Journal of Agricultural Economics*, **65** (1), 154-7.

Casey, J.F., T. Vukina and L.E. Danielson (1995), 'The Economic Value of Hiking: Further Considerations of the Opportunity Cost of Time in Recreational Demand Models', *Journal of Agricultural and Applied Economics*, **27** (2), 658-68.

Caulkins, P.P., R.C. Bishop and N.W. Bouwes Snr. (1986), 'The Travel Cost Model for Lake Recreation: A Comparison of Two Methods for Incorporating Site Quality and Substitution Effects', *American Journal of Agricultural Economics*, **68** (2), 291-97.

Cesario, F.J. (1976), 'Value of Time in Recreation Benefit Studies', *Land Economics*, **51** (2), 32-41.

Cesario, F.J. and J.L. Knetsch (1970), 'Time Bias in Recreation Benefit Estimates', *Water Resources Research*, **6**, 700-704.

Cheshire, P.C. and M.J. Stabler (1976), 'Joint Consumption Benefits in Recreational Site Surplus: An Empirical Estimate', *Regional Studies*, **10**, 97-104.

Clawson, M. (1959), *Methods of Measuring the Demand for and Value of Outdoor Recreation*, Reprint no. 10, Washington: Resources for the Future.

Clawson, M. and J.L. Knetsch (1966), *Economics of Outdoor Recreation*, Washington: Johns Hopkins University Press for Resources for the Future.

Clough, P.W.J. and A.D. Meister (1991), 'Allowing for Multiple-Site Visitors in Travel Cost Analysis', *Journal of Environmental Management*, **32**, 115-25.

Cummings, R.G., D.S Brookshire. and W.D. Schulze (eds) (1986), *Valuing Environmental Goods: An Assessment of the Contingent Valuation Method*, New Jersey: Rowman and Allanheld.

Freeman, A.M.III (1993), *The Measurement of Environmental and Resource Values: Theory and Methods,* Washington: Resources for the Future.

Gum, R.L. and W.E. Martin (1974), 'Problems and Solutions in Estimating the Demand for and Value of Rural Outdoor Recreation', *American Journal of Agricultural Economics*, **56**, 558-66.

Haspel, A.E. and F.R. Johnson (1982), 'Multiple Destination Trip Bias in Recreation Benefit Estimation', *Land Economics*, **58**, 364-72.

Hotelling, H. (1947), 'The Economics of Public Recreation', The Prewitt Report, Washington: National Parks Service.

Kealy, M.J. and R.C. Bishop (1986), 'Theoretical and Empirical Specifications Issues in Travel Cost Demand Studies', *American Journal of Agricultural Economics*, **68**, 660-7.

Kling, C.L. (1988), 'Comparing Welfare Estimates of Environmental Quality Changes from Recreation Demand Models', *Journal of Environmental Economics and Management*, **15**, 331-40.

Kling, C.L. (1989), 'A Note on the Welfare Effects of Omitting Substitute Prices and Qualities from Travel Cost Models', *Land Economics*, **65**, 290-6.

Knapman, B. and O. Stanley (1991), *A Travel Cost Analysis of the Recreation Use Value of Kakadu National Park*, Resource Assessment Commission, Kakadu Conservation Zone Inquiry Consultancy Series, Canberra: AGPS.

Knetsch, J.L. (1963), 'Outdoor Recreation Demands and Values', *Land Economics*, **39**, 387-96.

Krutilla, J.V. (1967), 'Conservation Reconsidered', *American Economic Review*, **57**, 777-86.

Kuss, F.R., A.R Graefe and J.J. Vaske (1990), *Visitor Impact Management: A Review of Research*, Washington: National Parks and Conservation Association.

Larsen, D.M. (1993), 'Joint Recreational Choices and the Implied Value of Time', *Land Economics*, **69** (3), 270-86.

Lime, D.W. and G.H. Stankey (1971), *A Selected Bibliography of Literature Related to Recreational Carrying Capacity Decision Making*, Forest Recreation Symposium, Syracuse, New York: School of Forestry.

Luzar, E.J., J.E. Hotvedt and C. Gan (1992), 'Economic Valuation of Deer Hunting on Louisiana Public Land: A Travel Cost Analysis', *Journal of Leisure Research*, **24** (2), 99-113.

McConnell, K.E. (1980), 'Valuing Congested Recreation Sites', *Journal of Environmental Economics and Management*, **7**, 389-94.

McConnell, K.E. (1992), 'On-Site Time in the Demand for Recreation', *American Journal of Agricultural Economics*, **74**, 918-25.

McConnell, K.E. and I. Strand (1981), 'Measuring the Cost of Time in Recreation Demand Analysis: An Application to Sportfishing', *American Journal of Agricultural Economics*, **63** (1), 153-6.

McKean, J.R., D.M Johnson and R.G. Walsh (1995), 'Valuing Time in Travel Cost Demand Analysis: An Empirical Investigation', *Land Economics*, **71** (1), 96-105.

Mitchell, R.C. and R.T. Carson (1989), *Using Surveys to Value Public Goods: The Contingent Valuation Method*, Washington: Resources for the Future.

Peters, T., W.L. Adamowicz and P.C. Boxall (1995), 'Influence of Choice Set Considerations in Modelling the Benefits from Improved Water Quality', *Water Resources Research*, **31** (7), 1781-7.

Ribaudo, M.O. and D.J. Epp (1984), 'The Importance of Sample Discrimination in Using the Travel Cost Model to Estimate the Benefit of Improved Water Quality', *Land Economics*, **60**, 397-403.

Rosenthal, D.H. (1987), 'The Necessity for Substitute Prices in Recreation Demand Analyses', *American Journal of Agricultural Economics*, **69** (4), 828-37.

Seller, C., J.R. Stoll and J. Chavas (1985), 'Validation of Empirical Measures of Welfare Change: A Comparison of Nonmarket Techniques', *Land Economics*, **61** (2), 156-75.

Shaw, W.D. (1992), 'Searching for the Opportunity Cost of an Individual's Time', *Land Economics*, **68**, 107-15.

Smith, R.J. (1971), 'The Evaluation of Recreational Benefits: The Clawson Method in Practice', *Urban Studies*, **8**, 89-102.

Smith, V.K. (1993), 'Nonmarket Valuation of Environmental Resources: An Interpretive Appraisal', *Land Economics*, **69** (1), 1-26.

Smith, V.K. (1988), 'Selection and Recreation Demand', *American Journal of Agricultural Economics*, **70**, 29-36.

Smith, V.K., W.H. Desvousges and M.P. McGivney (1983), 'The Opportunity Cost of Travel Time in Recreation Demand Models', *Land Economics*, **59**, 259-78.

Sorg, C., J. Loomis, D. Donnelly, G. Peterson and L. Nelson (1985), *Net Economic Value of Cold and Warm Water Fishing in Idaho*, Resource Bulletin, RM-11, Fort Collins: USFS.

Stoeckl, N. (1993), 'A Travel Cost Analysis of Hinchinbrook Island National Park', unpublished M. Econ. thesis, Townsville: James Cook University.

Ulph, A.M. and I.K Reynolds (1981), *An Economic Evaluation of National Parks*, Centre for Resource and Environmental Studies, Canberra: Australian National University.

Vaske, J.J., M.P Donnelly and D.L. Tweed (1883), 'Recreationist-Defined versus Researcher-Defined Similarity Judgements in Substitutability Research', *Journal of Leisure Research*, **15**, 251-62.

Walsh, R.G. (1986), *Recreation Economic Decisions: Comparing Benefits and Costs*, State College, Pennsylvania: Venture Publishing.

Walsh, R.G., L.D. Sanders and J.R. McKean (1990), 'The Consumption Value of Travel Time on Recreation Trips', *Journal of Travel Research*, Summer, 17-24.

Walsh, R.G., D.M. Johnson and J.R. McKean (1992), 'Benefit Transfer of Outdoor Recreation Demand Studies, 1968–1988', *Water Resources Research*, **28**, 707-13.

Ward, F.A. (1983), 'Measuring the Cost of Time in Recreation Demand Analyses: Comment', *American Journal of Agricultural Economics*, **65**, 167-8.

Ward, F.A. (1984), 'Specification Considerations for the Price Variable in Travel Cost Demand Models', *Land Economics*, **60**, 301-5.

Ward, F.A. and J.B. Loomis (1986), 'The Travel Cost Demand Model as an Environmental Policy Assessment Tool: A Review of Literature', *Western Journal of Agricultural Economics*, **11** (2), 164-78.

Ward, F.A., B.A. Roach and J.E. Henderson (1996), 'The Economic Value of Water in Recreation: Evidence from the California Drought', *Water Resources Research*, **32** (4), 1075-81.

Wetzel, J.N. (1977), 'Estimating the Benefits of Recreation under Conditions of Congestion', *Journal of Environmental Economics and Management*, **4**, 239-46.

Wetzstein, M.E. and J.G. McNeely (1980), 'Specification Errors and Inference in Recreation Demand Models', *American Journal of Agricultural Economics*, **62**, 798-800.

Wilman, E.A. (1987), 'A Simple Repackaging Model of Recreational Choices', *American Journal of Agricultural Economics*, **69**, 603-11.

Yen, S.T. and W.L. Adamowicz (1994), 'Participation, Trip Frequency and Site Choice: A Multinomial Poisson Hurdle Model of Recreation Demand', *Canadian Journal of Agricultural Economics*, **42**, 65-76.

Ziemer, R., W.N. Musser and R.C. Hill (1980), 'Recreational Demand Equations: Functional Form and Consumer Surplus', *American Journal of Agricultural Economics*, **62**, 136-41.

3. Demand Theory and TCM

We noted in the last chapter that early developers of TCM had a clear view that their goal to measure economic values of outdoor recreation and outdoor recreation policies should be based on the underlying theory of consumer choice and on the preferences of visitors and economic constraints that govern their choices. In this chapter we explain the basics of the theory of consumer choice and the concept of demand, discuss the determinants of demand and, importantly, constraints that limit demand. We also introduce elasticity of demand, discuss some pricing practises, and examine the bases of demand estimation using TC methodology. We include in the estimation section some discussion of important demographic variables.

DEMAND CONCEPTS

In this section, we examine consumer choice theory and the determinants of demand, and show how demand functions may be manipulated.

Consumer Choice and Utility

In building an understanding of consumer choice, we must first make a number of assumptions about people's behavior. These assumptions must be made so that we can build a model; if they are not plausible and testable for the general populace, then the model will have little explanatory power.

One assumption is that consumers have a set of tastes and preferences, which governs their choices among the multitude of goods (and services) on offer. It does not matter how those preferences are formed – for example, through cultural heritage, upbringing in the home, formal education, peer pressure or serendipitous encounters. Similarly, it does not matter whether others judge those preferences as worthy or despicable, altruistic or avaricious, lightly-held or ingrained.

A second assumption is that consumers will always prefer more of a good to less. This is really an assumption of rationality, not greed necessarily. Consumers who somehow receive more of a good than they can comfortably use or consume may be able to give some away and thus generate additional benefit for themselves from the act of giving. Thus having more of a good yields extra benefit over having less. Thirdly, economists assume consumers' preferences are transitive, in the sense that, if Andy prefers basketball to cycling, but prefers cycling to swimming, then Andy logically prefers basketball to swimming. If this assumption did not hold, then it would be extremely difficult to build a coherent theory about Andy's preferences.

Economists believe consumers make choices to maximize their utility. Utility is the amount of enjoyment or satisfaction, physical, intellectual or spiritual, that a consumer derives from using or having a good or a collection of goods. Rational consumers make choices among the thousands of goods on offer to decide which goods and the quantities of each that they will use. The driving force is the desire to gain the greatest possible satisfaction.

We noted above the assumption that more is better. There is another complicating factor that we must take into account in building this explanation. Generally, economists believe that willingness to substitute consumed amounts of one good for another decreases at the margin.

Why don't consumers have some of everything? As we noted above, consumers are constrained in their choices. The principal constraints are income, wealth and, particularly in the case of recreation, time. Generally we think of the economic constraint in terms of income, but some low-income consumers with wealth will in fact use that store of value to fund current consumption. So, to put the matter succinctly, consumers are thought to make purchase choices of the types and quantities of goods from the array available to maximize their satisfaction subject to monetary and time constraints.

The demand pressure exerted by all potential consumers of a good, such as visits to a national park, is called the market demand, and is equal to the aggregate value of all individual consumers' demand. Where goods of the same general type are slightly differentiated, such as motor vehicles, each firm supplies the whole market in that good. On the other hand, where the goods are not differentiated, such as wheat with 12 per cent protein, there are many firms supplying the market and the demand curves facing the firm and market are different. We can now examine market demand. You can decide later whether the good you are interested in is differentiated enough to form its own market or whether it is part of a larger multi-product market.

Demand Curves

A demand curve relates the quantities demanded to various prices. The formal definition of the demand for a good is the quantities that consumers are willing to buy at various prices within a stipulated time period, when all other factors apart from price are held constant. Graphically, a linear demand curve appears as in Figure 3.1; the curve has a negative slope which reflects the negative relationship between quantity demanded and price. The algebraic equation for the curve in this example is $Q = 1400 - 140P$.

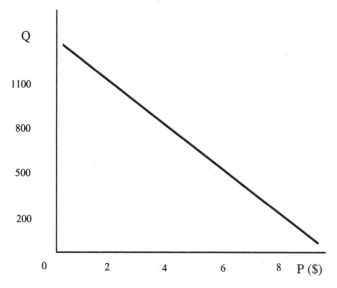

Figure 3.1 A linear Q-dependent demand curve

While price is an important determinant of demand, it is not the only determinant. We will thus move on to examine more closely the determinants of demand.

The Determinants of Market Demand and Demand Functions

The market demand for a product is a function of a number of factors including the price and design of the product, the number of distribution outlets, effectiveness of advertising, the price and availability of substitutes, the design and effectiveness of advertising of substitutes, the tastes and preferences of consumers, their income, their expectations of various aspects of the future and other factors such as government policy, population levels, weather conditions and so on. The first four of these variables are controllable by an organization for its own services or products; the other factors are controlled by others or not controllable at all. The demand function for a product at any given market area may be stated algebraically in terms of its determinants, a few of which are given here:

$$Qx = f(Px, Py, Oy, Ax, Ay, Y, T, N) + error \qquad (3.1)$$

Qx is the quantity demanded of x, Px is the price of x, Py is the price of a substitute y, Oy is the number of outlets for good y, Ax is the marketing budget for good x, Ay is the advertising budget for good y, Y is consumers' income, T represents tastes and preferences, and N is the population of potential consumers in the market.

The demand function may be estimated by regression analysis. If the algebraic form is linear, the population model may be stated as:

$$Qx = \beta_1 + \beta_2 Px + \beta_3 Py + ... + \beta_n N + \varepsilon \qquad (3.2)$$

where β_1, β_2 ... β_n are parameters for which estimates must be obtained. Data may be gathered for a sample from the population. For sample data, the regression model is written in the form:

$$Qx = b_1 + b_2 Px + b_3 Py + ... + b_n N \qquad (3.3)$$

where b_1, b_2, b_3...b_n are estimates of the parameters. The coefficients, b_2, b_3 ... b_6 , are partial slope coefficients, whilst b_1 is the intercept. Each regression coefficient measures the change in Qx for a one unit change in its respective variable, when the values of all the other independent variables remain constant. The b_1 coefficient is the constant or vertical intercept, and it gives the value of Qx when the values of all the independent variables in the equation are zero.

We would expect the regression coefficients for own price (Px), the number of outlets for the substitute good (Oy) and the advertising of the substitute good (Ay) to have negative algebraic signs because, when any of these three determinants increases, we would expect the quantity demanded of good x to decrease. It is most important to understand that there is a negative relationship between quantity demanded and price.

Whilst the collection of data on the values of the variables is a necessary precursor to the estimation of parameters and may appear to be an easy task, researchers often encounter considerable difficulties in both data collection and defining determinants of demand, especially in the case of TCMs.

Changing Demand Functions to Demand Equations

After estimating a demand function, economists and managers often find it useful to convert the function to a demand curve. This is achieved by holding all factors apart from price constant. This means that we assume certain values for those determinants, and those values do not change during our analysis.

Let's take a simple linear model and give it some values. Suppose we had estimated an equation by regression analysis of data and found:

$$Qx = 100 - 8Px + 12Py + 80N \qquad (3.4)$$

If Py is the price of the substitute good and currently is \$10, and if N is the population (measured in thousands) in the market area for good x and currently amounts to five, we could substitute these values into the equation and simply it, as follows:

$$Qx = 100 - 8Px + 12(10) + 80(5) = 100 + 120 + 400 - 8Px = 620 - 8Px \ (3.5)$$

We now have a demand curve which relates the quantity demanded to the price charged alone. All the other factors have been held constant at their observed values and incorporated into the value of the intercept. Thus, the intercept can be thought of as a catch-all, which shows the effect of all the variables except price, when those variables take values that do not change.

ELASTICITY OF DEMAND

Elasticity is the responsiveness of quantity demanded to a small change in one of its determinants. Demand elasticity is a very important concept and useful tool for managers, because knowledge of it allows managers to predict how quantity demanded will react to small changes in any one of the determinants of demand. In the case of outdoor recreation, some of those determinants are controllable variables, as we saw above, while some are influenced either by other people or by nature. Even where a determinant is not controllable, being able to predict its influence on demand is an advantage.

Probably the most commonly estimated elasticity is price elasticity, but cross price elasticity which refers to responsiveness to changes in prices of substitute or complementary goods, income elasticity and advertising elasticity are also useful concepts. For recreation planners, further elasticities such as age of people in the market area and water or site quality elasticities have relevance. Demand elasticities may be computed for any of the independent variables estimated in a demand function.

Price Elasticity

Price elasticity is therefore the responsiveness of quantity demanded to a small change in price. The formula for price elasticity (E_p) is:

$$E_p = \%\Delta Q / \%\Delta P \text{ or } E_p = \Delta Q / \Delta P \times P/Q \qquad (3.6)$$

Calculated values of E_p are always negative but, by convention, we ignore the negative sign when expressing price elasticity. Values range between zero and infinity. At values between zero and one, demand is said to be inelastic, because the percentage response in quantity demanded is smaller than the percentage change in price. Demand in these cases is relatively insensitive to price changes. At values greater than one, demand is characterized as price elastic. In percentage terms, the demand response is greater than the change in price. An estimated value of 3.0 means that a 1.0 per cent change in price will induce a 3.0 per cent change in quantity demanded.

If managers have knowledge of price elasticity, they can manage the setting of prices with much greater expertise. For example, managers can increase the price of inelastic services and be sure they will enjoy an increase in total revenue. This happens because the resultant drop in demand will not be sufficient to overcome the effect of the increase in price. Conversely, managers increasing the price of elastic goods will suffer such a decrease in demand that total revenue will fall. (A manager of an outdoor recreation site may be less interested in total revenue, and increase entry price anyway to gain the benefits of less congestion or slower ecological degradation.)

Inspection of the elasticity formulae will reveal that elasticity changes at different prices along a demand curve, even if the curve estimated is linear. The slope of a linear demand curve is constant and equal to $\Delta Q / \Delta P$. As the elasticity formula is $E_p = \Delta Q / \Delta P \times P/Q$, the value of E_p will depend on the value of P/Q. As price increases, Q decreases, so the value of P/Q increases. Thus for linear demand, elasticity must increase as price increases. This conclusion is consistent with expectations. We would expect consumers to be less sensitive to small changes in prices while prices are relatively low, but more reactive at high prices. Price elasticity also typically changes along the length of non-linear demand curves.

Why is price elasticity different for unlike goods? Firstly, the price elasticity of demand for a good depends on the number and characteristics of close substitutes. If a good has a large number of close substitutes, demand is likely to be very price elastic, because buyers are easily able to substitute other products. A good example concerns the large number of very similar reservoirs built for agriculture and flood control in California's Central Valley. They have recreation facilities with little difference between them.

Three points are worth noting here. One is the influence of habit on the part of consumers. If consumers are set in their ways and reasonably happy with a product, they are likely to be less price sensitive. Also implicated is the availability of information, about both the product in question and substitutes. Consumers may not substitute another product into their purchases, if they are not fully aware of other goods, their prices, characteristics, etc. Finally, the availability of substitutes depends on how closely the market is defined. For example, in relation to recreation, are consumers who picnic at a water-supply dam only interested in picnicking at water supply dams? Or are they happy to picnic beside small rivers as well as at water supply dams? Or are they content with water supply dams, small rivers, large rivers or open rural settings? The wider the definition of the product, in this context, the more elastic demand is likely to be. On the other hand, if we defined the product extremely broadly, say as 'recreation', then its demand is likely to be price inelastic, as 'food' or 'clothing' are not close substitutes for recreation. This matter of definition is not just a theoretical issue for researchers. It is also important for managers to try to be aware of how widely their consumers view the product category, because that will determine their appreciation of the number and types of substitutes, and inevitably consumers' sensitivity to price.

A second factor impacting on price elasticity is the significance of the good in the context of consumers' budgets. Do consumers spend small or large proportions of their budgets on the good? If the proportion is small, demand is likely to be less sensitive to small changes in price. An example is trips to a local suburban park

A third factor involves the character of the good in relation to having a comfortable and satisfying life. Is it a necessity or a luxury? Necessities exhibit greater price inelasticity than do luxuries, especially where income is low. Care must be taken with the necessity-luxury categorization, however, because one person's luxury can easily be classed by another person as a necessity. Baye, Jansen and Lee (1992) found the short term price elasticity of alcohol in the US to be 0.3. This is not an unexpected finding, given our knowledge of the use of alcohol. However, a previous study (Cook, 1982) had estimated price elasticity of alcohol as 1.8. Cook surmised that, because heavy drinkers account for a large proportion of the alcohol consumed, their limited budgets would constrain their alcohol consumption when prices rose. Even though alcohol was viewed by them as a necessity and accounted for significant shares of their budgets, their generally low incomes due to their difficulty in holding steady and well-paid jobs constrained their consumption and made their demand responsive to price changes.

Finally, price elasticity of demand is sensitive to the period of adjustment available to the consumer. The longer the period in question, the more likely that consumers will be able to find substitutes for a product of which the price has risen and the more price elastic demand will be. Consider the oil price rises of the early 1970s. As a reaction to those price rises, a good deal of research funding was directed towards alternative energy production and application systems. In the short term, users could find few substitutes, but in the longer term substitutes have been slowly developed.

Generally the price elasticity of demand for outdoor recreation activities in the US has been found to be relatively low. Gum and Martin (1975), for example, found rural outdoor recreation generally in Arizona to have price elasticities ranging from 0.12 to 0.56. They estimated the price elasticities for cold water fishing specifically to be in the range 0.38 to 0.97, depending on region.

Cross Price Elasticities

Demand for a good including a recreational activity, as we have already seen, depends on the prices of other goods, as well as on its own price. Cross price elasticity measures the responsiveness of quantity demanded of the good to small changes in the price of another good or, if data are available, a basket of other goods. In relation to recreation, we might be interested in the cross price elasticity between entry to one site and another substitute site, or the cross price elasticity between one activity and another activity.

The cross price elasticity formula is:

$$E_{xp} = \%\Delta Qx/\%\Delta Py = \Delta Qx/\Delta Py \times Py/Qx \qquad (3.7)$$

Just as we saw previously, $\Delta Qx/\Delta Py$ is the slope coefficient in a demand function. Computed values for cross price elasticities give the percentage change in demand for the good under review resulting from a 1 per cent change in the price of a related good. The algebraic sign of the estimated value may be positive or negative. Positive values indicate the two goods are substitutes; negative values indicate they are complements.

This concept is of use to managers who operate potentially competing facilities. For example, one administrative unit might control both primitive facilities and developed campgrounds. How will an increase in the price per night for the primitive facilities affect the demand for campground places? Similarly, a manager might administer two controlled-access walking tracks or two lakes with boating by permit. How will demand for one be affected by changes in price for the other? Kurtz and King (1980) estimated cross price elasticities for motor boating on some water supply dams in Arizona. They found the elasticities to vary between −1.5 to −4.4 and from 1.87 to 2.6. The dams with negative elasticities were complementary goods with their respective alternatives, which indicated that users desired to use both dams on a single trip. Positively signed elasticities, on the other hand, indicated that those pairs of dams were seen by users to be substitutes.

Income Elasticities

Income elasticity is another particularly useful concept for recreation managers. It is, of course, the responsiveness of the quantity demanded of a good to a small change in income. The formula follows the same format as explained above. Income elasticity is equal to $\%\Delta Qx/\%\Delta Y$. The calculated value is the percentage change in quantity demanded resulting from a 1 per cent change in consumers' incomes.

The calculated values for income elasticities may be either positive or negative. Positive values naturally mean that demand changes in the same direction as income changes; thus, an increase in income will promote an increase in demand. Negative income elasticities are possible and those goods which are found to exhibit this characteristic are called 'inferior' goods. It is worth noting, however, that the inferior good of one culture, social class or region is not necessarily that of another. The potato is a prime example. Demand for potatoes is commonly supposed to fall as incomes rise, as people substitute other foods into their diets. On the other hand, more health-conscious (and wealthier) people often increase their demand for potatoes, especially named varieties to enjoy their different flavors, because potatoes are rich in complex carbohydrates, non-fattening but filling.

Baye, Jansen and Lee (1992) found income elasticity of transportation in the US to be 1.80, but of food to be 0.80. Thus, demand for transportation can be expected to increase as incomes rise; demand for food will also rise, but not to the full proportional extent of the income increase. Kalter and Gosse (1969) investigated the income elasticities of a number of goods related to recreation. Wine and restaurant meals were found to have income elasticities of 1.4–1.5, live theatre nearly 2.0 and recreation in general 1.4. Specific recreation activities were estimated to have much lower income elasticities of 0.5 for skiing, 0.47 for fishing, 0.42 for camping and 0.34 for boating.

We are all aware that there is inequality in many societies with many employed people enjoying high standards of living and having high disposable incomes while the less well off are proportionately disadvantaged.

This suggests that income elasticities for recreation will differ at various income levels. Thompson and Tinsley (1978) found this to be so in relation to recreation in North Carolina. While overall income elasticity for recreation was estimated to be 1.4, it was calculated at 0.8 for low income families, 1.3 for middle income households, 2.0 for upper middle families and 1.4 for high income households.

While managers have no control over the incomes of their consumers and potential consumers, a knowledge of income elasticities will enable them to make informed decisions to projected changes in income. We are all aware that incomes have steadily risen over the last few decades for many people in western societies. This means that generally the demand for recreation will rise. However, aggregate incomes vary according to the economic cycle, and recreational managers can make use of their knowledge of income elasticity to prepare their recreational capacities to cope with expected demand, year by year, cycle by cycle.

Other Elasticities

Other elasticities which may be of interest to recreation site or activity managers are advertising, socioeconomic characteristics of the people living in or visiting the market area of the good, and characteristics relating to the quality of the natural environment such as water quality, water quantity in some circumstances, depth of snow, shade in campgrounds, noise levels in campgrounds and visual evidence of ecological degradation.

Fortunately, formulae for computing elasticities all follow the same format. All elasticities relating to demand determinants are equal to $\%\Delta Q/\%\Delta d$ or $\Delta Q/\Delta d \times d/Q$, where d is the demand determinant in question. They are essential to managers planning strategies and evaluating development proposals. Studies have been done estimating water and forest quality elasticities (see, for example, Bouwes and Schneider, 1979; Walsh and Olienyk, 1981). Kling (1988) estimated cross-quality elasticities in an analysis comparing models of recreation demand. While advertising does not always figure prominently in the planning of public sector recreation managers, it certainly does for commercial managers. It is of interest to note that advertising elasticity has been estimated at 0.25 for recreation in general (Baye, Jansen and Lee, 1992).

PRICING PRACTISES

Demand at Zero Price

What happens if the price for a good is zero? Put succinctly, there is sure to be overuse. We have no doubt all seen precious treated town water being wasted by consumers living in arid zones who, for example, use it to wash down driveways instead of using a broom or run it on a garden for hours until excess water runs away down the street. This happens in areas where water is not metered, and consumers are charged a flat fee for water supply. There is no direct charge per unit of water used. Similarly, city and state parks with no entry fees regularly attract more users than is desirable for the comfort of other users or the resilience of the natural environment. The results are congestion and worn grassed areas, degraded paths and loss of species diversity, respectively.

Why does this overuse occur? As we saw at the start of this chapter, consumers have internal systems of values which are quite separate from prices charged (or not charged) for goods in markets. These values may be characterized as utility or satisfaction. Individuals will value a given good differently.

Let's work through an example. Suppose there are nine individuals who weigh in their own minds the benefits gained from a day spent picnicking at a local park. Suppose the importance of picnicking to each person could be measured and we sorted them into descending order of value. Let's also assume the values ran, for simplicity's sake, from nine to one. We might characterize the picnickers with values greater than four as high-value users and the picnickers with values of four or less as low-value users. While there is no charge for entry to the park, all nine individuals will use the park. Now let's impose a charge of $5 for entry. It would be reasonable for the high-value users to continue using the park, because their personal benefits are greater than, or equal to, the cost of entry. The low-value users will now judge going to picnic in the park as 'not worth it' and will not go. Imposing a price has thus acted as a rationing mechanism and has screened out those users who did not put a high enough value on the use of the good. For most goods, there is a proportion of low-value users who will use the good if it is provided, but who will not gain enough value to continue using it once they are compelled to pay for its supply. Thus, congestion will be alleviated somewhat, and the natural environment of the park will not have to achieve so much repair.

Pricing to Achieve Particular Purposes

Is it desirable to charge for entry to parks and other outdoor recreation areas? We saw above that entry fees can help to ration use where congestion is a problem. One alternative as Clawson and Knetsch (1966, p. 305) acidly remarked is that the managing agencies could allow parks to become so crowded and dirty until enough people would be repelled that demand would be brought in line with supply.

Cullen (1985) examined the economic implications and effects of various rationing methods, and noted that the lottery system in particular required a good deal of administrative effort, which reduced its practicality. Fractor (1982) found non-price methods to be less efficient than pricing and all such methods reduced social benefits.

A knowledge of both demand and the cost structure is vital to making pricing decisions. The efficient allocation of resources, sometimes referred to as Pareto-efficient or Pareto-optimal, occurs when no more changes can be made to the allocation to improve the lot of any economic agent. Whilst the idea that a change might improve the lot of some people and harm no one is attractive in theory, in reality changes almost surely involve extra benefits to some people and losses to others. However, if the proposed change would result in the sum of the benefits of the gainers exceeding the sum of the losers' lost benefits, then the change is beneficial in the context of the whole of a society.

The efficient provision of public goods occurs when price is set at the point where marginal social cost equals marginal social benefit. Benefits are discussed in some depth in the next chapter. In the interests of optimal resource allocation, many economists have recommended that publicly-provided goods be priced at marginal cost (MC) (see, for example, Musgrave and Musgrave, 1984, p. 734). MC is the cost of the last unit produced. One problem which is immediately obvious is that, if the output is in the zone of operations where MC is less than average cost (AC) (i.e. AC is decreasing), the supplier will not recover total costs with price set at that level. Hence MC pricing would require a subsidy to sustain operations, and this may penalize non-users of a public good. If a subsidy is necessary, the quest to maximize net benefits to society in the allocation of resources may be defeated.

A pricing method which may be used to overcome the decreasing cost of production is average cost pricing. Price is set at the point where the demand curve cuts the average cost curve. Average cost pricing recovers all variable and fixed costs. However, the resulting output would be less than that suggested by marginal cost pricing, and the market-clearing price would be higher. No subsidy is required.

A theory of pricing which includes the condition that costs be recovered in the most efficient way is Ramsey or second-best pricing (Ramsey, 1927). The thrust of Ramsey pricing is that, in cases where the long-run average cost curve is decreasing, marginal cost is less than average cost and there is budget constraint, prices should be set to exceed marginal cost according to the following principles: the prices of goods with the most inelastic demands should be raised the most, and the ratio of mark-up percentages of any two such goods should equal the inverse of the ratio of their demand elasticities. It follows then that the optimal percentage mark-up of price over marginal cost varies inversely with elasticity (Wilman, 1988). This principle may be usefully applied in pricing different services within one site, for example, camping rights and day use, so long as they have different elasticities.

Two-tier pricing has been advocated by a number of workers as an almost efficient solution, generally for public utilities and specifically for public recreation facilities (Rosenthal, Loomis and Peterson, 1984; Wilman, 1988). Under this system, the entry fee is set at marginal cost and visitors are charged an additional license or permit fee, perhaps annually, to cover fixed costs.

A number of researchers have been concerned with the effects of pricing on revenue and equity. Huszar and Seckler (1974) reported a 20–25 per cent reduction in attendance at a museum when fees were charged, but a net increase in revenue. Adams et al. (1989) examined changes in participation rates, revenues and willingness-to-pay for a public pheasant-stocking program for hunters in Oregon and found a revenue-maximizing fee would not cover costs because of a substantial decline in participation by lower income groups. Walsh, Peterson and McKean (1989) found increased entry fees depressed local visitation rates and precluded the entry of low income earners.

The National Parks and Wildlife Service in New South Wales (NPWS) introduced a comprehensive schedule of new and higher entry fees to its most popular parks in June 1992. After a period of steady growth in estimated visitor numbers in the decade before, 1992, the NPWS regards visitation as having stabilized since 1992. Evaluation of the effect on demand of increased entry fees is impeded by the difficulty in collecting accurate visitor numbers where annual permits are sold and gatekeepers do not record such entries. Similarly, the management of the Powerhouse Museum in Sydney, a museum of applied arts and sciences, found it difficult to make a precise judgement on the effect of introducing fees for the first time, because records of attendance had not been kept before the introduction of fees. A pattern of an initial decrease after the introduction of new or higher fees followed by a gradual increase in use as time goes by, when potential users become accustomed to the fee structure, seems to be a reasonable expectation. To overcome any public perception of inequity, free entry may be offered on low-use days. For example, the Powerhouse Museum allows free entry on the first Saturday of each month (Museum, 1994).

Differential pricing may be practised. Parks often experience uneven demand. In Australia, for example, the peak periods for national park use are at Easter and other school holiday periods and long weekends, of which there are three or four each year. In this situation it is possible to split the market and charge economically efficient prices which vary between peak and off-peak periods. This is called peak-load pricing and it can be economically justifiable to charge a higher price in the peak period because marginal social costs will be higher due to increased ecological and congestion costs.

Another basis on which a market may be split to capture a greater share of consumer surplus is spatially. Bamford et al. (1988) reported an experiment offering a differential fee structure to campers at State parks in Vermont. They concluded that choice of campsite was price-responsive, with use more evenly distributed by differential pricing between highly desirable sites and others than it had been previously, and campsite revenue increased. Higher income campers chose to pay for more expensive sites. Whitehead (1990) was skeptical that revenue was enhanced. He suggested campers would substitute visits to lower-priced parks or fewer days at parks if campsite demand were elastic. ABARE (1991) investigated charging users of Australia's Great Barrier Reef Marine Park to raise revenue and to encourage visitors and commercial operators to use the park in an ecologically sustainable and efficient way. The authors recommended the use of annual permits to low demand areas and short-term passes to high demand areas with appropriate fees, the level of which would reflect the costs associated with operating the park.

From public policy or financial need, a manager may desire to maximize total revenue (TR) through collection of entry fees. The condition which must be satisfied to achieve this objective is to set prices so that marginal revenue (MR) is equal to zero. The MR curve always has the same relationship to its demand curve, when expressed in a P-dependent form, in any market situation where the firm has some degree of market power. In these cases, the demand curve is downward-sloping, as we have already seen. If the demand curve is linear and has the equation, $P = a - bQ$, the MR curve has the equation, $MR = a - 2bQ$. In other words, the MR curve shares the same intercept with its demand curve and has twice the slope. Thus, a manager wanting to maximize TR would estimate the demand curve, calculate the MR curve, set that equation equal to zero and solve for Q. After finding the TR maximizing output, that output value can be substituted back into the demand curve and the TR maximizing price to be charged estimated.

Managers wanting to maximize profits, on the other hand, would go through a similar exercise except that they would solve for Q when MR equalled MC. Thus, an MC equation or a value for MC would have to be estimated. After finding the profit-maximizing output, the Q value would be substituted back into the demand curve and the profit maximizing price to be charged estimated. A profit maximizing price will always be higher than a TR maximizing price, and a profit maximizing output will always be lower than a TR maximizing output, so long as costs are positive.

ESTIMATING DEMAND WITH A SIMPLE TCM MODEL

In the section above, we introduced some of the theory of demand together with some of the issues managers should consider when they are thinking about using their knowledge of demand strategically. In this part of the chapter, we focus on how a demand curve may be estimated using TC methodology and then examine more closely the demographic determinants of demand which are most likely to be of interest to managers of outdoor recreation areas.

A Simple Hypothetical TCM

TCM exploits the basic demand relationship that quantity demanded varies negatively with price, and this is reflected in the proposition that the quantity of visits by users of sites will decrease the further consumers must travel to a specific site due to the greater travel and time costs. Even where an entry fee is charged, travel costs impact on the use of a particular site and contribute (negatively) to the creation of demand. Other demand determinants also have an impact.

Briefly, the travel cost procedure involves two steps. A demand function for the recreation experiences at the site is estimated, and then a separate demand curve for the recreational use of the site is derived, using assumed increases in entry fees. (For simplicity, this example follows the zonal methodology and incorporates only one independent variable.) Hypothetical data provided in Table 3.1 illustrate the first part of the methodology. Using regression analysis, the line of best fit may be estimated to infer the relationship between the dependent variable, visitors per 1000 zonal population (V), and the independent variable, travel costs (TC). For the data in Table 3.1, the estimated equation is:

$$V = 8.19 - .0622\,TC \qquad\qquad (3.8)$$

The t test statistics for the estimated coefficients are 70.7 and −35.2 respectively, which indicate that the estimated coefficients are statistically significant at the 0.05 level. The coefficient of determination, R^2, for the equation is 0.999, indicating that 99.9 per cent of the variation in the dependent variable is explained by variation in the independent variable. More discussion of the meaning of these terms is given in Chapter 8.

Table 3.1 Hypothetical data illustrating the development of TCM variables

Zone	Population (1000)	Visitors	Visitors per 1000 population (V)	Travel cost per person ($) ($TC$)
1	50	350	7.0	20
2	250	1250	5.0	50
3	100	200	2.0	100

Using this equation in conjunction with travel costs which have been increased by the addition of various entry fees ranging from zero to ten, a demand schedule for entry to the site may be constructed. For an entry fee of $5 per person, for example, the travel costs per person from each of the three zones increase to, respectively, $25, $55 and $105. The equation predicts V to be 6.638, 4.770 and 1.658 for the three zones and the estimated number of visitors from each zone, when V is multiplied by the population of the zone, to be 332, 1192 and 166 respectively, making 1690 visits in all when the fee is $5.

For an entry fee of $8 per person, the estimated number of visitors is 1616, and for an entry fee of $10 per person, the estimated number of visitors is 1566, with their distribution by zone shown in Table 3.2. We continue to estimate the total predicted number of visitors for all possible entry fees, until predicted visits are zero from all zones of origin. With the incorporation of the 1800 visitors at zero increase in travel costs (the observed value for visitors), the estimated demand schedule for entry to the site is constructed.

These data may be graphed to give a typical downward-sloping demand curve. Another approach is to run a second regression with the predicted visits regressed on entry fees. The demand equation estimated from these data is:

$$Q = 1802.51 - 23.48\,P \qquad\qquad (3.9)$$

where Q is the number of visitors and P is the price of entry. Because this equation has been estimated for data generated by regression analysis, only the R^2 statistic is a relevant statistical test and, at .998, it indicates a good fit of the estimated equation to the data. Consumers' surplus or other measures of benefits can be calculated, but we will leave this until the next chapter.

Table 3.2 Estimated demand at various entry fees to the site

Entry fee per person ($)	TC plus fee ($)	Visitors per 1000 pop. (V)	Zonal population (1000)	Visitors (Q)	Estimated number of visitors
0	20	7.0	50	350	
	50	5.0	250	1250	1800
	100	2.0	100	200	
	25	6.638	50	332	
5	55	4.770	250	1192	1690
	105	1.658	100	166	
	28	6.451	50	323	
8	58	4.584	250	1146	1616
	108	1.471	100	147	
	30	6.327	50	316	
10	60	4.459	250	1115	1566
	110	1.347	100	135	

Variables included in Recreational Demand Estimations

Having estimated a simple demand curve, we will now examine some of the demographic and other variables which are thought to influence demand for outdoor recreation. Apart from the demographic variables, the most important variables which have been found to be statistically significant include travel cost, travel time, tastes and preferences, substitute and complementary goods, site quality and congestion. We have introduced these variables in Chapter 2 and will re-examine many of them later in this book. It is worth noting that some analyses completed quickly on a limited budget include travel cost as the only determinant.

Tastes and preferences have long been acknowledged as important in the determination of demand. Researchers attempting to quantify demand may try to measure a variable which describes adequately the tastes of consumers in the relevant market. However, this is often difficult to do, and analysts often fall back on measuring demographic characteristics in order to use these variables as proxies for tastes and preferences.

While we know that fit young men are more interested in outdoor recreation than elderly women, it is sometimes hard to prove it! We noted above that socioeconomic variables tend to be discarded from ZTCM analyses, because the averaging process to estimate one value for each variable for each zone in an analysis reduces the necessary amount of variation in the data. However, analyses incorporating ITCM often find demographic characteristics to be statistically significant. Thus, we will discuss some of the more important characteristics here.

Age of people in the market area

Intuitively, age would appear to be an important determinant of demand for outdoor recreation. Additionally, we would expect the relationship to be inverse. That is, as age increases, participation decreases. Confirming this expectation, one study completed in 1977 in the US found age accounts for 51 per cent of the variation in participation, with all other tested variables each accounting for less than 10 per cent (Walsh, 1986, p. 159).

Tested over 30 separate activities, participation rates in the US study were found to decrease generally with advancing age, the only exception to this pattern being 'driving for pleasure'. The age distribution of pleasure drivers, however, was skewed by the requirement to have a licence which reduced the number of people under 17 years old who could report participation (Walsh, 1986, p. 160). In contrast, a study conducted in Australia in 1996 found that participation rates for many outdoor recreational activities (for example, swimming, fishing, cycling and bushwalking) increased up to middle age and then decreased. Walking for exercise showed gradually increasing participation from 20 per cent of the 15–17 year old population to 50 per cent of the 65 years and over group. The only relevant activity which exhibited a typical US pattern in participation was visiting beaches, rivers, forests and national parks (ABS, 1998). The variation in these patterns suggests researchers should always try to incorporate the age variable if funding permits.

Sex

Sex has an influence on the types of recreational activities people undertake. In the US study noted above, men were far more likely to go camping, especially in primitive areas, canoeing, fishing, boating, hiking, hunting and to play golf. Women were found less likely to participate in most outdoor activities, with the exception of picnicking and nature study/birdwatching (Walsh, 1986 p. 166). In the Victorian study, men reported much greater participation rates in golf, fishing and cycling, while women were more likely to go swimming and walking for exercise (ABS, 1998).

While managers have no influence over the gender balance in their market areas, they should remain aware of the influence sex has on participation. Thus, when planning to introduce a new activity, for example, it could be worthwhile to include sex as one of the researched variables. Additionally, survey participants are used to providing this information and having it helps to check whether the sample is representative of the market population.

Education

Recreational consumers' levels of education have been found to be related to the types of activities undertaken. People with higher education appear to appreciate outdoor nature-based activities more than people with less formal education. Stoeckl (1993), for example, in her study of visitors to Hinchinbrook Island National Park near The Great Barrier Reef found 70 per cent of adult Australian visitors reported having a diploma or degree, whereas at the time only 28 per cent of the total Australian population held such qualifications. Walsh (1986) reported higher education being related to physically strenuous activities such as canoeing, sailing, swimming, hiking, backpacking, skiing and playing golf. On the other hand, fishing, hunting, snowmobiling and sledding were found to be inversely related to education.

Income

You were introduced to income as a demand determinant earlier in this chapter. Generally, it has been found that there is a positive correlation between income and participation in many recreation activities. However, the relationship is often not particularly strong. If an activity is expensive such as polo or golf in communities where the club membership fees are high, a correlation would be expected. Walsh (1986) reported statistically significant correlations between income and sailing, motor boating, canoeing, white water boating, sightseeing and cycling, and negative correlations for hiking and backpacking.

Whether income would be included in an analysis may depend on the particular purpose and available funding. There are also other factors to be considered when asking people by survey about their incomes. These will be discussed later.

Other demographic factors

Other characteristics of consumers which may be included in an analysis include occupation, leisure time, rural versus urban residence and family size. Obviously the more managers know about the characteristics of their markets the better, and the more able they are to make judgements whether particular variables should be included in analyses.

A Caution: Variables Must Vary

TCM employs regression analysis to quantify the relationship between a dependent variable and one or more independent or predictor variables. After that relationship is quantified, an analyst is able to predict the value of the dependent variable when the independent variables are given specified values.

To be able to estimate a relationship between two variables, however, both must vary. Without this variation, it is impossible to determine how one variable may relate to the other. Furthermore, the standard errors (a measure of the dispersion of values around a central value) of the coefficients and of the predictions are smaller when there is wide variation in the independent variable.

Remember in Chapter 2 the brief discussion about the use of ZTCM, ITCM or a hybrid? The lack of variability in the dependent variable, trips taken, when individuals visit a site is the reason that ITCM sometimes cannot be used. With distant sites or a lottery-rationed activity such as mammal hunting, many individuals take only one trip per period. Using ITCM, an analyst would have to specify that the demand determinants, all varying to a greater or lesser degree, combined to produce usually one trip per individual. This situation could not be successfully analysed using regression, because the methodology needs variation to explain variation. Hence, in these cases, ZTCM must be used to incorporate enough variation into the values of the dependent variable.

However, again as mentioned in the same section in Chapter 2, the averaging process solves one problem but creates another. The new problem is that averaging the values of demographic characteristics over zonal samples smoothes variations and leads to loss of information. As a result, many demographic characteristics are deemed statistically not significant as demand determinants.

CONCLUSION

Some important concepts of demand theory were introduced in this chapter together with a discussion of some of the determinants of demand generally and in relation to the demand for outdoor nature-based recreation. Techniques to analyze demand curves and to use estimated curves to determine prices for particular purposes were also examined. A simple two-stage TCM model was explained.

REFERENCES

ABARE (1991), *Charging Users of the Great Barrier Reef Marine Park*, Report to the Great Barrier Reef Marine Park Authority, Canberra: AGPS.

Australian Bureau of Statistics (ABS) (1998), *Leisure Participation, Victoria*, Report 4176.2, Melbourne: ABS.

Adams, R.M., O. Bergland, W.N. Musser, S.L. Johnson and L.M. Musser (1989), 'User Fees and Equity Issues in Public Hunting Expenditures: The Case of Ring-necked Pheasant in Oregon', *Land Economics*, **65** (4), 376-85.

Bamford, T.E., R.E. Manning, L.K. Forcier and E.J. Koenemann (1988), 'Differential Campsite Pricing: an Experiment', *Journal of Leisure Research*, **20**, 324-42.

Baye, M.R., D.W. Jansen, and J.W. Lee (1992), 'Advertising Effects in Complete Demand Systems', *Applied Economics,* **24**, 1087-96.

Bouwes, N.W. and R. Schneider (1979), 'Procedures in Estimating Benefits in Water Quality Change', *American Journal of Agricultural Economics,* **61**, 535-9.

Clawson, M. and J.L. Knetsch (1966), *Economics of Outdoor Recreation*, Washington: Johns Hopkins University Press for Resources for the Future.

Cook, P.J. (1982), 'The Effect of Liquor Taxes on Drinking, Cirrhosis and Auto Accidents', in M. Moore and D. Gerstein (eds.), *Alcohol and Public Policy*, Washington: National Academy Press.

Cullen, R. (1985), 'Rationing Recreation Use of Public Land', *Journal of Environmental Management*, **21**, 213-24.

Fractor, D.T. (1982), 'Evaluating Alternative Methods for Rationing Wilderness Use', *Journal of Leisure Research*, **14**, 341-9.

Gum, R.L. and W.E. Martin (1974), 'Problems and Solutions in Estimating the Demand for and Value of Rural Outdoor Recreation', *American Journal of Agricultural Economics*, **56**, 558-66.

Huszar, P.C. and D.W. Seckler (1974), 'Effects of Pricing a *Free* Good: a Study of the Use of Admission Fees at the California Academy of Sciences', *Land Economics*, **50**, 364-73.

Kalter, R.J. and L.E. Gosse (1969), 'Outdoor recreation in New York State; Projections of Demand, Economic Value and pricing Effects for the Period, 1970-1985', Special Series No. 5, Ithaca: Cornell University.

Kling, C.L. (1988), 'Comparing Welfare Estimates of Environmental Quality Changes from Recreation Demand Models', *Journal of Environmental Economics and Management,* **15** (3), 331-40.

Kurtz, W.B. and D.A. King (1980), 'Evaluating Substitution Relationships Between Recreation Areas' in D.E. Hawkins, E.L. Shafer and J.M. Rovelstad (eds), *Tourism Marketing and Management Issues,* Washington: George Washington University.

Museum (Museum of Applied Arts and Sciences) (1994), *Annual Report, 1993-1994*, Sydney.

Musgrave, R.A. and P.B. Musgrave (1984), *Public Finance in Theory and Practise*, New York: McGraw-Hill.

Ramsey, F.P. (1927), 'A Contribution to the Theory of Taxation', *Economic Journal*, **37**, 47-61.

Rosenthal, D.H., J.B. Loomis and G.L. Peterson (1984), 'Pricing for Efficiency and Revenue in Public Recreation Areas', *Journal of Leisure Research*, **16** (3), 195-208.

Stoeckl, N. (1993), 'A Travel Cost Analysis of Hinchinbrook Island National Park', unpublished M. Econ. thesis, Townsville: James Cook University.

Thompson, C.S. and A.W. Tinsley (1978), 'Income Expenditure Elasticities for Recreation: Their Estimation and relation to Demand for Recreation', *Journal of Leisure Research,* **10**, 265-70.

Walsh, R.G. (1986), *Recreation Economic Decisions: Comparing Benefits and Costs,* State College: Venture Publishing.

Walsh, R.G. and J.P. Olienyk (1981), 'Recreation Demand Effects of Mountain Pine Beetle Damage to the Quality of Forest Recreation Services in the Colorado Front Range', Report to the Forest Service by the Department of Economics. Fort Collins: Colorado State University.

Walsh, R.G., G.L. Peterson and J.R. McKean (1989), 'Distribution and Efficiency Effects of Alternative Funding Methods', *Journal of Leisure Research*, **21** (4), 327-47.

Whitehead, J.C. (1990), 'A Comment on Differential Campsite Pricing', *Journal of Leisure Research*, **22** (3), 276-9.

Wilman, E.A. (1988), 'Pricing Policies for Outdoor Recreation', *Land Economics*, **64** (3), 234-41.

4. Benefits Theory and TCM

This chapter deals with some aspects of benefits theory which provide the theoretical foundations of TC methodology. The first section introduces crucial benefits theory concepts. Welfare measures such as consumer surplus, compensating variation and equivalent variation are explained as are expenditure functions. The chapter then illustrates the use of these concepts in several TC models from simple single site models to more complex multi-site and variable site quality models.

BENEFITS CONCEPTS

A benefit is, as we all know, an advantage, a boon, a blessing or an increase in welfare. Benefits-based management is one research approach to measuring the benefits of outdoor recreation (see, for example, Allen et al., 1996; Driver et al., 1987; Stein and Lee, 1995). This path approaches outdoor recreation as a resource which promotes better health, reduced stress and improved understanding of nature. The field typically aims to discover more about the resource itself with less emphasis on its monetary value.

TCMs, on the other hand, attempt to translate the physical, psychological and social benefits produced by outdoor recreation into monetary terms so their benefits can be compared with costs using the common denominator of money. Measuring the benefits of proposed plans to change any aspect of recreational resources is achieved by estimation of how those proposals are expected to alter visitors' behavior, based on observation and analysis of past experience.

TCMs describe individual visitors' preferences for the resources that support outdoor recreation. Using a TCM requires translating the proposed policy, program or plan into one or more variables that influence individual visitors preferences for the sites involved. Policies to alter site characteristics or close sites typically stimulate more emotional responses than those that simply introduce new sites. While we still have relatively little understanding of how TCMs should be properly used to value these policies, it is just these policies that attract the most attention and need the support that appropriate economic analysis can provide.

The economic and cultural environments of visitors to outdoor recreation sites influence their choices on which sites to visit and the frequency of visits to each site. These environments are defined by visitors' personal economic conditions, including income, living costs and family structures, costs of travel including entry fees, available time and intensity of preferences. National economic conditions may have an impact. Environments are also affected by factors of nature, such as climate, weather on individual days and their influence on site characteristics such as trees and streamflow.

Any changes in the economic, natural or policy environments will cause visitors to be better or worse off. Site managers and policy analysts often want to measure how much better or worse off visitors who are affected by changes in any of these environments will be.

For individual visitors, changes in satisfaction measure how much better or worse off they are as a result of the change in the environment. However, satisfaction cannot be compared between different individual visitors, so the cardinal value of satisfaction has little use for policy analysis, since virtually all policy analysis deals with impacts on many visitors. Accordingly, economists have developed measures of welfare change, sometimes called benefits. These measures are based on individual satisfaction but are denominated instead in money terms, which are considerably more useful for policy analysis. Monetary impacts of proposed policies can be aggregated for many individuals.

The oldest and still most commonly used measure of visitor welfare change is consumer surplus (CS). CS is a traditional measure of net benefit to a consumer. With private goods such as apples, for example, consumers may be willing to pay a range of prices, starting with $10 for one apple and decreasing to $0.50 each for 20 apples. If the price of apples is set in the market at $1, then consumers gain net benefits of the amount above $1 that they had been willing but not required to pay.

Much careful work since the 1970s has shown that CS is a precise measure of welfare change only in very special conditions. Compensating variation (CV) and equivalent variation (EV) are additional measures of welfare change which were developed by Hicks in the 1940s. In some circumstances, all three measures provide equal estimates.

CV AND EV

CV and EV are both theoretically correct benefit measures for travel cost demand modeling work. CV is the amount of compensation, which is paid or received, that would return consumers to their original position after the change has been made. EV, on the other hand, is the amount of compensation, paid or received, that would bring consumers to their subsequent position had the change not occurred.

Any measure of change in welfare should be both useful to policy makers and 'democratic', in the sense that it should measure the impacts of all affected individuals. To ascertain whether all affected individuals are included in the measure requires thought about visitors' decision-making processes.

(Throughout this manual, we must necessarily deal with individual visitors, which means we often have to use singular, third person pronouns. Although we sympathize with the arguments against the unthinking use of 'he', 'his' and 'him', we found 'she' and 'her' sounded distinctly odd, so we settled on a standard set of masculine pronouns. The English language needs to evolve a new set of singular sexless pronouns, because it is not always possible to convert constructions to sexless plurals. In the meantime, please regard our masculine individuals as expressing as little sex as possible in their roles as visitors.)

A visitor's decision problem is choosing the combination of trips to the n-sites, $X_1 \ldots X_n$, that maximizes his satisfaction from travel, $u(X)$, subject to his recreational budget constraint, Y. We refer to Y as income throughout this chapter, but realize that it is just that part of total income the visitor allocates to recreation. We assume that Y is fixed, but in fact it could vary, possibly increasing or decreasing in the face of proposed policies that improve sites. When his choice of satisfaction-maximizing combination of trips, $X_1^* \ldots X_n^*$, exhausts his budget, we can write the visitor's problem as:

$$V(P,Y) = max \ u(X) \qquad (4.1)$$

such that $PX = Y$. The bold variable notation refers to a list (vector) of similar variables. For example, P, stands for $P_1, \ldots P_n$. The vector product, PX means P_1 multiplied by X_1 plus P_2 multiplied by X_2 and so on all the way to P_n multiplied by X_n, in short the sum of all prices per trip times trips taken summed over all n sites.

The mathematical function $V(P,Y) = V(P_1, \ldots P_n, Y)$, that produces the visitor's maximum satisfaction achievable at known prices and income is called the **indirect utility function**. The value of $X_1^* \ldots X_n^*$ that solves the visitor's optimization problem to *max* $u(X)$ is his demanded mix of trips. This is the number of trips to each site the visitor optimally takes at all possible combinations of prices and income. We did not write in a particular utility function for $u(X) = u(X_1, \ldots X_n)$, because we want to formulate this problem for any utility function a visitor may have. However, finding a real indirect utility function $V(P,Y)$, that can be used for policy analysis, requires having an actual mathematical function for $u(X)$. We discuss this later at some length.

The mathematical function that translates P and Y to the demanded trip mix is called the visitor's demand function. We summarize this demand function as

$$X = X(P, Y) \tag{4.2}$$

The bold fonts tell us that lots of things are going on. Namely, there is one demand function for each site, $X = X_1, \ldots X_n$. Furthermore, each site's demand function depends in principle on prices of all sites and income, that is, each $X_i = X_i(P_1, \ldots P_n, Y)$. So while equation (4.2) looks simple, it really contains n equations, and they tell us the factors that influence the demand for each of n sites.

One of the important properties of the demand function is that it is not altered by a proportional change in all prices and money income. For example, if all site prices double along with income, the demand function produces an unchanged demand mix of trips for all n sites. Such a proportional change has no effect on the budget constraint, so cannot possibly affect the satisfaction-maximizing package of trips to any of the sites.

Indirect Utility Function

The concept behind the indirect utility function introduced above and the mathematics that let us estimate and use it are pretty simple. The concept of optimal satisfaction is satisfaction the visitor gets after thinking about all possible combinations of trips he could take, then taking only the trip mix that maximizes satisfaction. We find it mathematically by substituting the visitor's demand function back into the original utility function on the right hand side of equation (4.1).

We can think of the indirect utility function as the visitor's conditional travel itinerary, a set of optimal travel plans. It produces an optimal number of planned trips to all possible sites of interest as a function of all things that could affect the plan. The indirect utility function summarizes the satisfaction outcome associated with each of the travel plans that could emerge. So it summarizes the outcome of the visitor's map covering all possible contingencies.

For every set of prices and available income, the indirect utility function translates those prices into a planned trip itinerary, then translates the trip itinerary into a satisfaction index. The mathematical function that summarizes that complicated two stage process is the indirect utility function. The indirect utility function $V(P, Y)$ has some important properties for travel cost modelers, especially those concerned with modelling multiple sites. It always increases with a larger visitor budget (Y) and it increases with decreasing prices (P).

The indirect utility function is really like the optimal income earned by a travelling sales representative. The sales rep's optimal income is the income earned after thinking of all possible travel routes then choosing the single route that maximizes total revenues minus total costs. That chosen route may not be the cheapest route, nor may it maximize gross revenue, but it maximizes net revenue. To be truly income-maximizing, the route is flexible, continually adapting to the economic variables regarding prices, costs and demand that may occur.

As we noted above, a welfare measure that correctly measure impacts on affected individuals should measure the change in satisfaction resulting from the proposed policy. We can imagine two budgets facing a visitor:

$$Budget\ 1 = (P_1^0,\ P_2^0,\ ...\ P_n^0,\ Y^0) = (P^0,\ Y^0) \qquad (4.3a)$$

$$Budget\ 2 = (P_1^1,\ P_2^1,\ ...\ P_n^1,\ Y^1) = (P^1,\ Y^1) \qquad (4.3b)$$

where $P_1^0,\ P_2^0,\ ...\ P_n^0 = P^0$ the first set of travel costs to each of the *1 ... n* sites, $P_1^1,\ P_2^1,\ ...\ P_n^1 = P^1$ the second set of travel costs to each of the *1 ... n* sites, Y^0 = old income and Y^1 = new income.

These two budgets measure the prices and income that the visitor faces under two different proposed policies. Each budget represents a different budget constraint line like the ones described previously. The visitor is always assumed to make site and visitation choices that maximize satisfaction for each budget constraint. For example, the first set of travel cost data may reflect low gasoline prices and no entry fees at the sites. The satisfaction-maximizing visitor would probably take trips to far-away sites since travel is so cheap. A second set of data could incorporate high gasoline prices and newly-established entry fees. The visitor would react by taking fewer and possibly shorter trips. We commonly think of (P^0, Y^0) as the status quo policy and (P^1, Y^1) as a proposed new policy or new conditions.

An estimate of the change in the individual visitor's welfare when moving from the optimal point on the first budget to a point on the second budget, from (P^0, Y^0) to (P^1, Y^1), is simply the difference in maximum satisfaction produced by the optimal visitation choices with one budget compared to the next. As stated above, the concept for expressing the maximum satisfaction reached when the visitor optimizes on one budget equation is indirect utility. Indirect utility can be measured for both old and new income.

Recall that the visitor's optimal choice is found by selecting which sites to visit and how many visits to take at each site by moving along his budget constraint so that he reaches the highest point on his utility function. This high point is defined by tangency between the budget constraint and utility function. That single point produces one observation on the indirect utility function. That point also produces one point to observe on his demand equation summarizing his optimal bundle of trips made to all sites. Some sites may receive zero visits. So each tangency point on one budget line produces a single point on the demand equation of all sites and a single point on the indirect utility function.

The complete indirect utility function is measured by substituting the demand function for visits to each site back into the original utility function. This produces the following indirect utility function:

$$V(P,Y) = U[(X_1(P,Y), X_2(P,Y), ... X_n(P,Y)] \qquad (4.4)$$

As suggested above, the values of the X_1, X_2, ...X_n terms inside the right hand side expression are not ordinary Xs, they are optimal Xs. To illustrate, suppose the visitor acts as if to optimize a Cobb-Douglas utility function (a functional form where the variables are raised to powers) at two sites. The general form of this utility function is:

$$U = X_1^{B1} X_2^{B2} \qquad (4.5)$$

The resulting demand functions that come from maximizing that function subject to income constraint are:

$$X_1 = B_1 Y / P_1(B_1 + B_2) \qquad (4.6)$$
$$X_2 = B_2 Y / P_2(B_1 + B_2) \qquad (4.7)$$

Substituting those demand functions back into the Cobb-Douglas utility function produces the following indirect utility function:

$$V(P,Y) = \left[\frac{B_1 Y}{P_1(B_1 + B_2)} \right]^{B_1} \left[\frac{B_2 Y}{P_2(B_1 + B_2)} \right]^{B_2} \qquad (4.8)$$

B_1 and B_2 are numbers between zero and one that indicate the visitor's relative intensity of preferences for sites one and two, respectively. Thus, the indirect utility the visitor receives after making his optimal visit choices depends on his budget (Y), his intensity of preferences (B_1 and B_2) and the travel costs (P_1 and P_2) to the two sites.

Notice that each site's price appears in the denominator while the budget is in the numerator. While equation (4.8) is only one example of an indirect utility function, it illustrates a pattern that holds for all of them. Namely, indirect utility increases with a higher income and decreases with any site's price increases. Visitors always prefer larger income and lower price of travel to their sites.

To return to our simplest definition of benefits, we define the visitor's benefits from a policy which moves him from (P^0, Y^0) to (P^1, Y^1) as:

$$\text{Benefit} = V(P^1, Y^1) - V(P^0, Y^0) \tag{4.9}$$

For the Cobb-Douglas indirect utility function in (4.8), this means the benefits of the proposed policy are measured as indirect utility at new prices and income minus indirect utility at old prices and income. If this difference is larger than zero, then the proposed policy change makes the visitor better off; if it is negative, the visitor is worse off. While this simple method tells us much about the benefits of the policy for an individual visitor, it is of limited use to policy analysts because it is measured in satisfaction units, and these cannot be usefully aggregated and compared.

Despite the difficulty of comparing satisfaction among visitors, policy evaluations made on this basis are quite common. Fishery managers often conduct surveys attempting to find angler satisfaction indices (e.g. a ranking of 1 to 10) to see how the indices change under various proposed management regimes. However, since most proposals increase some anglers' indices while decreasing others, managers struggle with overall evaluations based on these indices. One way out of the impasse is to target programs to increase satisfaction for certain anglers (e.g. low-income inner-city residents) and ignore the negative impacts of the displaced resources on the satisfaction of other anglers. In nearly all cases it is more productive to have a monetary measure of visitors' welfare changes. Policy analysts can use monetary estimates of welfare changes as practical measures of benefits gained or lost by groups of affected visitors.

While the indirect utility function sounds dusty and dry, with little serious use for practical people, its mathematical inverse is quite the opposite, and in fact lies at the entire heart of benefits estimation to support rational policy analysis.

Expenditure Function: Baseline Utility

The inverse of the indirect utility function is the expenditure function, described in greater detail in this chapter's appendix. We begin by recognizing that since the indirect utility function expresses maximum utility as a function of price and budget, we should be able to invert it. Its inverse is:

$$e = e(P, U) \qquad (4.10)$$

where e is the minimum income needed to sustain a given level of satisfaction, U, at site prices, P. We could have called this dependent variable Y, since we're interested in how money income varies with price and utility. However, we have consciously avoided calling it Y, because the visitor's actual income Y is assumed fixed. By contrast, the visitor's mathematical function e, equation (4.10), changes with policy proposals.

Recall how we defined the indirect utility function: optimal utility as a function of known prices and income. Its inverse should therefore be defined in the opposite way and it is. The expenditure function defines the minimum expenditure needed to achieve a known level of utility when facing known prices. It has some important properties for TCM practitioners. It increases with higher levels of P, thus higher prices require a higher minimum level of visitor expenditure to sustain a constant level of utility. It is also consistent in the sense that a doubling of all prices exactly doubles the minimum expenditure needed to sustain constant utility.

Observable Expenditure Functions

The expenditure function needs to be expressed in such a way that policy analysts can compare proposed policies to a current or baseline course of action. In addition, the function must characterize the satisfaction indices visitors achieve in either old or new policy conditions in such a fashion that the indices themselves do not require measurement. Fortunately, both barriers can be hurdled simultaneously with a single leap by posing the question: what determines the visitor's satisfaction under those baseline conditions? The answer is that the visitor's satisfaction comes from the set of baseline site prices acting in conjunction with visitor income. The visitor's baseline satisfaction comes from none other than the baseline conditions characterized by the visitor's indirect utility function, which itself is determined by his making the best decisions possible with his available income. So we can express the expenditure function in the following policy-compelling format:

$$e = e(\, P;\; V(P^0, Y)) = e(P;\; P^0, Y) \qquad (4.11)$$

This interpretation is much more useful to policy analysts, for it measures how much money income the visitor needs at new site prices P to be as well off as facing original prices P^0 with Y to spend on recreation. The most attractive feature of the expenditure function expressed in this way is that it contains only observable data. This feature is quite important when it comes to discussing policy evaluations of proposed programs influencing outdoor recreation resources. The significance stems from the fact that the expenditure function as expressed on the right is entirely measurable with no need whatsoever to measure satisfaction. Analysts need only to measure the initial conditions that influenced the visitor's satisfaction.

From Expenditure Function to Welfare Measures

From the above discussion of the expenditure function, we know that $e(P^1; P^0, Y)$ measures how much money income the visitor needs at prices P^1 to be equally as well off as he would be when facing P^0 and having income Y. The two most commonly used welfare measures for evaluating policy changes are the compensating variation (CV) and equivalent variation (EV). Assuming that the policy has no impact on money income, they are defined as:

$$CV = Y - e(P^1; P^0, Y) \qquad (4.12)$$

$$EV = e(P^0; P^1, Y) - Y \qquad (4.13)$$

The CV asks what income change is needed to compensate the visitor for the satisfaction change due to the price change the policy caused. Compensation takes place after the proposed change, so CV measures what income change has to occur after the visitor faces new conditions (P^1) to offset the welfare impacts of the price change from P^0 to P^1. The term Y is actual money income, while $e(P^1; P^0, Y)$ is the expenditure function $e(P^1, V(P^0, Y))$. The CV measures actual income minus the minimum expenditure needed at new prices (P^1) to support visitor satisfaction sustained by original prices (P^0).

Policy analysts who use the CV make strong assumptions about the distribution of property rights. Use of the CV to measure benefits of proposed policies assumes the visitor owns the rights to recreation at original prices P^0 and that policies that alter those rights by requiring him to face P^1 require compensation equal to the CV, either to or from the visitor. If new prices P^1 are low compared to the original prices, use of the CV assumes the visitor should pay the CV for the privilege of facing the lower P^1. If new prices are higher, use of the CV assumes the visitor should be compensated by the CV for the burden of facing those new prices. When new prices are lower, CV measures the willingness to pay (WTP) for access to the lower prices, since the visitor only has rights to original high prices. When new prices are higher, CV measures willingness to accept payment (WTA) for the burden of facing higher prices, since again the visitor has rights to buy at the original low prices.

In contrast, the EV asks what income change at the current prices is equivalent to the proposed change in terms of its impact on the visitor's satisfaction. The income change substitutes for the proposed policy change, so EV measures the income change under old conditions (P^0) which substitutes for (takes the place of) the welfare impacts of the price change from P^0 to P^1. The term $e(P^0; P^1, Y)$ is the expenditure function $e[P^0, V(P^1, Y)]$. So the EV measures minimum expenditure needed at old prices (P^0) to support visitor satisfaction produced by new prices (P^0) minus actual income.

Analysts who use the EV also make assumptions about the distribution of property rights. Use of the EV to value proposed policies assumes that the visitor has rights to recreation at proposed (new) prices P^1. Policies that would restrict the visitor to current P^0 and block him from buying at P^1 require compensation in the amount of the EV, either to or from the visitor. If new prices P^1 are lower than P^0, the visitor should receive the EV if he continues to have access to the resource at price P^1. If P^1 is higher, the visitor should pay the EV for a policy that lets him avoid buying at that price. When P^1 is lower, EV measures WTA payment for loss of access to his property at the lower price. Where P^1 is higher, EV measures WTP to avoid the burden of paying the higher price.

Table 4.1 illustrates several examples of how CV and EV are interpreted for analysis of recreation policy decisions. It shows the welfare measures for several policies that could influence site prices or characteristics. Table 4.2 provides a summary of the economic interpretation of the two benefit measures for various policies.

RECREATION BENEFITS: TRAVEL COST MODELS

Single Site Analysis

Single site TCMs are the cheapest to build, usually because of the low cost of on-site surveys. One important function of single site models is to predict visitor use. Use can be predicted for a future period under current or emerging conditions. Planners might like to know what new facilities to build to accommodate model-projected growth. Single site models can also be used to predict impacts of proposals affecting factors that would change use. For example, a proposed policy dealing with assisting endangered species, maintaining clean air or managing water pollution may have an impact on outdoor recreation use of a site. Having access to a tested and reliable TCM that predicts impacts on visitor use would provide important information for planners.

Table 4.1 *Economic benefits of selected policy proposals, based on a Cobb-Douglas utility demand system with visitor preferences summarized as $B_1 = 1.0$ and $B_2 = 2.0$. Old and new site prices and visits with constant income*

Policy	Dependent variables		Independent variables			Benefits of policy change	
	Visits, Site 1 (X_1)	Visits, Site 2 (X_2)	Income	Price Site 1 (P_1)	Price, Site 2 (P_2)	CV	EV
Old	3.33	5.00	100	10	20	0	0
New	3.33	5.00	100	10	20		
Old	3.33	5.00	100	10	20	20.6	26.0
New	6.66	5.00	100	5	20		
Old	3.33	5.00	100	10	20	37.0	58.7
New	3.33	10.00	100	10	10		
Old	3.33	5.00	100	10	20	50.0	100.0
New	6.67	10.00	100	5	10		

$$CV = Y\left[1 - \left(\frac{P_1^I}{P_1^0}\right)^{\frac{B_1}{B_1+B_2}}\left(\frac{P_2^I}{P_2^0}\right)^{\frac{B_2}{B_1+B_2}}\right] \qquad EV = Y\left[\left(\frac{P_1^0}{P_1^I}\right)^{\frac{B_1}{B_1+B_2}}\left(\frac{P_2^0}{P_2^I}\right)^{\frac{B_2}{B_1+B_2}} - 1\right]$$

Table 4.2 Economic interpretation of CV and EV for selected policy proposals

Policy class or measure	Definitions and examples
IA	**Introduce one or more sites at known prices and qualities**
CV	Monetary compensation paid by visitor that offsets benefits of gaining site access rights. Example: (gain) Boater's maximum willingness to pay for the right to use a state park's boating facilities.
EV	Monetary compensation paid to visitor equivalent to the benefit of gaining site access rights. Example: (gain) Boater's minimum willingness to accept payment to avoid losing right to use a state park's boating facilities.
IB	**Withdraw one or more sites that were priced at known prices and qualities**
CV	Monetary compensation paid to visitor that offsets costs of losing site access rights. Example: (loss) Boater's minimum willingness to accept payment for loss of right to use a state park's boating facilities.
EV	Monetary compensation paid by visitor equivalent to the cost of losing site access rights. Example: (loss) Boater's maximum willingness to pay to avoid loss of right to use a state park's boating facilities.
II	**Change one or more site prices, holding qualities unchanged**
CV	Monetary compensation paid by (or to) visitor that offsets welfare impacts of the price changes. Example: (gain) Boater's maximum willingness to pay compensation for benefits of policy that reduces entry fees at all state parks. Example: (loss) Boater's minimum willingness to accept payment as compensation for costs of policy that raises entry fees at all state parks.
EV	Monetary compensation paid to (or by) visitor equivalent to the welfare impact of price changes. Example: (gain) Boater's minimum WTA payment equivalent to benefits of a policy that reduces entry fees at all state parks. Example: (loss) Boater's maximum WTP equivalent to costs incurred from policy that raises entry fees at all state parks.
III	**Change or more sites qualities, holding prices unchanged**
CV	Monetary compensation paid by (or to) visitor that offsets welfare impact of quality changes. Example: (gain) Boater's maximum WTP compensation for benefits of policy that upgrades launch lanes at all state parks. Example: (loss) Boater's minimum WTA payment as compensation for policy that lets launch lanes depreciate at state parks.

III	**Change or more sites qualities, holding prices unchanged**
EV	Monetary compensation paid to (or by) visitor equivalent to the welfare impact of quality changes. Example: (gain) Boater's minimum WTA payment equivalent to benefits of a policy that upgrades launch lanes at all state parks. Example: (loss) Boater's maximum WTP equivalent to costs incurred by policy that lets launch lanes depreciate at state parks.
IV	**Change one or more site prices and one or more sites qualities**
CV	Monetary compensation paid by (or to) visitor that offsets welfare impact of price and quality changes. Example: (gain) Boater's maximum WTP compensation for benefits of policy that reduces entry fees and upgrades launch lanes at state parks. Example: (loss) Boater's minimum WTA payment as compensation for costs of policy that raises entry fees and depreciates launch lanes at state parks.
EV	Monetary compensation paid to (or by) visitor equivalent to the welfare impact of price and quality changes. Example: (gain) Boater's minimum WTA payment equivalent to benefits of a policy that reduces entry fees and upgrades launch lanes at state parks. Example: (loss) Boater's maximum WTP equivalent to costs of a policy that raises entry fees and depreciates launch lanes at state parks.

Table 4.3 shows the formulas for computing demand and benefits for three of the most widely used models. These are the linear, the log-linear and the semi-log models. For all three model forms, use is assumed to be influenced by travel cost per trip (P), income (Y) and all other variables such as demographic or on-site factors, which we lump in the category (N). The single site model can be expanded to include as many factors that influence visitation as the analyst's budget will allow data to be collected.

We begin with a policy of changing a site's price. The TCM measures travel cost per trip as the relevant price, so both travel and on-site prices are included. Viewing price in this way permits us to use a TCM to evaluate policies that affect both entry fees and the cost of travel, such as energy or transportation policy. However, it is unlikely that many energy or transport planners have been exposed to the beauties of TCM!

Proposals to change entry fees receive a great deal of attention. Outdoor recreation facilities are commonly under-funded so the question of financial solvency is often answered with proposals to raise entry fees. Elected representatives, however, are often loath to incur the ire of groups of voters over what is seen to be a relatively minor amount of funds. It is easier to allow insidious degradation to occur. On the other hand, park visitors are often low-income people, so we often see proposals to lower entry fees to keep such recreation affordable.

The linear model

With the linear model given in Table 4.3, the use-predicting equation is a linear function of all the variables. As discussed in an earlier chapter, this means that the effects of changes on any variable on visitor use is linear. For example, a $5 increase in a site entry fee has one half as much effect on visits as a $10 increase. With the linear model, further fee increases ultimately drive visits to zero. Zero visits will occur at the so-called 'choke' price, the price at which all visits cease. The same holds true for changes in any of the other visit predictors.

Linear models are attractive because they're easy to estimate using ordinary least squares (OLS) regression. None of the variables need to be transformed to squares, square roots, logs and the like, thus minimizing potential coding errors. They are also easy to manipulate when managers wish to use the knowledge about visitation that they present. We would expect therefore that more linear demand models would been estimated than any other mathematical form. However, the last 20 years of published research in TCMs have seen relatively few, mostly because nonlinear forms seem to fit the data better. This is particularly the case where there is still some visitation left at very high prices and very high visitation at near-zero prices. It is those extremes, however, that are very important for outdoor recreation policy.

Sites that show a large increase in use for the very closest visitors are typically local parks and recreation areas, which may be candidates for special political attention. Sites that attract visitors from very great distances are typically important from the national and natural heritage points of view. Often these sites are also important for local economic reasons such as employment and investment in accommodation in the area. One needs only to pay a short summertime visit to Yellowstone National Park to see the boost to the local economy produced by the reserve. We suspect that a linear demand curve for that attraction would fit badly at the extremes.

Figure 4.1 shows a linear demand curve and the very large consumer surplus (CS) accruing to the visitor who buys at a low price and takes many trips per year. We have not discussed the CS in great detail yet, but for now we define it as a close approximation to the correct welfare measures, CV and EV. Typically the low price visitor is the person who lives very close to the site. For the sake of simplicity and illustration, we present examples of two kinds of two policies that would affect the price.

Table 4.4 presents numerical examples of how the CV, EV and CS can be calculated using the formulas in Table 4.3. We continue to assume a linear model and that a TCM has been estimated in which the parameters are as follows: B_1, the price coefficient, equals -2.28; B_2, the income coefficient, equals 0.10; and B_3, representing effects of all other variables, equals 0.72.

Table 4.3 Formulas for visitor demand and benefits from adding a site or lowering its price: three common algebraic forms for single site models[a]

Functional form	Measure and formula
	Visits demanded
Linear	$X = B_0 + B_1 P + B_2 Y + B_3 N$
Log-linear	$X = B_0 P^{B_1} Y^{B_2} N^{B_3}$
Semi-log	$X = exp(B_0 + B_1 P + B_2 Y + B_3 N)$
	CS
Linear (Add/drop a site if available at P_1)	$(X_1)^2 / (-2B_1)$
(Change price from P_0 to P_1)	$\left[(X_1)^2 - (X_0)^2\right] / (-2B_1)$
Log-linear (Add/drop a site if available at P_1)	$P_1 X_1 / (-B_1 - 1)$
(Change price from P_0 to P_1)	$\left[P_1 X_1 - P_0 X_0\right] / (-B_1 - 1)$
Semi-log (Add/drop a site if available at P_1)	$X_1 / (-B_1)$
(Change price from P_0 to P_1)	$\left[X_1 - X_0\right] / (-B_1)$
	CV[b]
Linear (Add/drop a site if available at P_1[b] or change price from P_0 to P_1)	$\left[\dfrac{X_1}{B_2} + \dfrac{B_1}{B_2^2}\right] - exp\left[B_2(P_1 - P_0)\right]\left[\dfrac{X_0}{B_2} + \dfrac{B_1}{B_2^2}\right]$

Table 4.3 (cont.)

Log-linear
(Add/drop a site if available at P_1 [b] or change price from P_0 to P_1)

$$Y - \left[Y^{1-B_2} + T_1 B_o \ N^{B_3} T_2 \right]^{\frac{1}{1-B_2}}$$

$where$

$$T_1 = \left[\frac{B_2 - 1}{1 + B_1} \right]$$

$$T_2 = \left[P_0^{B_1+1} - P_1^{B_1+1} \right]$$

Semi-log
(Add/drop a site if available at P_1 [b] or change price from P_0 to P_1)

$$\frac{1}{B_2} ln \left[1 + \frac{B_2}{B_1} \left(X_0 - X_1 \right) \right]$$

EV[b]

Linear
(Add/drop a site if available at P_1 [b] or change price from P_0 to P_1)

$$exp\left[B_2 (P_0 - P_1) \right] \left[\frac{X_1}{B_2} + \frac{B_1}{B_2^2} \right] - \left[\frac{X_0}{B_2} + \frac{B_1}{B_2^2} \right]$$

Log-linear
(Add/drop a site if available at P_1 [b] or change price from P_0 to P_1)

$$\left[Y^{1-B_2} + T_1 \ B_o \ N^{B_3} T_2 \right]^{\frac{1}{1-B_2}} - Y$$

$where$

$$T_1 = \left[\frac{B_2 - 1}{1 + B_1} \right]$$

$$T_2 = \left[P_1^{B_1+1} - P_0^{B_1+1} \right]$$

Semi-log
(Add/drop a site if available at P_1 [b] or change price from P_0 to P_1)

$$-\frac{1}{B_2} ln \left[1 + \frac{B_2}{B_1} \left(X_1 - X_0 \right) \right]$$

Notes:

[a]P is price, Y is income, N represents all other demand predictors, such as demographic factors or site characteristics. The Bs are estimated from the data.

[b]For CV and EV one formula is used for both policies. Calculate whatever price P_0 (the choke price) makes predicted visits equal 0 (or as close to it as we'd like) to value introducing it at P_1. Generally P_0 depends on the value of all variables; conditions producing high use need a high P_0 to eliminate use.

Table 4.4 Demand and benefits from building a site or lowering its price: three common algebraic forms for single site models[a]

Linear	Log Linear	Semi-Log
Value of parameters, constants and non-price variables:		
$B_0 = 13.06$; $B_1 = -2.28$;	$B_0 = 1$; $B_1 = -2$;	$B_0 = 2.37$; $B_1 = -0.28$;
$B_2 = 0.10$; $B_3 = 0.72$	$B_2 = 0.9$; $B_3 = 1$	$B_2 = 0.012$; $B_3 = 0.10$

Value of constants and non price variables:

exp (...) means e (2.7183) raised to the power of (...); $Y = 100$; $N = 10$

Value of P_0 that reduces visits (X) to 0 (0.1 for log linear and semi-log)

13.29	79.43	24.54

Predicted visits at price:

7.5	18.9	6.3	25.2	5.9	23.9
at $P_0 = 10$	at $P_1 = 5$	at $P_0 = 10$	at $P_1 = 5$	at $P_0 = 10$	at $P_1 = 5$

Consumer Surplus:

Add site at $P_1 = \$5$ (P_0 set to make visits $= 0$)[b]

78	126	85

Reduce price from ($P_0 = 10$ to $P_1 = 5$)[c]

66	63	64

Compensating Variation:

Add site at $P_1 = 5$ (P_0 set to make visits $= 0$)[b]

60	72	59

Reduce price from ($P_0 = 10$ to $P_1 = 5$)[c]

54	48	47

Equivalent Variation:

Add site at $P_1 = 5$ (P_0 set to make visits $= 0$)[b]

138	206	Infinite

Reduce price from ($P_0 = 10$ to $P_1 = 5$)[c]

88	84	122

Notes

[a] For all three demand models, X is visits; which are predicted from tabled independent variables, parameters and constants.

[b] P_0, computed to simulate site closure by reducing visits to zero (to 0.1 for log linear and semi log forms).

[c] When site is open, it's assumed accessible to visitors at $P_1 = 5$.

The intercept, B_0 equals 13.06, which accounts for the effect of all important variables not included in the model.

We must know the value of all the independent variables before we can use the model to predict visits. The values of the coefficients given above are assumed to remain constant. Table 4.4 provides values of all the non-price variables. They're assumed to equal 100 for income (Y) and 10 for other variables (N). If the price (travel cost per trip) is $5 with zero entry fee, use of the linear equation predicts our visitor takes 18.7 trips per year, using the assumed values of the coefficients and the independent variables.

Predicting future use   Travel cost models are usually applied to predict trips by the 'typical' visitor who lives at a known distance from the site. The same model is then re-applied to visitors at different travel distances who face different values of the other independent variables but the same values of the coefficients. The model when applied to people facing different conditions produces predicted trips for all the visitors in the market area.

Opening or closing a site   A policy question which could be posed concerns the impact on benefits, if measured as CS, of removing this site from the visitor's available opportunities. Removal of a site could mean either raising the entry fee to a high enough level so nobody could afford to enter or closing down the site, possibly temporarily for repairs or permanently because there isn't enough funding to keep it in business. There is actually another way of looking at this question, which sounds different but produces an identical consumer surplus. We could ask what is it worth in CS to build a site that currently does not exist and then make it accessible to our visitor at a travel cost of $5. This is a very common question posed by recreation planners who consider developing new facilities such as hiking trails and golf courses. An economic interpretation of this question involves both the price which is high enough that the visitor just does not visit ($P_0 = \$13.29$) and the price at which he will use it ($5).

Setting P_0 equal to $13.29 may seem arbitrary but it has good economic logic. It comes from solving the linear use equation for the value of price at which predicted visits are zero ($X = 0$) for the given values of the parameters and all the non-price variables. As we would expect, the higher the visitor's income and values of other factors contributing to potential visitation, the higher will be the price needed to reduce visits to zero. This price, currently at $13.29, increases with increased values of B_0, B_2, B_3 or any of the non-price variables. It also increases as the price coefficient goes closer to zero.

Table 4.4 shows this policy produces a CS of $78, from the consumer surplus formula. In that formula, X_1 means the number of trips taken at the price when the site is open for business ($5), while X_0 is the trips when the

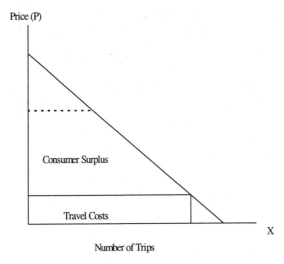

Figure 4.1 Consumer surplus for private recreational use of a public recreation site

site is closed, namely zero. That consumer surplus is the area of the large triangle shown in Figure 4.1

Local versus distant visitation One interesting application of TCMs is to estimate use and benefits for visitors whose cost of access is near zero. As stated above, a single TCM is typically applied to all visitors, including those who live so close to the site that they have effectively a zero price. Although not shown in Table 4.4, we can apply the same linear demand function to the visitor who faces a zero price. In terms of Figure 4.1, this visitor receives the area under the entire demand curve as his consumer surplus. Assuming the value of the other parameters and variables are the same as those for a more distant visitor, we see his choke price is unchanged at $13.29. However, by applying the formula in Table 4.4 to the visitor who lives at the site, his consumer surplus due to the site's presence is $200.

This example illustrates an important principle underlying all TCMs. The greatest benefit accrues to visitors who live nearest the site. However, most of their benefit accrues as consumer surplus. Analysts can expect unenthusiastic reception from local businesses who are shown results of TCMs predicting high benefits for proposed sites, where the benefits accrue largely as consumer surplus to close-by visitors. Understandably, they are more interested in benefits that accrue as additional local spending.

How to deal with visitors who live close to a site can be a very confusing point for some analysts who may instinctively wish to assign higher benefits to visitors who are seen coming from great distances. After all, aren't these visitors willing to travel a long way to visit the site? Therefore they must value it highly. These are good instincts, but only partly right.

Sites that attract visitors from large distances will indeed show demand functions that are very steep. In terms of price elasticity, which we discussed in Chapter 3, these sites will show very low price elasticities (price inelasticity). The Grand Canyon and Yosemite Park, both of which receive over 4 million visitor days per year, are two good examples. People travel from around the world to visit these western American icons. But the most distant visitor does not necessarily receive the highest benefits. Their high-cost visits cause the estimated TCM to have low price elasticity and a demand schedule that is shifted far to the right. However, in comparing any two visitors, other things being equal, the visitor with the lowest price always enjoys the biggest CS as well as the biggest CV and EV.

Effect of price decreases   Another policy question sounds rather different, but is really a special case of the first. It concerns the impact on consumer surplus of actions that lower the price of access from $10 to $5 per trip. Public recreation policies do not typically lower entry fees. However, external policy decisions do increase the efficiency of transportation networks, such as building tunnels or roads, expanding airports or otherwise lowering the cost of access to outdoor recreation areas. Still other examples are measures to reduce the cost of travel to the driving public. Policies that reduce energy import barriers could also lower the cost of travel through their impact on the price of gasoline.

This policy question asks what is the impact on CS of reducing the price from $10 to $5. Figure 4.1 shows effects of a policy moving the visitor from a price of ($P_0 = 10$), shown as a dotted line, to a price of ($P_1 = 5$). This policy increases the visitor's benefit from a small triangle to the larger triangle, the complete area of which we know to be $78. The difference in area between the little triangle and big one is the area of a trapezoid. This trapezoid area is the horizontal slice bound by the prices of $10 and $5. The area of the trapezoid is the average of the numbers of visits at the high and low prices multiplied by the price reduction of $5. The CS formula shows this policy is worth $66, as shown in Table 4.4.

Table 4.4 also presents formulas and shows examples for the same two policies using the CV and EV welfare measures. Both the CV and EV formulas are complex. Details on their derivation can be found on some postgraduate microeconomic theory texts, for example Varian (1992). Bockstael, Hanemann and Strand (1989) present additional documentation. Even though the formulas are complicated, they can be coded into a spreadsheet once, then applied as many times as desired every time a new study is undertaken or for each policy application in a given study. Additionally, for all the reasons discussed above, the CV and EV have precise interpretation in terms of WTP and WTA payment, while the CS has no welfare interpretation at all. Its saving grace is that it is usually close to the two correct measures.

Opening or closing a site   The CV for the policy of introducing the site at a price of $5 is $60 and $54 for reducing its price from $10 to $5. As expected, these CV welfare measures are both slightly smaller than the CS. For this case the CV has a welfare interpretation as the WTP for the privilege of accessing the site at a price of $5. The CV is the correct benefit measure to use if we assume that the visitor has no property right to access the site at the old price.

The policy analysis takes on a rather different tone if the visitor is accustomed to using the site at a price of $5, taking 18.9 trips per year. Suppose the proposed policy would close it down or otherwise take it out of use. Then the same $60 becomes the visitor's EV, namely the income loss that would be equivalent to losing access to the $5 site. Table 4.4 describes the $60 as the CV because it assumes the policy lowers price. On the other hand, if the policy raises the price from $5 to $10, the $60 now becomes the EV. In any case the $60 is still the visitor's WTP to continue his access to the site and is correctly used as a welfare measure if the visitor is presumed to lack a property right to access it.

The EV for the policy of building and introducing the site at the $5 price is $138. As all microeconomic theory textbooks show, EV is larger than both the CV and CS, whenever income elasticity is greater than zero. For the case of a price reduction, the EV has an interpretation as the willingness to accept payment (WTA) as a substitute for access to the site. While the $138 is considerably higher than the CV of only $60, one can imagine that it could be quite high indeed, possibly infinite, if the visitor considers the site a necessity that utterly lacks substitutes. The EV is the right benefit measure when one presumes the visitor has a property right to access the site at the $5 price, and that he must be compensated for a policy that fails to maintain the site. As property owners have the right not to sell at any price, high or infinite EVs should be common for sites held to have no substitutes.

Again this policy has an interesting parallel for the case of the visitor who already uses the site at $5. If the proposed policy would shut it down, $138 is now the CV and no longer an EV. It's still $138, but it's now the income compensation that would take the place of lost site access by raising the site's price from the current $5 to the $13.29 choke price. That $138 income payment is still the visitor's WTA money to take the place of lost access. It is

correctly used as a welfare measure if the visitor is assumed to have a right to
the low cost access.

Other functional forms

Table 4.4 also shows how to compute the various welfare measures for two
other widely-used functional forms, the log-linear and semi-log demand
functions. Although not discussed here in detail since the same steps are used
for welfare calculations, both these functions have the property that no finite
price can reduce visits to zero, so the TCM modeler typically must select a
choke price.

One common method is to use the maximum price (travel distance) at
which visitors consistently come for the sole purpose of visiting the site.
Another method is to select an arbitrarily low number of visits, such as 0.1,
then mathematically solve the demand function for the price that would
produce that predicted number visits. The second method is the one we chose
to illustrate the welfare measures from these forms.

Note that for the semi-log model, the price that would reduce visits to 0.1
for the semi log model is $24.54, and the EV is infinite. This means that the
site must be so valued by the visitor that it would take an infinite addition to
income to take the place of simply reducing the price from $24.54 to $5. One
suspects that the semi-log form would provide good fits to sites that have
unique characteristics and for which closure or environmental damage would
impose major burdens to large numbers of visitors.

Multiple Sites

Measuring the theoretically correct CV and EV from observed data requires
observing actual trips taken, site prices (travel costs), income and finally the
expenditure function itself. For the standard utility functions used in most
microeconomic texts and in most applied research, the multiple site
expenditure function is also measurable from observed data. As explained
above, measuring the expenditure function requires inverting the indirect
utility function, which itself comes from substituting the demand function
back into the original utility function. For the example of the two sites Cobb-
Douglas utility function, the expenditure functions are:

$$e(P^1; P^0, Y) = Y \left(\frac{P_1^1}{P_1^0} \right)^{\frac{B_1}{B_1 + B_2}} \left(\frac{P_2^1}{P_2^0} \right)^{\frac{B_2}{B_1 + B_2}}$$

(4.14)

$$e(P^0; P^1, Y) = Y \left(\frac{P_1^0}{P_1^1} \right)^{\frac{B_1}{B_1+B_2}} \left(\frac{P_2^0}{P_2^1} \right)^{\frac{B_2}{B_1+B_2}}.$$

$$(4.15)$$

where the subscripts in the price (P) terms refer to the site number and the superscripts refer to new (1) and old (0) policy levels. Equation (4.14) is used to find the CV while (4.15) is for the EV. The two ratios refer to our two sites. For more than two sites, two adjustments are made. First, each extra site has its own B_i reflecting intensity of the visitor's preferences towards that site. Second, we insert more ratios farther out to the right, with each ratio taking an exponent equal to $B_i / \Sigma B_i$. However, no matter how many sites are in the system there are only two equations. So the complete formulas for the CV and EV are calculated as:

$$CV = Y \left[1 - \left(\frac{P_1^1}{P_1^0} \right)^{\frac{B_1}{B_1+B_2}} \left(\frac{P_2^1}{P_2^0} \right)^{\frac{B_2}{B_1+B_2}} \right]$$

$$(4.16)$$

$$EV = Y \left[\left(\frac{P_1^0}{P_1^1} \right)^{\frac{B_1}{B_1+B_2}} \left(\frac{P_2^0}{P_2^1} \right)^{\frac{B_2}{B_1+B_2}} - 1 \right]$$

$$(4.17)$$

Both of these welfare measures can be estimated from observed data on income, visitation and the two site prices. See Appendix 4.1 for more details. The two welfare formulas can be generalized to as many sites as are being analyzed by adding more terms in ratios and modifying the exponents as described above.

Remarkably, OLS regression can be used to estimate the B_i parameters. The trick is to divide the first site demand equation by the other, both the independent and dependent variables. The dependent variable is the log of the ratio of visits of site 1 to site 2. After taking ratios and logs for the independent variables, there are two intercept parameters and two variable parameters. The parameters for the log of P_2 must be 1 while the one for (natural) log of P_1 must be -1.

Both the CV and EV welfare measures above are unchanged if both B_1 and B_2 are doubled. This is referred to as independence of a scale change. So we typically choose a number for B_1 (assumed here to be 1.0) and the regression software estimates the other (assumed to be 2.0 for this case). Note that this method is based entirely on observed data, with no need to measure satisfaction. For a many-site Cobb-Douglas demand system, the parameters can be estimated with OLS. The left and right hand sides of each site's demand equation are divided by the demand of a base site. This procedure produces *n-1* ratios of site demand to demand for visits at the baseline site. The estimation produces $n-1$ parameters B_i.

Effect of price changes   Referring back to Table 4.1, note that it shows the application of equations (4.16–4.17) by computing the welfare impacts for four hypothetical policy changes. The first policy is the policy of no change, which as expected shows that CV and EV are zero. The second policy halves the first site's price from $10 to $5, holding the second sites price at a constant price of $20, and assumes income is a constant $100. The CV of this policy is $20.6, while the EV is about 25 per cent larger at $26.0.

The third policy holds the first site's price constant at $10, while reducing the second site's price from $20 to $10 with a constant income. Both welfare measures show a much larger gain compared to the second policy. The reasons are, firstly, site 2 is more preferred (e.g. it has better trout fishing and the visitor is a trout fisherman). Secondly, the halving of site 2's price is applied to a much higher initial price. This could happen with a policy that reduces entry fees at the preferred site.

Policy 3 produces a CV of $37 and an EV of $58.7. This means that the angler is willing to pay up to $37 for the right to access policy 3, but he would need to be compensated $58.7 to substitute for lacking access to this policy. Use of the CV of $37 assumes that the visitor lacks property rights to the lower price produced by the policy. Use of the EV is the appropriate welfare measure if polluters have to compensate fishermen for blocking anglers' access to the lower priced fishing to which they have a right.

The last policy halves both sites' prices. For a constant income of $100, this has the effect of doubling the effective power of income, had original prices not changed. As expected, the EV, added income needed to take the place of the policy, is an even $100. Likewise, the CV is the change in income to offset the satisfaction gain, had the visitor had access to the cheaper site prices. As expected, the CV is $50. That is, the original recreational budget would need to be cut by $50, from $100 to $50, if the visitor has access to the new cheaper site prices to gain zero satisfaction from those cheaper prices.

Closing a site This example vividly shows the importance of presumed property rights for measuring benefits of proposed policies. Suppose the proposed policy would dam a previously wild river, thus removing a previously available rafting opportunity. The welfare impact (benefits) of the proposed policy depends on who has the presumed property rights to the wild river.

If we assume visitors have no property right to raft the river, we measure their WTP to avoid building the dam and keep the river wild. Their WTP to avoid the loss of access to a river which is someone else's property is their EV. What's interesting is that we tend to find low numbers for these people because rafters often don't have much money. In fact, mathematically the WTP has an upper bound equal to the visitors' incomes. When we measure rafters' WTP to avoid loss of the wild river, we're assigning the property right of developing the river to the power companies (Gaffney, 1997).

However, we could just as easily assume the rafting public already owns the right to a wild river. Then we would not ask people for their WTP to keep their own river wild. We ask them their WTA compensation to allow the power company to change the river from wild to tamed and developed. In this case, we're asking rafters their CV to compensate for loss of their wild river and not their EV. The last 30 years of research has shown what we'd expect. For WTA, we usually get very high numbers. Many people won't sell their river at any price and, in some cases, where environmental resources are perceived as necessities, the WTA is infinite. Mathematically, the WTA has no upper bound, as shown for the Cobb-Douglas example in Table 4.1.

For situations where the proposed policy improves welfare, the CV offsets the gains so it is a WTP and the EV is a WTA. On the other hand, where the proposed policy reduces welfare, the CV offsets the losses, so it is a WTA and the EV is a WTP. Regardless of whether we use the CV or EV, the WTA is always at least as large as the WTP and often much larger. Table 4.1 shows examples of policies that would improve welfare, so the CV is a WTP for the gain and the EV is a WTA payment in lieu of the gain.

From the simple results of this table, it is easy to imagine that the WTA can be very large indeed since, for example in the table, a simple halving of prices to all recreation sites requires a WTA as large as the total budget itself. For proposed policies that would preserve an environmental resource people perceive as a necessity (e.g. restrict power companies' emissions that cause air pollution at the Grand Canyon or prohibit oil drilling on the Great Barrier Reef), it is easy to imagine an infinite WTA required to compensate for loss of the asset.

The Welfare Approximation: Consumer Surplus

The classic apparatus for measuring welfare change in TCMs is consumer's surplus (CS). If $X(P,Y)$ is the mathematically correct visitor's demand for a single site, as a function of its price and income, then the CS associated with a price change is measured as the area to the left of the demand curve and between those two prices. This is shown in Figure 4.1, as we saw above, as the large triangle. CS is also shown in Figure 4.2 as the trapezoid-like area A + B between the prices P_0 and P_1. This second figure represents a policy in which a public resource agency lowers the site entry fee. It is the CS approximation of the theoretically correct welfare measures, shown in Figure 4.2 as CV and EV, that Hotelling's original 1947 suggestion attempted to measure.

The consumer surplus is nothing more than the area to the left of the demand curve between the old-policy and new-policy price. Still, it turns out that under a remarkably wide range of conditions the single site CS is a very good approximation for the correct measures. In fact, the CS measures neither the willingness to pay for the site nor the willingness to accept payment as compensation for no site, but it's often close to both. As shown in Figure 4.2, for the case of a price decline, the following relationship holds among the three for a normal good for which income elasticity exceeds zero:

$$|CV| < |CS| < |EV| \qquad (4.18)$$

Figure 4.2 shows that the CV is equal to the area beneath a very special demand curve that is compensated to the old price situation. By this we mean that income continually adjusts in the face of price changes so that the visitor is held to the same level of satisfaction he received under the old price. The function that continually adjusts income is, as we would expect, the expenditure function for old price conditions. Similarly, the EV is equal to the area beneath a similar compensated demand curve compensated to new price satisfaction and is equal to A + B + C. This time income adjusts in the face of price changes to hold the visitor at the level of satisfaction he receives under new prices. Again, the income adjuster is the expenditure function for new price conditions. For the case of a price increase for the single site, all three measures are negative since welfare goes down. However, in absolute terms, the opposite relation holds for a normal good, namely:

$$|CV| > |CS| > |EV| \qquad (4.19)$$

This says the CV is absolutely larger than CS, farther away from zero, which in turn is absolutely larger than the EV.

The interested reader would find it entertaining to pursue this very old, sometimes amusing, and very often confusing literature. Questions have been raised and re-raised regarding the CS since the time of Marshall's original *Principles of Economics* (1890). Marshall had developed an earlier suggestion made by the French engineer Jules Dupuit in 1844 that the CS may be a tool for measuring the benefits of a proposed bridge.

One of the more widely quoted summaries of the CS is Hicks (1956). In his classic treatise *A Revision of Demand Theory*, Hicks concluded that for the CS to be a good measure, 'one thing alone is needful ... that the income effect should be small'. In fact if the income elasticity is zero, all three are identical. Probably the clearest and most compelling statement for its use was done by Willig (1976). In his article, he established bounds describing how far apart those three can be. Thus, the CS measures no welfare concept at all, but we can take considerable comfort by knowing it is close to the other two.

Nevertheless, travel cost modelers for years have estimated ordinary demand curves and presented CS as their best estimate of welfare effects of proposed policies. Since 1976 they have been able to do it with considerably less apology than before. It is our view that CS is a safe measure to use for the single site demand curve for the case of price change. However, for those who are less trusting of the CS, we present formulas in Table 4.3 to show how to find all three measures for three commonly used demand functions. These formulas show that the EV has no upper bound but the CV is strictly bounded by the visitor's income and the CS lies somewhere in between.

It is less safe to use the CS for a single site where policy-induced quality changes shift the demand curve left or right. This is so because for very little rigorous work in the literature has updated Willig's CS error bounds for the case of quality changes. For multi-site systems, it is probably safe to use the multi-site CS, which is simply the area beneath an appropriately sequenced system of ordinary demand functions when needing to approximate the CV and EV for the case of price changes. Conversely, it is quite inappropriate to

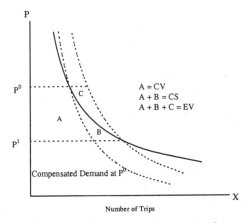

Figure 4.2: Three welfare measures from a price change

use changes in the multi site CS to approximate welfare change for quality change at systems of sites, as illustrated in this chapter's appendix. You will compute a number but, like reaching under a rock to pick up something that rattles, you will get something you may not like.

BENEFITS OF QUALITY CHANGES

Maler's (1974) pathbreaking work described conditions he labeled 'weak-complementarity' that provide the theoretical justification for measuring the benefits of environmental quality changes from observable single site demand functions. These conditions, described by Maler and elaborated on by Freeman (1979), explained the required conditions for valuing a quality change by using the area behind the compensated demand curve for a single market good affected by changes in quality. If Figure 4.1 were drawn to show a shift to the right of compensated demand in the face of increased site quality, Maler's method values the higher quality by the increased CS traced out through the shifted compensated demand. The compensated demand is described in this chapter's appendix.

As an example, the market good could be an outdoor recreation trip to picnic at a lake, the price is the visitor's travel costs, and the quality could be the water quality at the destination lake. The difference in the area behind this demand curve for the market good was shown by Maler to be a good estimate of the value of the improved water quality as long as the change in water quality had no effect on the visitor's benefits when the market good was not consumed. This is his weak complementarity condition.

Numerous authors since that time have used these results when estimating the benefits of environmental improvements through TCMs. Bockstael and McConnell (1983) generalized Maler's result for the case of the household production function. They found that the same principle applies, namely that the increased area beneath an input demand function into a household production process is a good measure of the benefits of an environmental quality change under two conditions. The quality must be a weak complement to the commodity produced by the household, such as water-based recreation trips. Additionally, the input that is being valued, such as cleaner beaches, must be required in the production of that commodity.

We therefore have a limited knowledge of how to incorporate quality properly into single site models to measure CV and EV from observed data. However, in the realm of major national policies, single site models have limited appeal. Environmental quality changes due to actions by national agencies, such as the US Environmental Protection Agency or US Forest Service, are usually huge in geographical scope and many sites are typically affected. To deal appropriately with multiple sites, it is essential to find data with enough variability in it to trace out impacts on visitor behavior. Ignoring multiple site interactions neglects important substitution possibilities for visitors. Thus, trying to account for all the impacts with a series of single site models is simply too limited in scope. Furthermore, there is an interest in modeling demand for recreation activities that can occur at a large number of competing sites. For all these reasons and also because observed recreation behavior is typically defined over a large number of choice alternatives such as different activities or different sites, resource economists have turned to multiple site recreation demand models with quality incorporated.

There are several recreation policy problems for which the simple single site TCM is misleading for yet another reason. There is usually not just one isolated site and therefore one travel cost that enters into the visitor's decision to participate in an activity at that site. Rather there are commonly many alternative sites and activities that offer both very similar and very different experiences. In any case, sites are rarely identical and rarely the same distance from the visitor's residence. The qualities and prices of the many alternatives often show so much variability that the researcher who needs to value site characteristics naturally wants to use that variability to advantage.

An Example of a Demand System with Quality Incorporated

Table 4.5 provides an example of a model of a demand system with incorporated quality changes. It is the familiar Cobb-Douglas utility function in which quality is this time allowed to enter the picture. The algebraic form looks quite similar to the Cobb-Douglas demand system without quality which was shown in Table 4.1. That is, it predicts demand at each of many sites. Different values of the right hand side variables apply to each site so predicted X_i can be different for each site. What's new is that what we previously called intensity of the visitor's preferences for a site, the B_i independent variables, now appear as explicit functions of the site quality. This means that each site's B_i is a function of its quality, hence $B_i = B_i(Q_i)$.

There are many ways to incorporate site qualities into the visitor's utility function and, through its effect on visitor's choices, into his demand function. This is a very active area of research and will likely continue to be so for many years. One of the more comprehensive treatments of methods for bringing quality into demand systems is that of Bockstael, Hanemann and Strand (1989). A more flexible way of doing it is to insert the quality variables directly into the place in the utility function normally occupied by parameters in models without quality. So what is normally a constant in the utility function for the demand system without quality becomes some mathematical function containing both parameters (constants) and quality. So long as the analyst does not insert prices or incomes into this function, and leaves it only a function of quality and constants, the system of demand equations with quality held constant looks essentially identical to the system without quality entering at all. Site quality will not directly affect either the price or the budget constraint, when a site's quality is not a function of price (travel distance).

Although site characteristics occupy the places formerly held by constant parameters, their mathematical functions of qualities still have parameters to estimate. Table 4.5 shows that we assume each site's quality function has two parameters, one that accounts for the level of the site's quality, and the other to account for changes in quality. We illustrate by using the following simple function:

$$B_i = b_{0i}(Q_i)^{b_{1i}}$$

(4.20)

This equation (4.20) is fairly flexible, permitting observed data on each site's visits to adapt to both the level of quality (b_{0i}) and changes in quality (b_{1i}). As described in this chapter's appendix, this demand system and its related quality parameters can be estimated with ordinary least squares regression, as long as we're willing to make some convenient assumptions about the errors.

This system of demand functions has two major uses, the prediction of visitation and, through estimation of its parameters, measurement of benefits. After estimating the demand system equations, we can use it to predict use at any given site in the system. This prediction is done by substituting in travel costs (prices) facing the visitor at all sites in the system, the visitor's income and all sites' qualities.

This functional form lacks price substitution but has much quality substitution. This means that each site's demand is affected only by its own price, but not by the price of any substitutes. However, any given site's demand is affected by its own quality and by the qualities of all other sites. That is, decisions such as buying water rights, building hiking trails, stocking fish and reducing pollutants at each site affects the demand for all substitute sites. It is typically policies affecting quality at several sites for which policymakers want to know the changes in benefits.

Table 4.5 shows the formulas used to compute the various welfare measures associated with four classes of policies. The first two classes of policies have already been discussed in the single site case. Class I considers policies which would introduce sites, while Class II is a more general case of Class I in which prices of one or more sites could be changed. These classes also have already been discussed for the Cobb-Douglas utility demand system above. We now discuss the remaining classes of policies.

Quality Changes with Constant Prices

The third policy class is quite different from anything discussed in the single site model or the multi-site model for price changes. This class explicitly permits evaluation of policies that would change qualities from their old levels, Q_1^0, Q_2^0, ... Q_n^0 to a new proposed level Q_1^1, Q_2^1, ... Q_n^1 at each site while holding the sites' prices unchanged. This policy class represents the complete range of decisions in which the quality characteristics of several sites are simultaneously affected by a single action. National pollution control proposals that would restrict emissions into air or waterways over large regional areas are good examples. Others are a state conservation department's decision to upgrade trout hatchery capacity so that significantly greater numbers of fish can be stocked statewide or a legislative appropriation to build boat ramps, buy water rights or build hiking trails throughout a large region.

A further example of the Class III policy is a policy involving major reallocation of fixed resources among competing sites, such as a decision by a national park service to reallocate its budget from buying new sites to maintaining an existing national park system better. In any case, Class III policies permit evaluation of quality changes at several sites; some sites may get increased quality, while others may get less. However, since prices are assumed unchanged, Class III policies could be described as unfunded or at least mandates for change not directly charged to visitors.

The fourth policy class evaluates welfare impacts of simultaneous quality and price changes at all sites. This means that old quality and price levels, Q_1^0, Q_2^0, ... Q_n^0 and P_1^0, P_2^0, ... P_n^0 can be changed to new quality and price levels Q_1^1, Q_2^1, ... Q_n^1 and P_1^1, P_2^1, ... P_n^1. Class IV policies are proposals for quality changes in which the visitors are charged to finance some or all of the investments. Boat ramps, camping facilities and boat docks all come to mind as examples. For the case of environmental damage, we would imagine policies that compensated resources users. Visitors are rarely reimbursed for a deteriorating environment through lower prices, but one could imagine a legislative body enacting a policy that reduced fishing license prices where fishing waters have suffered contamination.

Derivation of the expenditure function and CV and EV welfare measures for the case of simultaneous price and quality changes is shown in the Appendix 4A. The appendix shows only the case of the Cobb-Douglas utility function with quality embedded in the quantity exponents. However, exactly the same steps are followed for any other utility function chosen, such as the CES or other well-behaved utility function typically explained in microeconomics textbooks. The appendix shows the case of simultaneous changes, which is the most general problem. Although the appendix does not

*Table 4.5 Demand and benefit formulas using a 'multi-site TCM,
based on a Cobb-Douglas utility function*[a] *with quality*

Class		CS	CV	EV
I	Introduce one or more sites at prices[b] P_1^1, P_i^1 ...P_n^1 holding qualities at initial levels			
	$\left(\dfrac{Y}{\sum_i B_i^0}\right)\sum_i B_i^0\left[\log P_i^m - \log P_i^1\right]$		$Y - A$	$D - Y$
II	Change several sites' prices from P_1^0, P_i^0 ...P_n^0 to P_1^1, Pi^1 ... P_n^1 holding qualities at initial levels			
	$\left(\dfrac{Y}{\sum_i B_i^0}\right)\sum_i B_i^0\left[\log P_i^0 - \log P_i^1\right]$		$Y - A$	$D - Y$
III	Change several sites' qualities from Q_1^0, Q_i^0 ... Q_n^0 to Q_1^1, Qi^1 ... Q_n^1 holding their prices constant at P_1^1, Pi^1 ... P_n^1			
	Not reliable		$Y - B$	$E - Y$
IV	Change several site's qualities from Q_1^0, Q_i^0 ... Q_n^0 to Q_1^1, Qi^1 ... Q_n^1 and change their prices from P_1^0, P_i^0 ... P_n^0 to P_1^1, Pi^1 ... P_n^1			
	Not reliable		$Y - C$	$F - Y$

Algebraic Formula for Demand: $X_i = \dfrac{B_i Y}{P_i \sum_i B_i}$ where: $B_i = b_{0i}(Q_i)^{b_{1i}}$

$Q_i = ith$ site's measured quality

$b_{0i}, b_{1i} =$ estimated parameters

Notes:

[a] This functional form has quality substitution but lacks price substitution. The only price affecting the demand for a site is its own; however, all sites' qualities affect its demand. Thus, the demand for site 1 falls when site 1's price rises, site 1's quality falls or when any other site's quality increases. The reason rests with the budget constraint. With a limited visitor budget a quality increase in site 1 causes its own demand to increase, but that increased demand must come at the expense of visits to one or more substitutes.

[b] The price P_i^m is the 'choke' price, the theoretical price that reduces a sites's visits to zero. For this algebraic form no price reduces visits to zero, so a high but finite price must be used.

$$A = e(P_i^1, Q_i^0 ; P_i^0, Q_i^0, Y) = Y \prod_i \left(\frac{P_i^1}{P_i^0} \right)^{\left(\frac{B_i^0}{\Sigma B_i^0} \right)}$$

$$B = e(P_i^0, Q_i^1 ; P_i^0, Q_i^0, Y) = Y^{\left(\frac{\Sigma B_i^0}{\Sigma B_i^1} \right)} \left(\frac{\sum_i B_i^1}{\left(\sum_i B_i^0 \right)^{\frac{\Sigma B_i^0}{\Sigma B_i^1}}} \right) \left(\frac{\prod_i \left(B_i^1 \right)^{\frac{-B_i^1}{\Sigma B_i^1}}}{\prod_i \left(B_i^0 \right)^{\frac{-B_i^0}{\Sigma B_i^1}}} \right) \left(\frac{\prod_i \left(P_i^0 \right)^{\frac{B_i^1}{\Sigma B_i^1}}}{\prod_i \left(P_i^0 \right)^{\frac{B_i^0}{\Sigma B_i^1}}} \right)$$

$$C = e(P_i^1, Q_i^1 ; P_i^0, Q_i^0, Y) = Y^{\left(\frac{\Sigma B_i^0}{\Sigma B_i^1} \right)} \left(\frac{\sum_i B_i^1}{\left(\sum_i B_i^0 \right)^{\frac{\Sigma B_i^0}{\Sigma B_i^1}}} \right) \left(\frac{\prod_i \left(B_i^1 \right)^{\frac{-B_i^1}{\Sigma B_i^1}}}{\prod_i \left(B_i^0 \right)^{\frac{-B_i^0}{\Sigma B_i^1}}} \right) \left(\frac{\prod_i \left(P_i^1 \right)^{\frac{B_i^1}{\Sigma B_i^1}}}{\prod_i \left(P_i^0 \right)^{\frac{B_i^0}{\Sigma B_i^1}}} \right)$$

$$D = e(P_i^0, Q_i^0 ; P_i^1, Q_i^0, Y) = Y \prod_i \left(\frac{P_i^0}{P_i^1} \right)^{\left(\frac{B_i^0}{\Sigma B_i^0} \right)}$$

$$E = e(P_i^0, Q_i^0 ; P_i^0, Q_i^1, Y) = Y^{\left(\frac{\Sigma B_i^1}{\Sigma B_i^0} \right)} \left(\frac{\sum_i B_i^0}{\left(\sum_i B_i^1 \right)^{\frac{\Sigma B_i^1}{\Sigma B_i^0}}} \right) \left(\frac{\prod_i \left(B_i^0 \right)^{\frac{-B_i^0}{\Sigma B_i^0}}}{\prod_i \left(B_i^1 \right)^{\frac{-B_i^1}{\Sigma B_i^0}}} \right) \left(\frac{\prod_i \left(P_i^0 \right)^{\frac{B_i^0}{\Sigma B_i^0}}}{\prod_i \left(P_i^0 \right)^{\frac{B_i^1}{\Sigma B_i^0}}} \right)$$

$$F = e(P^0, Q^0 ; P^1, Q^1, Y) = Y^{\left(\frac{\Sigma B_i^1}{\Sigma B_i^0} \right)} \left(\frac{\sum_i B_i^0}{\sum_i \left(B_i^1 \right)^{\frac{\Sigma B_i^1}{\Sigma B_i^0}}} \right) \left(\frac{\prod_i \left(B_i^0 \right)^{\frac{-B_i^0}{\Sigma B_i^0}}}{\prod_i \left(B_i^1 \right)^{\frac{-B_i^1}{\Sigma B_i^0}}} \right) \left(\frac{\prod_i \left(P_i^0 \right)^{\frac{B_i^0}{\Sigma B_i^0}}}{\prod_i \left(P_i^1 \right)^{\frac{B_i^1}{\Sigma B_i^0}}} \right)$$

derive it, welfare values for price changes only and quality changes only are
special cases of the simultaneous change of both.

   Table 4.5 presents the welfare formulas for all three, for both the CV and
EV. The CS welfare approximation formula is also shown in Table 4.5 for
the case of price changes only. The CS formula comes from finding the area
between two price horizontals summed over all of the sites' demand
equations. Sites that have no price change have no area to be computed. For
the case of the Cobb-Douglas utility function, the CS is independent of the
order in which the price changes occur, simply because each site's demand
depends on only its own price. This would not be the case for other multi-site
utility function demand systems. Moreover, even if the demand system
comes from an underlying utility function, the multi-site consumer surplus
depends on the order in which the price changes are evaluated. That is, it is
path-dependent.

   Path dependence is never a problem with the CV or EV, no matter how
many sites are in the system or how many price and quality changes are being
evaluated, as long as they come from an underlying utility function. We do
not show the CS for quality changes or for price and quality changes, since
they have no foundation in welfare theory. We do not know if they are close
to the EV and CV. For example, a policy that spends resources to double all
site qualities may leave visits at all sites unchanged and show a total
consumer surplus of zero, since the slope and position of all demand
functions are not changed for the Cobb-Douglas function. However the CV
and EV would both show a huge gain in benefits.

   We now present a few numerical examples of the last two classes of policy
proposals, illustrating application of the rather formidable-looking welfare
formulas shown in Table 4.5. For quality changes and constant prices, Table
4.5 shows that policies that change qualities at one or more sites without
affecting price produces a CV which the table defines as $Y - B$ and EV is
defined as $D - Y$. These formulas come from the following definitions for CV
and EV respectively:

$$CV = Y - B = Y - e(P^0,Q^1; P^0,Q^0,Y) \qquad (4.21)$$

$$EV = E - Y = e(P^0,Q^0; P^0,Q^1,Y) - Y \qquad (4.22)$$

That is, CV is actual income (Y) minus the expenditure function (B), which is
the minimum income needed at qualities Q^1 (new quality conditions) for the
visitor to be as well off as he would be facing qualities Q^0 (old qualities).
Since prices do not change for this evaluation, we include them at constant
levels. For the case where new qualities are better, CV measures the visitor's

WTP for the better quality. In contrast, where new qualities are worse, CV measures the visitor's WTA payment for the imposition of the worse quality.

The EV is the expenditure function referenced at old conditions (E) minus actual income (Y). That expenditure function continually adjusts money income to changing quality so that it produces minimum income needed at qualities Q^0 so that the visitor is as well off as when facing qualities Q^1. Again prices don't change.

We discuss the CV in detail since the formulas for EV are similar. The expenditure function B includes four terms to be multiplied together, including an income term raised to a quality power, a ratio of summed new qualities to summed old qualities, a ratio of a product of new qualities to a product of old qualities and a ratio of a product of old prices to a different product of old prices. For the simple two site-case, there are only two elements for both sum and product terms. Note that the demand function never explicitly appears in the expenditure function, although the same terms that affect visits affect the expenditure function. Although it is hard to tell by looking at the formula, small increases in quality at small numbers of sites will reduce the expenditure function slightly. Large quality increases at larger numbers of sites will decrease it more. Since the CV is measured by subtracting B from actual income, greater quality and/or quality increases at larger numbers of sites produce CVs that approach total income as an upper limit. For a given number of total visitors, their summed income is the upper limit of their CVs. If they are all poor, it will be a small number.

Table 4.6 shows results for several proposed policies using the two site example, in which several pairs of policies applied as old and new prices and quality changes are considered. This table illustrates all four policy classes.

We begin with policy Class III, in which the old prices for site 1 and site 2 are $10 and $30 respectively, while the old qualities for these two sites are 100 and 20 respectively. These old price and quality conditions applied to the demand function in Table 4.5 produce 5.81 visits at site 1 and 1.40 visits at site 2. The proposed new policy holds everything constant except increase quality at site 2 from 20 to 50. Its effect, as expected, is to increase visits at the new higher-quality site, diverting them from the constant quality site. New visits at the higher quality site 2 are 1.85 while new visits at the constant quality site 1 are 4.45.

One interesting outcome of this policy experiment is that the higher quality site gained only 0.45 visits while the constant quality site lost 1.36 visits. Does that mean that the visitor lost benefits by reducing his total number of visits? Absolutely not. He gained. He gained a CV equal to 11, because everything stayed the same except for his access to better facilities at a site he was already using. He reduced use at the constant quality site by an amount equal to 3 times as many visits as he increased at the gaining quality site, because of his budget constraint. The site with increased quality has a price that is three times as high.

Thus it is not necessarily a bad public investment to spend money on remote sites with higher travel costs. However, everything else being equal, it is a better investment to spend money at the more accessible sites with lower travel costs. For example, if the same resources could have been allocated to increase quality at the lower priced site by a factor of two and a half, from 100 to 250, while holding site 2's quality constant at its initial 20, the visitor would gain more, with a CV of 20 (not shown in the table).

The EV story is similar except, in the case of a welfare improvement, it is interpreted as the visitor's WTA payment to take the place of the site quality improvement, and it assumes a property right to that improvement. Improving site 2's quality from 20 to 50, holding everything else constant, produces an EV of 16. Increasing site 1's quality from 100 to 250, holding site 2's quality constant, produces an EV of 29 (not shown in the table).

Another interesting example of policy Class III is shown as the second to last set of policy experiments in Table 4.6. This time we have intentionally enacted a policy whose net effect has a zero impact on overall visits, to illustrate the great dangers of using the multi-site CS with quality. We have allocated site improvements among the two sites quite carefully, increasing quality at site 2 by one third, from 20 to 30. Then we simultaneously increased quality by a much greater amount at the low priced site 1. In fact we gave site 1 enough extra resources that all the diverted visits due to site 2's quality improvement are pulled back to the cheap site. In terms of the demand equation system shown in Table 4.5, we have effectively found just the right mix of quality improvements over the two sites so that each site's numerator increased by the same percentage as its denominator, thus leaving visits at both sites where they were at the beginning. While a CS application of a TCM could show unchanged welfare, since visits are unchanged by the policy, the theoretically correct CV and EV tell a very different story, the right one. This policy produces a CV WTP of 22 and an EV WTA of 38.

Simultaneous Price and Quality Changes

Our last example considers a Class IV policy. The policy changes qualities and prices at both sites. This seems like a fundamentally different analysis from the quality change case by itself, but it really isn't much different, as long as a few things are kept in mind. For simultaneous quality changes and price changes, Table 4.5 shows that policies that change qualities at one or more sites without affecting price should have a measure for CV which the table defines as $Y - C$ and that EV is defined as $F - Y$, in which C and F are defined in the table as expenditure functions. These formulas come from the following definitions for CV and EV:

$$CV = Y - C = Y - e(P^1, Q^1; P^0, Q^0, Y) \qquad (4.23)$$

$$EV = F - Y = e(P^0, Q^0; P^1, Q^1, Y) - Y \qquad (4.24)$$

CV is actual income (Y) minus the expenditure function (C) defined as minimum income needed at prices P^1 and qualities Q^1 (new price and quality conditions) to be as well off as he would be facing prices P^0 and qualities Q^0 (old prices and qualities). Table 4.6 and the appendix show the details. Since both prices and qualities change for this evaluation, notice that equations (4.23) and (4.24) show different terms before and after the semicolon. Again, for the case where new prices and qualities produce better conditions, CV measures the visitor's WTP for these better opportunities. In contrast, where new prices and qualities produce worse circumstances, CV measures the visitor's WTA payment to compensate for inferior conditions.

The EV is the expenditure function referenced at the old price and old quality conditions (F) minus the actual income (Y). That expenditure function continually adjusts money income to changing price and quality conditions so that it produces minimum income needed at old conditions (P^0 and Q^0) to be as well off as when facing completely new conditions (P^1 and Q^1).

The fourth policy class is also much different from anything discussed in the single site model or the multi-site model for price changes. This class permits evaluation of policies that would change qualities and prices from their old levels, Q_1^0, Q_2^0, ... Q_n^0 to new levels Q_1^1, Q_2^1, ... Q_n^1 that occur jointly with price changes from P_1^0, P_2^0, ... P_n^0 to P_1^1, P_2^1, ... P_n^1. The last pair of rows in Table 4.6 shows an example of a Class IV policy. Site 1's price is increased from \$10 to \$20, while site 2's price increases from \$30 to \$40. Presumably both prices are increased for the purpose of paying for the quality improvement at the two sites. Site 1's quality increases from 100 to 200 and site 2's from 20 to 50. The net effect of this complex policy applied to the demand function is to reduce visits at both sites, from 5.81 to 2.40 at site 1 and 1.40 to 1.30 at site 2. Interestingly, the effect of the increase in price causes a greater welfare loss than the gains from improving the sites. Both the CV and EV fall by about 32.

Of course what's most attractive about estimating welfare measures for simultaneous price and quality change from travel cost demand systems is that very large numbers of combinations of price and quality change proposals can be evaluated within a consistent framework. Once the formulas are placed into a spreadsheet, they can be run for as many policy proposals as needed. The ultimate use of such measures is to allow resource managers

Table 4.6 Example of impacts on demand and benefits from selected policy proposals, using a two site TCM with quality.
Data are based on Table 4.5 demand and benefit formulas using parameters below.

Class	Old/New	Prices		Qualities		Income	Visits		Benefits of policy proposal		
		P_1	P_2	Q_1	Q_2	Y	X_1	X_2[a]	CS	CV	EV
I	Old	–[b]	30	100	20	100	0.58	1.40			
	New	10	30	100	20	100	5.81	1.40	134	74	281
II	Old	10	30	100	20	100	5.81	1.40	–52	–69	–41
	New	20	40	100	20	100	2.91	1.04			
II	Old	10	30	100	20	100	5.81	1.40	–40	–50	–33
	New	20	30	100	20	100	2.91	1.40			
III	Old	10	30	100	20	100	5.81	1.40	–[c]	11	16
	New	10	30	100	50	100	4.45	1.85			

III	Old	10	30	100	20	100	5.81	1.40	—[c,d]	22
	New	10	30	338	30	100	5.81	1.40		38
IV	Old	10	30	100	20	100	5.81	1.40	—[c]	-32.1
	New	20	40	200	50	100	2.40	1.30		-32.2

Values of site quality parameters are as follows: $b_{01} = 1.0$; $b_{11} = 0.2$; $b_{02} = 0.3$; $b_{12} = 0.6$.

Notes

[a] Predicted visits under the various proposed policies are based on a system of two demand equations with four parameters values assigned in the table. Quality is assumed to be the number of fish stocked at the site.

[b] No finite price reduces either site's visits to zero for this demand system. A maximum price of $100 is used, presumably reflecting the longest observed travel distance of visitors for whom the site is the main purpose of the trip. Another solution is to set price to a level that reduces visits to some arbitrarily low level.

[c] Multi-site CS from quality changes at several sites can be computed. One way is to measure the summed areas beneath the demands under old qualities and compare the sum under new site qualities. This method gives a number, but unfortunately, it bears no consistent relationship to the correct CV or EV. This is why we show no CS formula for quality changes. Maler (1974) suggested a method for computing multi-site CS based on careful sequencing of price changes that approximate the CV and EV under restrictive conditions.

[d] For this policy, we selected the two sites' quality increases to produce zero change in both demands compared to pre-policy qualities. This odd result can occur with the Cobb-Douglas utility demand system because each demand is an increasing function of its own quality, a decreasing function of the other site's quality, and is unaffected by the other site's prices. Since both demands are unchanged from old- policy site qualities and both demand price slopes are unaltered by the quality changes because both demand quantities are identical to conditions under pre- policy site qualities and both demand price slopes are unaltered by the quality changes. This little example shows why measured multi site consumer surplus with quality change (zero) should be avoided for demand systems analysis.

and other decision makers to analyze and carry out decisions that are consistent with the economy's production possibilities.

CONCLUSION

This chapter has examined the theoretical foundations of TCM which stem from welfare concepts and benefit theory. TCM is based entirely on observed behavior. CS, CV and EV have been examined and many outdoor recreation policies analyzed. The CV and EV are theoretically correct welfare measures that can be applied with confidence to any combination of price or quality changes at any number of recreation sites. Where the income effect is small, the CS approximation is close to both the CV and EV for one or more price changes. Formulas for a vast array of policy analyses are given.

REFERENCES

Allen, L.R., B. Stevens and R. Harwell (1996), 'Benefits-Based Management Activity Planning Model for Youth in At-Risk Environments', *Journal of Park and Recreation Administration*, **14**, 10-19.

Bockstael, N.E. and K.E. McConnell (1983), 'Welfare Measurement in the Household Production Framework', *American Economic Review*, **73** (3) 806-14.

Bockstael, N.E., W.M. Hanemann and I. Strand (1989), 'Measuring the Benefits of Water Quality Improvements Using Recreation Demand Models', Report to the U.S. Environmental Protection Agency.

Driver, B.L., R. Nash and G. Haas (1987), 'Wilderness Benefits: A State-of-the Knowledge Review', in R.C. Lucas (ed), Proceedings B National Wilderness Research Conference: Issues, State-of-knowledge, Future Directions, General Technical Report INT-220. Ogden, UT: USDA Forest Service.

Freeman, A.M. (1979) *The Benefits of Environmental Improvements: Theory and Practice*, Baltimore: Johns Hopkins Press for Resources for the Future.

Gaffney, M. (1997), 'What Price Water Marketing: California's New Frontier', *American Journal of Economics and Sociology*, **56** (4), 475-520.

Hicks, J. (1956), *A Revision of Demand Theory*. New York: Oxford University Press.

Maler, K.G., (1974), *Environmental Economics: A Theoretical Inquiry*, Baltimore: Johns Hopkins Press for Resources for the Future.

Marshall, A. (1890), *Principles of Economics*. Reprinted 1961, London: Macmillan.

Stein, T.V. and M.E. Lee (1995), 'Managing Recreation Resources for Positive Outcomes: An Application of Benefits-based Management', *Journal of Park and Recreation Administration*, **13** (3) 52-70.

Varian, H. (1992), *Microeconomic Analysis*, New York: Norton.

Willig, R. D. (1976), 'Consumers' Surplus Without Apology', *American Economic Review*, **66** (4), 589-97.

Appendix 4A Derivation of a Demand System with Quality

In this section, we derive the ordinary demand, indirect utility and expenditure functions, welfare measures and compensated demand functions for the Cobb-Douglas direct utility function with variable site characteristics. These site characteristics are assumed unpriced from the view of the visitor's budget. However, they are directly influenced by proposed policies, projects and programs. Estimation of these relationships is also discussed. This procedure can be applied to other standard direct utility functions described in microeconomic theory texts.

THEORY

We assume the visitor chooses a number of trips to *each* of *1... n* recreation sites, in which each site has an objectively measurable site characteristic level equal to B_i, which in turn is a mathematical function of that site's quality Q_i. We seek a monetary measure of the welfare consequences of decisions that alter these qualities and/or their prices. Using the familiar Cobb-Douglas example, we specify the visitor's utility as:

$$U = \prod_i X_i^{B_i}$$

(4A.1)

in which U = utility and X_i = number of trips the visitors take to the *i*th site.

What we are doing is inserting a mathematical function of site quality in the position normally occupied by the fixed parameters, B_i. When quality does not vary, we typically think of this fixed parameter as measuring intensity of preferences. But with quality, we assume that intensity of preferences now depends at least partly on what's at the site. This presumes a relation between the visitor and the site's characteristics in which decisions that influence what's at a site directly affect the visitor's preference for that site. Other methods of incorporating quality into utility functions are possible (e.g. Bockstael, Hanemann, and Strand, 1989).

The visitor is assumed to maximize ordinal utility subject to a budget constraint, in which the utility function depends on each site's quantity of trips and its quality. Quality is a choice variable for recreation managers and policymakers. It is not a choice variable to the visitor. The visitor optimizes by choosing trip numbers to each site for given prices, qualities, and budget by solving the following problem:

$$Max \ L = \prod_i X_i^{B_i} - \lambda(\sum_i P_i X_i - Y),$$

$$(4A.1a)$$

where Y is the visitor's income allocated to these recreation sites. This maximization leads to a partial demand system and not a complete system, since it is presumed the visitor has other income to spend on other things. We refer to the constant Y as income, to avoid confusion with the expenditure function, which is variable.

The following LaGrangian expression characterizes the rules that govern the visitor's optimizing behavior:

$$\frac{\partial L}{\partial X_i} = \frac{B_i}{X_i} \prod_i X_i^{B_i} - \lambda P_i = 0, \ for \ all \ n \ sites,$$

$$(4A.1b)$$

and

$$\frac{\partial L}{\partial \lambda} = (\sum_i P_i X_i - Y) = 0.$$

$$(4A.2)$$

From equation (4A.1b) we can make the following substitution:

$$\lambda = \frac{P_i X_i}{B_i} = \frac{P_j X_j}{B_j} \ for \ all \ n \ sites.$$

$$(4A.3)$$

Equations (4A.2) and (4A.3) can be solved as a set of simultaneous equations describing the visitor's series of ordinary demands. These demands are:

$$X_i = \frac{B_i Y}{P_i \sum B_i} .$$

$$(4A.4)$$

This series of equations predicts the visitor's behavior, namely how many trips he takes to each site according to all sites' prices, qualities, and income. Trips to any *i*th site depend on its price, income, and *all* sites' qualities.

One unexpected result comes from applying equation (4A.4). A doubling in all the B_i through increasing all sites' qualities, with no change in their prices, has no influence on the visitor's demand to any site. This is because both numerator and denominator double. However, it has an enormous impact on his total benefits as we will see later.

Indirect Utility Function

Substituting the series of demand equations (4A.4) back into the original utility function (4A.1) produces the indirect utility function, which measures the ordinal utility received by the visitor who successfully optimizes, given his aims and resource limits. That function is:

$$V = (Y)^{\Sigma B_i} \prod_i P_i^{-B_i} \prod_i B_i^{B_i} \left(\sum_i B_i \right)^{-\Sigma B_i}.$$

(4A.5)

The level of indirect utility reached under old prices and qualities is:

$$V^0 = (Y)^{\Sigma B_i^0} \prod_i \left(P_i^0\right)^{-B_i^0} \prod_i \left(B_i^0\right)^{B_i^0} \left(\sum_i B_i^0 \right)^{-\Sigma B_i^0}.$$

(4A.5a)

in which the zero superscripts indicate old prices and qualities. Using superscripts of one for new prices and qualities, the indirect utility level reached under new conditions is:

$$V^1 = (Y)^{\Sigma B_i^1} \prod_i \left(P_i^1\right)^{-B_i^1} \prod_i \left(B_i^1\right)^{B_i^1} \left(\sum_i B_i^1 \right)^{-\Sigma B_i^1}.$$

(4A.5b)

Expenditure Function

The expenditure function is the holy grail of applied benefit cost analysis. It's what we all look for. Successfully measuring it lets us perform a huge range of important policy evaluations. Most travel cost models are estimated with the primary intent of measuring benefits of one proposal or another. When done right, measuring those benefits depends on finding the expenditure function.

Inverting the indirect utility function (4A.5) allows us to solve for the expenditure function, as it depends on prices *and* qualities. It expresses minimum visitor expenditure as a function whatever level of utility the visitor reaches. We write it as $e(P,Q,U)$. The bold fonts P and Q refer to $P_1,...P_n$ and $Q_1,...Q_n$. For the Cobb Douglas utility function, the expenditure function is:

$$e(P,Q,U) = (U)^{\frac{1}{\Sigma B_i}} \prod_i P_i^{\frac{B_i}{\Sigma B_i}} \prod_i B_i^{\frac{-B_i}{\Sigma B_i}} \sum_i B_i$$

(4A.6)

in which U is the visitor's level of utility reached.

Equation (4A.6) is now applied to find the minimum level of expenditure the visitor needs when facing new prices and qualities, P^1 and Q^1, to sustain the same utility, U^0, that he reached under old prices and qualities, P^0 and Q^0. That expenditure level is

$$e(P^1,Q^1,U^0) = (U^0)^{\frac{1}{\Sigma B_i^1}} \prod_i (P_i^1)^{\frac{B_i^1}{\Sigma B_i^1}} \prod_i (B_i^1)^{\frac{-B_i^1}{\Sigma B_i^1}} \sum_i B_i^1 .$$

(4A.6a)

Note that the first right hand side term is ordinal utility reached under <u>old</u> prices and qualities, while the remaining terms refer to <u>new</u> prices and qualities. It is used to compute the CV.

Next, we derive the formula for a considerably more useful version of equation (4A.6a). Its usefulness comes from totally purging equation (4A.6a) of ordinal utility, and in its place substituting in the original prices and qualities confronting the visitor that produce U^0. This substitution produces an expenditure function with all the utility terms gone, leaving nothing but entirely observable variables and parameters. The resulting function measures the minimum expenditure when facing new prices and qualities, which achieves the same level of ordinal utility as was reached under initial prices, qualities, and money income. That substitution produces:

$$e(\,P^{\,1},Q^{\,1};\ P^{\,0},Q^{\,0},Y\,)=$$

$$\left(\left(Y^{\left(\frac{\Sigma B_i^0}{\Sigma B_i^1}\right)}\right)\frac{\sum_i B_i^{\,1}}{\left(\sum_i B_i^{\,0}\right)^{\frac{\Sigma B_i^0}{\Sigma B_i^1}}}\left(\frac{\prod_i\left(B_i^1\right)^{\frac{-B_i^1}{\Sigma B_i^1}}}{\prod_i\left(B_i^0\right)^{\frac{-B_i^0}{\Sigma B_i^1}}}\right)\left(\frac{\prod_i\left(P_i^1\right)^{\frac{B_i^1}{\Sigma B_i^1}}}{\prod_i\left(P_i^0\right)^{\frac{B_i^0}{\Sigma B_i^1}}}\right)\right).$$

$$(4A.6b)$$

This expression consists entirely of terms that are observable, with no need to measure cardinal or ordinal utility.

In an analogous way from applying equation (4A.6) to derive equation (4A.6a), minimum expenditure needed to reach the visitor's utility reached under new price and quality conditions, U^1 when he faces old prices and qualities, P^0 and Q^0, is:

$$e(\,P^{\,0},Q^{\,0},U^{\,1}\,)=\left(U^{\,1}\right)^{\frac{1}{\Sigma B_i^0}}\prod_i\left(P_i^0\right)^{\frac{B_i^0}{\Sigma B_i^0}}\prod_i\left(B_i^0\right)^{\frac{-B_i^0}{\Sigma B_i^0}}\sum_i B_i^0.$$

$$(4A.6c)$$

This expenditure function is used to compute the equivalent variation (EV).

Substituting into (4A.6c) new prices and qualities facing the visitor that produced U^1 lets us purge utility from (4A.6c), using instead the conditions that produced that utility. This very useful and observable expenditure function is:

$$e(\,P^{\,0},Q^{\,0};\ P^{\,1},Q^{\,1},Y\,)=$$

$$\left(\left(Y^{\left(\frac{\Sigma B_i^1}{\Sigma B_i^0}\right)}\right)\frac{\sum_i B_i^{\,0}}{\left(\sum_i B_i^{\,1}\right)^{\frac{\Sigma B_i^1}{\Sigma B_i^0}}}\left(\frac{\prod_i\left(B_i^0\right)^{\frac{-B_i^0}{\Sigma B_i^0}}}{\prod_i\left(B_i^1\right)^{\frac{-B_i^1}{\Sigma B_i^0}}}\right)\left(\frac{\prod_i\left(P_i^0\right)^{\frac{B_i^0}{\Sigma B_i^0}}}{\prod_i\left(P_i^1\right)^{\frac{B_i^1}{\Sigma B_i^0}}}\right)\right).$$

$$(4A.6d)$$

Expenditure functions (4A.6b) and (4A.6d) look imposing, for they involve much tedious algebra. But once they're coded into a spreadsheet, they can be used at virtually zero cost for as many policy analyses as desired. They can also be summed over visitors or visitor classes then coded as an objective function for programming models. Such programming models might optimize over a management, policy, or other decision space to allocate limited resources for improving quality.

A classic use of equations (4A.6b) or (4A.6d) is to confront the problem of how to optimally allocate a limited number of hatchery-produced fish among many competing fishing sites. The fisherman allocates trips among many sites from a limited travel budget assuming that the fishing quality is set beyond his control. The anglers' decisions show that either equation (4A.6b) or equation (4A.6d) is the impact on his welfare from various ways of altering stocked fish. The fishery manager can optimize over equation (4A.6b) or equation (4A.6d), after summing over relevant anglers, to allocate fixed numbers of stocked fish among competing sites. The manager assumes the fisherman's travel budget is set by forces beyond the manager's control.

Welfare Measures

Armed with the two useful expenditure functions obtained entirely with observed data, equations (4A.6b) and (4A.6d), we can now compute the desired welfare measures from the range of proposed policies. The CV and EV measures of welfare change from a price *and/or* quality change at one or more sites are, respectively:

$$CV = Y - e(P^1, Q^1; P^0, Q^0, Y)$$
(4A.7a)

$$EV = e(P^0, Q^0; P^1, Q^1, Y) - Y$$
(4A.7b)

Both these welfare measures can be measured entirely from observable data, i.e. from the parameters and variables found by estimating the series of demand equations (4A.4).

Compensated Demands

The system of compensated demand functions for each ith site is obtained by differentiating the expenditure function in its most general form (4A.6) with respect to changes in the site's price (travel cost). While the compensated demands are not needed to find the CV and EV once we already have the expenditure function in hand, they continue to receive much attention in the travel cost research literature. This attention is for a good reason. Areas behind the compensated demands from price changes between the relevant price horizontals are exact measures of the CV and EV. Furthermore when the income effect is small, the compensated demands are close to the ordinary demands (4A.4). This demand system is:

$$X_i^* = U^{\frac{1}{\Sigma B_i}} \left(\frac{B_i}{P_i} \right) \prod_i P_i^{\frac{B_i}{\Sigma B_i}} \prod_i B_i^{\frac{-B_i}{\Sigma B_i}} = \frac{B_i\, e(\, P, Q, U\,)}{P_i \sum_i B_i}.$$

(4A.8)

We write equation (4A.8) so that the site's compensated demand formula has a star superscript, to distinguish it from the observed demand (4A.4). The compensated demand formula is the same as for the ordinary demand (4A.4), except that the expenditure function from (4A.6) appears in place of Y. Think of the expenditure function as the mathematical operation that continually reduces (increases) Y by as much as possible whenever prices decrease or qualities increase, while holding utility constant at old (new) levels. When you know the amount by which the expenditure function reduces nominal income, you know the visitor's benefit of the proposed policy. If nominal income is $100, and the expenditure function pulls income down to $40 after a policy implementation, the visitor with no utility loss has received a money benefit of $60, i.e. the CV is $60.

Estimating the expenditure function from real data requires estimating the system of ordinary demand equations (4A.4). After the parameters from this demand system are estimated with those data, the estimated parameters and variables are inserted into the appropriate places in equations (4A.6b) and (4A.6d).

The compensated demands can be expressed for either old or new conditions. From the indirect utility function (4A.5a) and Hicksian demand formula in equation (4A.8), we write the compensated demands that would emerge under any possible prices and qualities, but conditioned on *old* prices, qualities. It is:

$$X_i^*(P,Q;\ P^0,Q^0,Y) = \frac{B_i e(P,Q;\ P^0,Q^0,Y)}{P_i \sum_i B_i} =.$$

$$\left(Y^{\left(\frac{\Sigma B_i^0}{\Sigma B_i}\right)}\right)\left(\frac{B_i}{P_i}\right)\left(\frac{1}{\left(\sum_i B_i^0\right)^{\frac{\Sigma B_i^0}{\Sigma B_i}}}\right)\left(\frac{\prod_i (B_i)^{\frac{-B_i}{\Sigma B_i}}}{\prod_i (B_i^0)^{\frac{-B_i^0}{\Sigma B_i}}}\right)\left(\frac{\prod_i (P_i)^{\frac{B_i}{\Sigma B_i}}}{\prod_i (P_i^0)^{\frac{B_i^0}{\Sigma B_i}}}\right)$$

$$(4A.8a)$$

This produces identical quantities demanded as the ordinary demands in (4A.4) when prices and qualities are set at old levels. Note that all utility terms are gone.

The equation for the sites' compensated demands using *new* prices and qualities as the starting point are similarly based on the indirect utility function under new conditions defined in (4A.5b), along with (4A.8). It is:

$$X_i^*(P,Q;\ P^1,Q^1,Y) = \frac{B_i e(P,Q;\ P^1,Q^1,Y)}{P_i \sum_i B_i} =$$

$$\left(Y^{\left(\frac{\Sigma B_i^1}{\Sigma B_i}\right)}\right)\left(\frac{B_i}{P_i}\right)\left(\frac{1}{\left(\sum_i B_i^1\right)^{\frac{\Sigma B_i^1}{\Sigma B_i}}}\right)\left(\frac{\prod_i (B_i)^{\frac{-B_i}{\Sigma B_i}}}{\prod_i (B_i^1)^{\frac{-B_i^1}{\Sigma B_i}}}\right)\left(\frac{\prod_i (P_i)^{\frac{B_i}{\Sigma B_i}}}{\prod_i (P_i^1)^{\frac{B_i^1}{\Sigma B_i}}}\right)$$

$$(4A.8b)$$

Equation (4A.8b) produces identical observed quantities demanded as the ordinary demands (4A.4) when prices and qualities are at *new* levels.

Marginal Benefits of Quality Change

Differentiating the expenditure functions (4A.6b) or (4A.6d) with respect to quality changes, produces a result that summarizes marginal benefits of the quality changes, since nominal income does not change. Results are slightly different for the old and new policy situations. If, for example, new conditions consist of installing large numbers of boat ramps at a heavily-used reservoir, the marginal benefit of further added boat ramps is much less at that site with new conditions than with old.

Specification of Site Quality

Suppose each of the site's B_i terms is a function of one or more site quality characteristics as described above. The term B_i need not be limited to a single quality index, and could even include non-quality variables. It normally would be a function of the site's measured quality (Q_i) and possibly of other demand predictors (N_i). It could include demographic variables or variables characterizing the site beyond managers' control, e.g. the weather. A typical formulation is

$$B_i = b_{0i}(Q_i)^{b_{1i}} N_i^{b_{2i}}.$$

(4A.9)

ESTIMATION

Calculating the welfare functions requires estimating the above-described demand system in (4) with actual data on travel costs, visitation, site quality, and other demand shifters. We repeat (4A.4), which is

$$X_i = \frac{B_i Y}{P_i \sum_i B_i}.$$

(4A.10)

This demand system has the amenable property that it can be linearized to permit estimation by simple regression methods. Taking the log of the ratio of X_i to some baseline X_j produces:

$$\log\left(\frac{X_i}{X_j}\right) = \log\left(\frac{B_i}{B_j}\right)\left(\frac{P_j}{P_i}\right)$$

(4A.11)

in which both income, Y, and the B_i terms inside the summation of the (4A.10) denominators cancel.

We now make use of well-known properties of logarithms to simplify. If, for example, each ith site's characteristic term, B_i, can be expressed as a simple product of its measured quality Q_i, then

$$B_i = b_{0i} \, Q_i^{\,b_{1i}}$$

(4A.12)

and equation (4A.11) applied to (4A.12) results in

$$\log\left(\frac{X_i}{X_j}\right) = \log \, (b_{0i}) - \log \, (b_{0j}) \, +$$

$$b_{1i} \, \log \, (Q_i) - b_{1j} \, \log \, (Q_j) + 1.0 \, \log\left(\frac{P_j}{P_i}\right).$$

(4A.13)

This equation has the happy property that all terms to be estimated are linear in the parameters. Note that the first term on the right is a difference of two intercepts, so we can only estimate a single parameter for it. Finally, the parameter for the logged price ratio is restricted to be 1.0, because of price variable in (4A.10) has an exponent of 1.0. There are two parameters per quality characteristic to be estimated at each site minus the scale factor at the base site.

For an n-site model, there will be $n-1$ equations to estimate to produce equations (4A.13). For all $n-1$ equations, the same variable on observed visits, X_j, will appear in the denominator of the left hand side for whatever baseline jth site is chosen. So it's best to choose a base site that receives heavy visits to avoid unadjusted zeros in the denominator.

Applying OLS to each of the $n-1$ equations in (4A.13) will produce 4 times $(n-1)$ estimated parameters. But only $2n-1$ are independent. These are $b_{01} \ldots b_{0n}$ and $b_{11} \ldots b_{1n}$, minus the scale parameter required for b_{0j} at the base jth site. There will be $n-1$ estimates of the single quality coefficient for the jth reference site, b_{1j}, all likely to be slightly different. These $2n-1$ coefficients in total provide enough information to evaluate any number of policy proposals desired that would influence prices and/or qualities at any of those n sites.

Applying this procedure to the case of a three-site demand system, there are two quality parameters to be found for each site, minus the scale factor, for a total of five. If site 1 is the base site, there are two estimates of the quality coefficient, b_{11}.

Expressions for site characteristics other than shown in (4A.12) can be imagined. The single quality term could be expanded into a series of quality terms, e.g. one for fishing quality and one for water quality. The terms would be logically multiplied together, and each term raised to its own exponent. For each extra demand shifter added, the equation to be estimated gets one more positive and one more negative log term. For the case of two quality attributes per site, we have:

$$log\left(\frac{X_i}{X_j}\right) = log\ b_{oi} - log\ b_{oj} + b_{1i}\ log\ (Q_{1i}) - b_{1j}\ log\ (Q_{1j}) +$$

$$b_{2i}\ log\ (Q_{2i}) - a_{12j}\ log\ (Q_{2j}) + 1.0\ log\left(\frac{P_j}{P_i}\right),$$

(4A.14)

which is also linear in all estimated parameters.

Other variations on this theme are possible. If there is a large number of interrelated but similar sites for which to evaluate policy proposals, say more than ten, various restrictions on the quality coefficients could be imposed and tested. One example is requiring all fishing quality coefficients to be equal for one class of sites and all water quality coefficients to be equal for another.

REFERENCE

Bockstael, N.E., W.M. Hanemann and I. Strand (1989), 'Measuring the Benefits of Water Quality Improvements Using Recreation Demand Models', Report to the US Environmental Protection Agency.

5. Design Principles for TCMs

We study history to learn from past experience. To a recreation demand modeler this means we build TCMs to analyse what visitors did, so we can learn what they will do in the future. But we don't build a TCM just to predict what visitors will do if current trends continue. We build it to find out what they will do under one or more proposed policies. Then, if we are good listeners and good communicators, we explain those predictions to decisionmakers so that they can formulate an appropriate set of decisions among the many possible choices they face.

Building models ensures that our data are organized so that we can exploit its relationships. We then use our knowledge of those historical relationships to predict the past and thus check the usefulness of the model by comparing the predictions with our knowledge of what actually occurred. If the predictions are good, we are able to design better futures provided the structure doesn't change.

This book assumes that models will normally be quantitative and estimated through regression models. What it means to predict the past accurately needs little elaboration. We use the independent variables of our TCM regression model in conjunction with its algebraic function to predict the behavior we actually saw. We want to estimate a TCM for which price, income, site characteristics and demographic factors predict recorded trips. We can use the model then to construct counterfactual histories of the past by posing questions like: 'if the past price at a site had been doubled, how many fewer visits would we have seen?' We normally use elasticities to perform these experiments. In this chapter, we cover some model design requirements and provide some simple examples of estimated models. In addition, we present a regional model in some detail.

MODELS THAT ANSWER A POLICY QUESTION

This section describes a few basic principles for designing and building TCMs for better decision support. In all cases we assume that the modeler wants to build a TCM to answer the questions policy makers are actually posing.

Building, Closing, or Rehabilitating a Single Site

One common class of policy proposals in the realm of the environment and natural resources deals with actions that would build, close, or rehabilitate a single site. These can involve all levels of government from local to national as well as commercial builders. Building a site is a major undertaking in terms of its drain on a budget. Closing a site may have less direct cost, but it may permit other activities to take place on the land or with its funding. A planner confronting a decision on providing new site facilities to meet a growing demand for recreation will also be interested in evaluating the benefits of use against their cost.

Accounting for closing or opening a site in a TCM is typically done by including a price variable based on travel costs per trip then, after estimating the model, raising the price until predicted visits become suitably close to zero. The variation in price gives a range of quantities of visits demanded and, from these data, a demand curve and benefits measure may be computed. Sufficient detective work is also required to get data on and include as visit predictors all important variables other than price that would cause observed visits to change. Otherwise, the TCM researcher risks falling into the trap of falsely ascribing variation in visits to price alone, when the variation is really due to something else that varies such as substitute site prices, income, demographic factors, weather or site facilities.

Efficient Management of a Single Site

How to manage existing resources at a facility is an important related policy issue. An example is how to determine the optimal carrying capacity of a facility that has the potential for physical or economic congestion due to too many visitors. (Ecological congestion may occur at a different level of output.) For TCMs to deal with this problem, the researcher must find data on how total visits by certain individuals are altered by the direct presence of other individuals or by evidence of that presence, such as trampling of hiking trails.

Measuring the benefits and costs of congestion through use of a TCM as a way to find the optimal carrying capacity of a site is more difficult than it seems. The obvious way to measure congestion is the number of people who use the site, which is the same as the dependent variable. However, the mechanics of building a regression model that aims to predict total use, the dependent variable, as a function of, among others, total use as an independent variable presents problems that have yet to be resolved. This problem has been discussed by Cicchetti and Smith (1973), Deyak and Smith

(1978), Dorfman (1980), Smith and Desvousges (1986) and many others.

Pricing a Single Site

Outdoor recreation pricing is an important policy issue. The decision of whether or not to impose a price or alter an existing price has important economic and financial implications. While outdoor recreation on federal or state lands is typically priced at or near zero, the use of these resources is commonly strongly competitive with other uses of the same resources, especially commercial uses.

Ranchers who are charged grazing fees, irrigators who pay for federal water and logging companies who are charged fees for commercial use of forests are quick to point out the asymmetric policy associated with free recreational uses of the same resources. Protests especially occur in situations where scarcity is compelling, for example, in a prolonged and severe drought when decisions are made to hold water behind a federal reservoir for free recreation rather than release it for priced irrigation. Politicians listen.

When a TCM is estimated to answer a pricing policy question, it's obvious that the researcher needs to include observed data on price as a predictor of visits. In fact TCMs cannot be built without a price variable, because increases in prices are used to compute consumer surplus. The best way to find out more about the impact of a proposed future price change is to have lots of information on the impact of past price changes, preferably with variability in prices at each site. However, those data are rarely available, because prices at most recreation sites change infrequently. So the TCM modeler is typically forced to make the assumption explained previously that increased travel costs due to distance have the same effect on reducing visit rates as an increase in site prices would have on people visiting from a given distance.

Building, Closing, or Rehabilitating Several Sites

Many classes of policies have simultaneous impacts at more than one site. Endangered species policy, hydroelectric dam relicensing, toxic spills that lead to natural resource damage assessments, river basin management, forest policy and commercial fisheries policy are just a few examples. When changes in any of these policies effectively open or close a series of sites, TCM modelers are faced with the challenges of dealing with multiple site models.

Failure to estimate an integrated demand system when the proposed change in policy would simultaneously affect many sites may produce estimated benefits which are nonsensical. The recreation benefit of a program that limits water drawdowns in droughts depends on programs that set lake levels, fish stocks and facilities at substitute reservoirs. Similarly a contamination episode that damages an important stream increases the value of policies that keep its substitutes clean. We would expect policymakers to be acutely aware of the importance of analytical techniques that facilitate comprehensive analysis of policies over the large numbers of sites that make up a regional or national resource.

The earliest TCM innovators to deal with multiple site models were Burt and Brewer (1971) and Cicchetti, Fisher and Smith (1976). Both studies estimated a demand system that recognized explicitly the substitution possibilities among large numbers of heterogeneous recreation sites. Modeling an integrated recreation demand system is no small task. Building it requires computing the price for each recreation site (or type of site) for each visitor or visitor class. For each site (or site class) the number of trips to those sites are regressed on the price of that site and on the price of all its substitutes. The result is a set of demand functions, one for each of the *n* sites, that look like:

$$X = f_1(P_1, P_2, \dots P_n, N) \quad = f_1(\boldsymbol{P}, N)$$
$$X_2 = f_2(P_1, P_2, \dots P_n, N) = f_2(\boldsymbol{P}, N)$$
$$\cdot$$
$$\cdot$$
$$X_n = f_n(P_1, P_2, \dots P_n, N) = f_n(\boldsymbol{P}, N) \tag{5.1}$$

where X_i is the number of trips to site i, P_i is the travel cost to site i and N is a series of other demand shifters such as income and demographic factors. Demand for each site depends on prices of all sites. The importance of an integrated demand system is that close substitutes can be directly recognized and modeled in the demand system, thus answering a wider range of policy questions.

One kind of policy question that multi-site demand analysis can examine is the impact on visits and total benefits of building or developing some combinations of sites and excluding others. Another question involves the impact on numbers of visits, benefits and gate receipts of various packages of changes in current prices. If the interdependence of demand for visits to a range of sites is ignored, analysts can come to the false conclusion that the total benefits of the package of policy elements is simply the sum of the value of the individual parts. For a system of strong substitutes, this independent aggregation of independent benefit components inflates the change in total recreation benefits. Gains are overstated as are losses.

Policies Affecting Qualities of Many Sites

Where policymakers want to know the impact of potential packages of quality changes over a system of sites, TCM modelers need something like a multiple-site model discussed above, but it needs to account for even more complexity than price substitution across sites.

Now the TCM must account for both price substitution and quality substitution across sites. Again, there must be a set of demand functions, one for each of the n sites. In this case, the demand function for each site must incorporate prices and qualities for all sites in a way that looks like the following.

$$X_1 = f_1(P_1, P_2,...P_n; Q_1, Q_2, ... Q_n; N) = f_1(P, Q, N)$$
$$X_2 = f_2(P_1,P_2,...P_n; Q_1, Q_2, ... Q_n; N) = f_2(P, Q, N)$$

$$X_n = f_n(P_1, P_2,...P_n; Q_1, Q_2, ... Q_n; N) = f_n(P, Q, N) \qquad (5.2)$$

All variables are defined as in (5.1), with the addition of Q_i as an indicator of the ith site's overall quality. Examples of quality indicators are fish density, biological oxygen demand of water, water temperature, camping facilities, numbers of boat docks, discolored trees, acres of wildlife habitat, trees per acre with diameter at breast height (dbh) greater than 12in or 30cm, area of wilderness, average streamflow, reservoir volume and length of hiking trails.

TYPES OF TCMs

TCMs can be built to account for a wide variety of conditions. People who legislate natural resource policies or operate natural resource sites typically do so under a wide range of natural resource, demographic and economic conditions. Because conditions rarely repeat themselves, information on recreation benefits that is used for a policy or management decision needs to be correct under a wide variety of conditions to be reliable and believed.

For example, suppose that the average visitor recreation day at all US Army Corps of Engineers reservoir sites produces x dollars in direct benefit to the visitor. These are sometimes called national economic development (NED) benefits in the language of US federal water agencies.

Information on the numerical value of x is of some use to a planner.

However, the value of x should be adjustable according to recreational preferences of the regional population, scarcity of substitutes, reservoir operating conditions and population characteristics. For example, an additional acre foot of water held behind a dam for a month to produce fishing benefits may produce $1 in additional recreation benefits when the reservoir has few facilities, draws visitors from a limited market area and has several recreational substitutes. However, an acre foot of water held at a reservoir with more facilities, a larger market area and fewer substitutes may produce $25 in additional recreation economic benefits. For these reasons, information on recreation benefits should be adaptable to the wide range of conditions in which natural resource facilities operate and under which natural resource policy decisions are made.

Single Site Models

Early TCMs were typically specified only for single-destination visits to a single site. Such a model is useful only for a limited number of policy issues, such as the current per-day or per-trip value of recreation under existing facility levels. The single site demand function can only reflect distance to the site and demographics of the visitors.

Because all visitors to a given site may experience the same facilities, especially over a relatively short period such as a season or year, a separate variable cannot be estimated to account for the impact on visits of changing site characteristics. If the analyst wishes to tell the decision maker how recreation use and benefits change with the addition of new recreation facilities or by maintaining a higher or lower than historical average reservoir water level, a single-site model is of little use. This is because a single-site model only reveals average behavior under current average conditions at that single site.

Predictions of the single-site model are based on travel costs from each zone of visitor origin in the market area to the site destination. Because a site-specific TCM predicts visitation based on variables unique to that site, it has limited capability to transfer accurately visit and benefit predictions to other sites to support analysis of a policy issue. The only way to transfer predictions from one site-specific TCM to a different site is to find a TCM estimated for a similar site.

Transferring an existing single-site model to an unstudied target site requires the use of the 'most similar site' method. Application of this method requires access to estimated price and possibly other elasticities such as those referring to facilities and demographic factors applied to a per capita use model. Price elasticity was discussed in Chapter 3. Thus, if price elasticity is known to be −3.0, a 1 per cent increase in travel cost reduces visits from a given visitor origin by 3 per cent.

Table 5.1 provides hypothetical data for a single site model estimated with ordinary least squares regression and the parameter estimates are in Table 5.2. Table 5.2 shows estimation of a TCM with the hypothetical dataset using the three most common functional forms employed by TCM researchers. Examples of welfare measures associated with these three forms based on the estimated parameters were shown in Chapter 4.

Table 5.1 Single site data for TCM estimation and estimated visits

Price (P)	Income (Y)	Other (N)	Visits (X)
10	100	10	6.31
5	100	10	25.23
10	50	10	3.38
5	50	10	13.53
10	100	5	3.15
5	100	5	12.62
10	50	5	1.69
5	50	5	6.76
10	100	20	12.62

Table 5.2 Estimated single site TCM for three common algebraic forms

Model	Visit estimator	Logged variable
Linear	$X = B_0 + B_1 P + B_2 Y + B_3 N$	none
Log Linear	$X = B_0 P^{B1} Y^{B2} N^{B3}$	all
Semi-Log	$X = exp(B_0 + B_1 P + B_2 Y + B_3 N)$	X only

	B_0	B_1	B_2	B_3
Linear	13.06	−2.28	0.10	0.72
Log Linear	1.00	−2.00	0.90	1.00
Semi-Log	2.37	−0.28	0.01	0.10

The US Water Resources Council's Principles and Guidelines (1983, p. 73) discuss application of TCMs to a target policy site for which there are no existing estimates of price elasticity. For a single-site model, one presumes that the facilities and other characteristics in comparing one site with the next are what makes the price elasticities unique.

The analyst must make a subjective decision on which existing site is most similar to the target site. Mechanically, the analyst selects the most similar site, uses its estimated elasticity and applies it to the target site. Per capita use estimates are then computed for the target site from each zone of origin in the market area. Results of per capita visitor use estimated in this manner are multiplied by population in each zone. The result produces an estimate of total visits. Recreation benefit is estimated by computing the increase in per trip travel costs from any zone of origin needed to reduce that zone's visits to zero. An important limitation in implementing the similar-site method is the considerable subjectivity required to match conditions at the target site to those at the most similar site.

Multiple Site Demand Systems

As described earlier, a site-specific multiple-site model is an advance on the single site-specific model described above. The site-specific multiple-site model attempts to predict demand at each of several sites in a region. Predicted demand to any given site is based on travel distances from several zones of origin in the market area to the given site.

The multi-site model is considerably more ambitious than the single-site model because it accounts for prices to all relevant substitute sites as a demand predictor, not just the price to the given site. Similar models to the Burt and Brewer (1971) and Cicchetti, Fisher and Smith (1976) studies have been estimated recently. One example is the model estimated for water-based recreation in a three-county region in New Mexico (Ward, 1989). Despite their desirability, use of such models still requires the analyst to employ the most similar-site method when predicting demand and benefits at an unstudied target site. The analyst still must make a subjective decision on which of those sites in the region has site characteristics that most closely approximate the target site.

The strength of the multiple site-specific model is that it predicts demand for all sites in the region for which the study was done. Unfortunately, the model is not directly applicable to other unstudied sites of interest to managers. Moreover, even in the site-specific multiple-site model, looking for the similar site from which to transfer predictions to a target site introduces unavoidable arbitrariness. For this reason, planners often want something more versatile than the various site-specific models.

Regional Models

We define a regional recreation demand model (RRDM) as a model that estimates direct recreation economic benefits produced at one or more site locations that is accurate under a wide range of conditions. By conditions we mean management actions, on-site facilities, population demographics and economic trends. Accomplishing this objective is the primary aim guiding the formulation and estimation of a RRDM.

Regional models offer considerably more to decision makers than either the single-site or multiple-site specific models. By combining data on visitors with varying demographics from several origins to many site locations that have different amounts of recreation facilities, one can observe how visitors change their use rates in the face of varying facilities and quality characteristics or changes in the demographic patterns. Thus, a more comprehensive demand equation that contains coefficients for each of the variables that affect visitation patterns throughout the region can be estimated.

Relatively few regional recreation demand models have been built, we suspect because of the high cost of getting consistent visitation data across many sites in the region. These models typically identify the determinants of recreation visits and use these determinants to develop predictive models for recreation use and benefits.

In 1983, the WRC recommended developing regional recreation models to promote consistency and efficiency in evaluation of water resources sites. In addition, such models would reduce the cost of these evaluations. WRC's criteria for model development provide the purpose and scope of regional demand models.

Specifically, regional recreation models should yield an empirical estimate of demand based on demographic characteristics of market area populations, quantitative characteristics describing the recreation opportunities, costs and characteristics of substitute opportunities. Models should allow managers to evaluate economic gains and losses associated with various proposed policies.

The WRC (1983) asked that attention be given to maximizing net economic benefits in formulating water policies. TCM provides a way to bring public recreation services, usually an unpriced resource, into this analysis.

Information provided by the TCM can support several kinds of natural resources planning decisions. A TCM can be used to determine the net economic value of an existing recreation site, provide estimates of the economic value of creating a new site or modifying an existing site, contribute to more efficient allocation decisions among programs, explain visitors' travel behavior and forecast changes in the use of a recreation site resulting from charging fees or changing fees.

A final advantage of regional models is that they can be transferred to unstudied areas. Transferability without the need for estimating new parameters for the unstudied site or region is desirable because site-specific data on benefits are typically scarce. So transferability saves the very high cost of carrying out an entirely new study for every new region.

For example, the regional TCM might predict trips to any site per unit of population from any zone of origin as:

$$(Trips_{ij}/Pop_i) = B_0 + B_1(Price_{ij}) + B_2(Income_i) + B_3(Acres_j)$$
$$+ B_4(Tables_j) + B_5(Sub_i) + B_6(Subprice_i) \qquad (5.3)$$

where $Trips_{ij}$ = trips from visitor origin i $(i = 1, ... n)$ to site j $(j = 1$ to $m)$, Pop_i = total population from visitor origin i, $Price_{ij}$ = travel cost per trip, based on distance from visitor origin to site j, $Income_i$ = per capita income of visitors living in origin i, $Acres_j$ = the average recreation season surface acres at site j, $Table_j$ = the number of picnic tables at site j, Sub_i = the extent of substitutes facing origin i visitors, $Subprice_i$ = travel cost per trip to substitute opportunities facing origin i visitors.

The term B_0 is an intercept, while B_1 to B_6 are constants, estimated from the historical relationship between changing levels of each independent variable and the impact of each variable's change on the dependent variable. These constants have a very important interpretation to decision makers as the incremental effect on recreational use resulting from an increase of one unit in the independent variable.

With this kind of model that combines facility, demographic and substitute factors, the analyst can predict by how much visits to any one of the sites would change with the addition of the right-hand side variable. For example, B_4 is the additional trips per capita with the addition of one picnic table. The same interpretation holds for changes in outside forces that affect future changes in demographic factors such as income or substitutes. If the estimated value of B_3 is 0.20 then each additional acre foot of water in the recreation season produces 0.20 more visits to any one of the regional sites per unit of zone-of-origin population.

Regional models estimate recreation benefits under existing conditions and they can predict how use and benefits change with changes in management-controlled site variables. These models can be used to simulate effects on recreation use and benefits resulting from management actions at existing recreation sites.

A major advantage of an RRDM is that it can provide an estimate of recreation use and benefits at a target site even though the target site does not match perfectly any of the existing sites used to estimate the model. This rather remarkable feature of a RRDM is possible because the regional demand equation allows analysts to estimate recreation use and benefits for numerous combinations of facilities and demographic factors at the target site not directly observed at any of the existing sites or visitor zones of origin used to fit the model.

As long as the facilities at the target site and demographic factors within the market area lie within the range of observed facilities and demographics at the existing sites in equation (5.3) decision makers can estimate the effects of proposed policies. For example, if they were interested in impacts on visitation from changes in area or in numbers of picnic tables, there are coefficients $(B_1 - B_6)$ to reflect the effects of these variables. Thus in principle, an unstudied site can be described by a combination of its location $(Price_{ij})$, its area $(Acres_j)$ and its facilities (here illustrated by $Tables_j$). Similarly, the market area in which the unstudied site is located can be described by its population (Pop_i), per capita incomes $(Income_i)$, extent of substitutes (Sub_i) and substitute prices $(Subprice_i)$.

In summary, a RRDM reduces the subjectivity in applying site-specific models to unstudied sites, unstudied market areas, planned but unbuilt sites, unstudied decisions for studied sites or several combinations of these.

Regional models consistent with choice theory

Many policy decisions are designed in an environment where site characteristics at many sites simultaneously compete for limited manpower, money and other resources. In this situation, policymakers need analytical techniques that facilitate comprehensive analysis of policy over large numbers of sites. To do this, they need to know the incremental benefits from altering any characteristic of any site.

It is even more desirable if this measure of the benefits is flexible enough to measure benefits from altering any characteristic of any site as a function of each characteristic of each important related site. For example, the benefits of investing in cleaner rivers is higher where there are many polluted rivers than where most area rivers are clean. What this adds up to is that benefit-cost analysis based on TCMs should measure the benefits of a wide range of policies that reconfigure characteristics of a system of goods that contain interdependent elements of value.

A RRDM system of demand equations consistent with choice theory guarantees that proposed policies changing many sites' characteristics by large amounts avoid predicting absurd visitor behavior. Behavioral predictions are plausible because that behavior is based on a visitor's budget constraints that limit his behavioral response to proposed policy changes.

Consistency with choice theory assures that visitor response, for example, to a proposed drought-coping plan that increases lake levels at several high mountain reservoirs will avoid increasing visits at all those reservoirs without reducing visits elsewhere. More generally, RRDMs consistent with choice theory guard against the inflation of the benefits of policies that improve the environment or the costs of policies that damage the environment.

Many proposed policies are designed in an environment where the choice is movement around various possible points on what amounts to a production possibilities frontier. In this case, demand systems consistent with choice theory (not simply individual demand curves taken one site at a time) are required to correctly measure benefits of movements around that surface.

For example, a fish hatchery allocation program may examine proposals to alter the quality of sport fishing through stocking fish at hundreds of waters that compete for the same limited fish hatchery capacity. The production possibilities frontier across fishing waters measures all possible combinations of stocked fish allocated to these waters for a fixed total hatchery capacity.

Efficiency-minded fishery managers search for the one point on that frontier that produces the greatest possible total fishing benefits. This frontier has many 'total benefit contours' intersecting it, for which the aim is to find the single point on the frontier that is tangent to the highest total benefits surface.

While 'social indifference curves' defined over stocked fish are not measurable, total benefit contours can be. When a demand system is consistent with choice theory, individual monetary welfare gains are based on visitors' budget constraints and behaviors enforced by that constraint. These individual welfare measures can be aggregated into total benefit surfaces. What this means is that use by analysts of RRDM demand systems consistent with choice theory assures that proposed policies maximize total benefits to the resource-using public for available public resources.

Finally, demand systems consistent with choice theory treat all sites in the system in a consistent yet comprehensive way. For any given site in the system, the demand for that site increases with decreases in its price and with increases in any of its quality characteristics. However, its demand also may decline with decreases in any substitute site price but increases with any increase in a quality characteristic at any substitute site.

Two examples of RRDMs consistent with choice theory are the Cobb-Douglas utility system and the CES utility system. One example of the Cobb-Douglas model (see Appendix 4A), using surface area of water and picnic tables, as an examples, is:

$$Trips_{ij} = ((Income_i)\ Q_j\ )/(Price_{ij}\ Q_j\ ) \qquad (5.4)$$

where $Q_j = B_1 + B_2 (Acres_j) + B_3 (Tables_j)$, an index of a site's characteristics. Note that for the Cobb-Douglas form, substitute prices do not appear anywhere in equation (5.4), which means that policies that influence the price of substitute sites have no impact on any given (*j*th) site. However the presence of substitute sites does influence visits to each site through the substitute characteristics which appear in the denominator. That is, any increase in a substitute site's characteristics (not the *j*th site in question) will reduce the number of trips to the *j*th site. For more details, with slightly different notation, see Appendix 4A. For an example illustrating estimation of the parameters of the Cobb-Douglas utility form using OLS regression with hypothetical data, see Table 5.3. This table has slightly different notation from equation (5.4), a single quality attribute for each site and an exponential elasticity for the single quality variable.

Table 5.3 Estimated multiple site TCM for Cobb-Douglas utility function with varying quality: two sites

Model estimated (OLS, logged ratios)	Parameter	Estimate
$X_i = (Y B_i)/(Pi Bi)$ where $B_i = b_{0i} + b_{1i} Q_i$ for sites $i = 1$ and 2	b_{01}	1.0
	b_{11}	0.2
	b_{02}	0.3
	b_{12}	0.6

Data (hypothetical) for two sites						
Site 1			Site 2			
X_1	P_1	Q_1	X_2	P_2	Q_2	Y
6.57	10	4	3.43	10	4	100
13.14	5	4	3.43	10	4	100
6.56	10	4	6.85	5	4	100
12.00	5	4	7.99	5	6	100
6.18	10	6	3.81	10	6	100
12.40	5	6	3.80	10	6	100
6.75	10	6	6.52	5	4	100
13.50	5	6	6.49	5	4	100

The CES utility demand system model with quality shown below is more flexible in adapting to observed visitor data. However, greater flexibility is bought at the price of slightly messier algebra and more transformations required to estimate it with OLS regression methods. The CES form is:

$$Trips_{ij} = (Income_i)(Q_j^{\sigma-1})(Price_{ij})^{-\sigma}/\Sigma_j [(Q_j^{\sigma-1})(Price_{ij}^{1-\sigma})] \quad (5.5)$$

where σ, the elasticity of substitution, accounts for price substitution among sites. Higher values of σ magnify the effects on demand at a given site and its substitutes from a change in the site's price or quality. With a higher elasticity of substitution, a given price increase at a site translates into a greater reduction of trips to that site and a greater increase of trips to substitute sites. Similarly, with a higher elasticity of substitution, a given quality increase at site translates into a greater increase of trips to that site and a greater decrease of trips to substitute sites. The expenditure function based on quality and price for the CES demand system is described elsewhere (Ward, Cole, Green-Hammond and Deitner, 1997).

The CES may be more realistic because both price and characteristics of substitute sites appear in equation (5.5). For the given 'own' site, Q_j and $Price_{ij}$ appear in the numerator, which means that increases in the own site price reduce visits to it while increases in the own site characteristics increase its visits. Note that the sum of all sites' prices and characteristics appear in the denominator, including the own site. However the own site price and characteristics effects in the numerator always outweigh their effects in the denominator as long as the total number of sites in the system exceeds one. Increases in substitute site prices raise visits to the own site, while increases in substitute site characteristics reduce visits to the own site.

Equations (5.4) and (5.5) are quite remarkable because both are reasonably simple in mathematical form, but both also constrain the visitor not to violate his budget constraint thus producing plausible visitor behavior and hence plausible benefit estimates under a very wide range of proposed policies. Consistency with the budget constraint can be demonstrated in either equation by multiplying prices times quantities demanded for any set of prices or characteristics at all sites. The result exactly equals total income. A disadvantage of both these regional demand model forms is that neither predicts corner solutions, i.e. zero trips at finite prices. For an excellent discussion of corner solution issues and some of the many attempts to deal with them, see Bockstael, Hanemann and Strand (1989).

For both the Cobb-Douglas and CES forms, consistency with choice theory is most plausible if $Trips_{ij}$ are interpreted as trips per household, which assumes the household is the decision making unit. Either model can be applied to origin zones of varying populations. Application of equations such as (5.4) or (5.5) to regional policy analysis requires multiplication by the number of households in each zone of origin if trips per household is the independent variable.

Regional recreation demand model performance standards

A RRDM aims to predict demand and benefits of potential management actions at one or more existing study sites or at unstudied target sites. Overcoming the limits imposed by site-specific models requires that a regional model should meet several criteria. The first four criteria below are described in WRC's Principles and Guidelines (1983) and the fifth is ours. If a RRDM meets the following five criteria, it allows policy analysts to evaluate a wider range of possible actions quantitatively, based on the wide range of information from which the model was estimated.

A RRDM should be based on measurable demographic characteristics of market area populations and on measurable factors that characterize the uniqueness of recreation opportunities at the site. The model should rely on measurable costs and characteristics of substitute opportunities in the region facing area populations. Demand and benefit estimates over time and over the range of potential management actions should be based on observed changes in underlying determinants of demand. Finally, where limited public resources for improving or restoring sites are allocated among several sites in a region, the model should be based on choices and economic constraints facing visitors.

Comparisons of Site-Specific and Regional Models

RRDMs may be used to provide a resource to identify the site attributes and user characteristics that determine recreation use at sites and site substitutes. Additionally, RRDMs predict changes in recreational use and can translate changes in recreation use to changes in benefits for management actions.

A RRDM is generalizable to a wide range of management actions, site locations, visitor populations and substitute opportunities. By contrast, site-specific models, even multiple site-specific models, have little generalizability beyond conditions observed when visitors were sampled.

Next, a RRDM generalizes patterns of observed behavior to a wider range of potential future on-site conditions than is possible with site-specific models. That range could include changes in natural conditions or in management actions. Examples of changes in natural conditions are those brought about by prolonged drought not previously observed at a given site but observed somewhere in the region. Management actions include modifying reservoir levels for flood control, irrigation or hydropower production, improving fish habitat, stocking fish, restoring recreation areas or providing critical habitat (such as land, water, or forests) for endangered species under the US *Endangered Species Act*.

Third, a RRDM has a greater potential for accurately transferring predicted visits or benefits to unstudied sites in the study region or to unstudied regions. The potential for accurate transfer of the RRDM is especially improved if measured value of facilities at the unstudied target sites and demographic characteristics at the unstudied market areas are numerically bracketed by those already studied.

Fourth, a RRDM is preferable to a site-specific model because it bypasses the subjectivity inherent in selecting a similar site at which to apply the model. This decrease in subjectivity reduces a potentially important source of investigator bias.

Finally, use and benefit predictions at target sites are likely to be more accurate than those from site-specific models. In addition, visit predictions at existing study sites are likely to be more accurate. The greater accuracy is expected because a RRDM is based on observed behavioral responses to a wide variety of operating conditions at numerous sites throughout the region.

THE DEVELOPMENT OF AN RRDM: AN EXAMPLE

This section describes how a model can be developed and estimated. The illustration is based on a recently estimated RRDM, completed for the US Army Corps of Engineers (CE). For more details, see Ward et al. (1995), Loomis et al. (1995) and Ward, Roach and Henderson (1996).

All TCMs are estimated using regression methods. As previously noted, OLS is most commonly used. Further examination of this technique is given later in this book. The principle underlying regression analysis is that past observations on the dependent variable are used to isolate the separate impacts on that dependent variable produced by observed changes in the various independent variables. The dependent variable is typically some indicator of visitor participation, typically measured as visitor days, visitor trips and the like. For zonal models, the visitor participation data are typically summed for a given zone of origin, such as a county, then deflated by the total population in that zone. The independent variables need only include travel cost per trip (price), possibly site characteristics and anything else our instincts or the site managers' experience suggest should be good predictors of visits.

Dependent Variable: Visitor Participation

In this study, the dependent variable was an estimate of visitation from the total market area from county i to site j during year k. CE visitor surveys provided visitor samples. However, sampled visits could not be used directly as dependent variables, because sites were surveyed at significantly different sampling rates. Failure to account for different sampling rates would result in higher visit predictions at some sites merely because they were surveyed at higher rates.

Sampling rate differences across sites were corrected by using variable sampling expansion factors. Sample expansion factors are defined as the ratio of total estimated visits at a site to visits sampled by the survey. By multiplying the sampled visits from a county by the appropriate sample expansion factor, an estimate of total visitation from the county was obtained.

It was known for some time in advance of the model estimation that the dependent variable would be related in some way to total site-level visit counts. A site visit was selected as the dependent variable for modeling purposes and defined as the entry of one person into any recreation area on a CE site to engage in one or more recreation activities. A visit was simply a head count of a visitor. A trip to a site by a person to go fishing for one hour and a two week camping trip to a site by one person, even though they are substantially different experiences, each counted as one visit.

Visits were further divided into camping visits and day-use visits, because each was expected to reveal significantly different behavior. A required model input was historic camping and day-use visit records for the period 1983-6. Site visitation data recorded in the CE Natural Resource Management System (NRMS) were obtained from each CE district office.

The total visitation specification was preferred to a per capita visitation dependent variable as being less restrictive (Rosenthal, 1987; Knetsch et al., 1976). Use of a per capita dependent variable, i.e., total visits divided by total population, restricts the exponent on population as a predictor of a county's total visitation to a site to be exactly 1.0. Rather than imposing such a restriction, use of total visitation as an independent variable tests whether visitation increases proportionally as population increases.

We suspected rural counties, common for CE sites, might exhibit different recreation use patterns from more urban counties. An exponent of less than 1.0 on population indicates that visitation rates per unit of county population are higher in less populated counties. An exponent of greater than 1.0 reveals that urban populations, on a per capita basis, contribute more visits to the site.

All data on visitation were collected from CE exit surveys conducted during 1983-6. Surveys were conducted during the years 1983-5 in the Sacramento District, 1983-6 in the Nashville District and 1985 in the Little Rock District.

At the end of their trips to sites, survey respondents were asked to indicate their zip code of origin. The Little Rock District surveys included zip codes of origin for 48 629 day-user surveys and 4724 camper surveys. The Nashville District produced 17 562 day user surveys and 2094 camper surveys. In the Sacramento District, 81 306 day-user surveys and 17 040 camper surveys indicated zip codes. Thus, the size of the origin destination data set was large by conventional standards of travel cost recreation studies.

A national zip code county directory was used to assign a county and state to each survey zip code of origin. Any national database that cross references zip codes and associated counties and states can be used for this purpose. Numerous similar databases are widely available from commercial vendors at costs under $500. Surveys were aggregated to obtain the total surveys sampled by day-use and camper category from county i to site j during year k for all counties of origin producing at least one sample survey.

Sample expansion factors unique to each site and year were necessary to magnify sampled visitation to an estimate of total visitation. The process of sample expansion was begun by estimating actual total day-use and camper visitation numbers for each site during each year. Visitation data were obtained from two sources: the individual CE districts and the Waterways Experiment Station (WES). The object was to obtain an estimate of the total number of day-use and camper visitors during the surveyed years.

Based on the presumed correct total use estimates and assuming a random sample, sampled visitation totals for each county i to site j in year k can be multiplied by the appropriate expansion factor. The estimate of total visitation from origin i to site j in year k is then corrected for the effect of different sampling rates at different sites.

An estimate of total visits was calculated for sampled visits in each county, site and year. Those total visits were used as the dependent variable. The model thus attempts to explain total visitation from any county to any site and any year by travel cost, various facility variables, substitutes and various county demographic variables.

Independent Variables

Economic theory and the considerable experience of recreation managers have shown that four classes of independent variables affect recreation visitation: demographic variables, site variables, travel costs and substitutes. Demographic variables characterize zone-of-origin populations. There are several kinds of site variables, including installed site facilities, fishing quality, water quality and water level variability.

Demographic variables
Populations of visitor counties of origin were characterized by several

demographic variables, which generally were obtained from US Census sources. US Census sources are widely available, consistent across the US, available for zones-of-origin much smaller than counties if needed and, since the late 1980s, available at a very low price.

Because the dependent variable is visitation from county i to site j during year k, all demographic independent variables are ideally defined specific to county i during year k. However, census data are typically unavailable at a county level for every year. Because the on-site surveys were conducted between 1983-6, the 1980 census was the most appropriate source to use for demographic data. Also, data from the 1990 census were unavailable when the demographic database was constructed during 1991.

County population was the only demographic variable available from the US Department of Commerce for every year in the 1983-6 period. Year-specific data on population seemed especially important because visitation rates at CE sites can change during the period of analysis simply due to population changes. While many of the other demographic variables, such as income and unemployment, mostly exhibited little change during the period of analysis, population did change in many counties. A changing annual population variable is useful when applying the model results to years outside the study period.

Demographic variables for population and average income per capita by county were used in all models. Other variables may induce collinearity problems and were chosen according to the statistical contribution to the model performance. The average per-capita county wage rate was included as part of the calculation of travel costs, in order to calculate the monetary costs of travel time. Additional demographic variables included the age structure and ethnic composition of the county.

Few consistent hypotheses regarding the influence of demographic variables on recreational visitation have been published. While population size should have a positive effect on visitation, visitation may not increase proportionally to population. As described elsewhere, including population as an independent variable allows us to test for differences in recreational behavior between rural and urban counties.

Similar ambiguity exists on the effect of other demographic variables on recreational visitation. The effect on visits of age structure can change from one CE facility to another. Some sites may be popular with families and thus a high proportion of children would have a positive influence on visitation. Other sites may be popular with mature visitors using recreational vehicles.

In general, income is expected to have a positive affect on visitation. However, income could have a negative effect if the site in question is a low-cost substitute for higher quality recreation opportunities. Reduced demand in the face of higher incomes was expected with the Sacramento District reservoirs because other recreation possibilities, such as the Sierra Nevadas, various commercial theme parks, the Pacific Ocean and several national parks, are popular among high income California households.

Site facilities

TCMs have been estimated for a huge range of outdoor recreation sites and one could imagine fitting them over the range running all the way from a wilderness experience to some kinds of urban facilities. CE sites are typically accompanied by large investments in site facilities.

Each of the site facility variables were expected to have a positive influence on visitation. Where facilities are excessive compared to demand (overbuilt), additional quantities would have a small or no effect on added visitation. Information on facilities at each reservoir is available from the CE NRMS database.

Numbers of day-use picnic tables, boat launch lanes, total parking spaces, camp sites, swimming beaches, full-service marinas and recreation pool surface acres of the reservoir were collected. Some facilities attract particular kinds of people but deter others. A good example of this is privately owned boat docks, which may allow greater lake access to some visitors, but private development along a lakeshore may detract from the recreation experience of others. The net effect can only be estimated by examining the visitation data.

Alternatively a dataset could be split by class of visitor, with a separate TCM estimated for each. As a general principle, it is good to split up a dataset as long as what's left has enough observations on all variables to provide a reliable statistical fit. However, we've found that this kind of splitting is expensive, either in the expense of additional sampling or in the cost of having too little data.

Estimating coefficients on the separate effect on visitation of each of these variables was a central objective of the CE study because these coefficients were used to estimate benefits gained from installing more facilities, or benefits lost by their depreciation. However, collinearity between these facility variables was quite high because they are often constructed in approximately constant proportions to vary with the size of the site. It's impossible to use a TCM based on observed data to isolate the separate impacts of different kinds of facilities if those facilities were always constructed in constant proportions, e.g. one picnic table per campsite, or one cabin per acre of beach front property. Recreation site designers and builders don't usually think about pleasing the TC modeler who comes along 20 years later.

Fishing quality

Many natural resource policies have influences on aquatic life, such as fish. Thus, fish density is a very commonly used variable in TCMs. For the CE study we expected visitation to increase with improvements in fishing quality. After many unsuccessful attempts to estimate fish density in a consistent manner across the reservoirs, we used a proxy measure. We selected the morphoedaphic index (MEI) as an indicator of overall fishing quality. The MEI is defined as total dissolved solids (TDS) divided by the mean depth of a reservoir. MEI is a proxy for overall biological productivity of a reservoir.

Water quality

Water quality is an important factor affecting recreation benefits of CE reservoirs. Like the fishing quality data, water quality data proved difficult to acquire. Because consistent data were not obtainable on many water quality measures, only two variables were included in this study's database, water clarity and total dissolved solids.

The impact of water quality on visitation may be a result of visitors' perceptions rather than actual water quality. Steins (1992) studied the economic value of the effect of several water quality measures on the value of lakeside lots in Minnesota. Lake clarity, as measured by secchi disk readings, had the largest positive influence on land values. Because visitors typically have no access to objective measures of water quality, secchi disk levels of CE reservoirs were used in this study to represent visitor water quality perceptions.

Data on secchi readings for the study years were available in each CE district. The value of secchi depth was the average of all readings taken at site j during year k, measured in feet of depth. Visitation is expected to be positively influenced by secchi depth if visitors prefer reservoirs with high clarity. However, anglers may prefer less clarity if it leads to greater fish production and increased catch rates.

The other water quality variable included in the database was total dissolved solids (TDS), measured in milligrams per liter. Normally, several TDS readings were available for a reservoir for each year surveyed. TDS is needed to calculate the value of MEI, as described. TDS had the potential to enter the visit predictor equation as a separate water quality variable.

Water quantity and variability

For CE reservoirs, visitation was expected to increase as the water level at a reservoir rises towards the designed recreation pool. Also, visitation was expected to be greater at reservoirs with a steady water level than those which fluctuate widely. This effect should be most evident in the dry Sacramento District where some reservoirs fluctuate greatly during a recreation season due to agricultural and municipal demands. These competing demands for water cause water levels to fall toward the end of summer.

Data on water levels at each reservoir were available from recreation managers at each CE district. All water level variables are based on readings of surface acres because visitors have been found to respond more to surface area than volume or elevation. Monthly average surface acre readings were recorded for all sites during the study years. Using an annual average of these monthly readings to represent water levels obscures the fact that most visitation occurs during the summer months. In order to correct for summer use, estimates of monthly recreation use at each reservoir were obtained from the CE national visitor database and the proportion of visitors by month was used to weight the importance to recreation visitors of water levels in that month. Thus, water levels during the summer months receive the highest weights.

The resulting variable, weighted surface area, measured the weighted average of monthly recreational surface acres of site j during year k. This variable was then divided by the designed recreation pool surface area to determine whether a reservoir is full for recreation purposes.

Reservoirs with low water levels were hypothesized to have a negative effect on visitation. Water levels above the recreation pool level may also impact on visitation. However, preliminary specification of a variable to express water levels above the recreation pool produced poor recreation predictions. Thus, the application of model results to flood conditions will produce unreliable results.

An additional indicator of reservoir water level was specified in an attempt to account for lake level fluctuations. Because lake level fluctuations during the winter should have a minimal impact on visitation, winter lake levels were not considered in calculating lake fluctuations. For the Sacramento District, the three months with the lowest visitation (November to January) were excluded from the specification of water surface area. For the Little Rock District, the months of December to February were excluded. Because winter in the Nashville District is slightly longer, the four months with the lowest visitation were eliminated (November-February).

A common choice for measuring lake level fluctuations is a variance or standard deviation. However, the variance numbers did not standardize for overall lake size. Thus, a given variance in surface area may have a large impact on a small reservoir but a negligible effect on a large reservoir. To calculate a standardized measure, the coefficient of variation (COV) was used for this study. The value of COV, defined as the standard deviation divided by the mean, used the standard deviation of non-winter monthly average surface acres at reservoir j during year k. COV was hypothesized to have a negative effect on visitation in the models.

The final water variable specified was shore miles of the reservoir. Holding other factors constant, visitation may vary between circular reservoirs and those with many branches. Branching reservoirs may allow boaters a more secluded experience and could affect fishing quality. On the other hand, circular reservoirs may allow more open space for water sports. The expected effect of the SHORE variable on visitation was therefore ambiguous. Although not done for this study, an index of circularity could also be specified as the ratio of shore miles to area. A smaller ratio would indicate greater circularity.

Travel cost

Travel distances from county i to site j were calculated using a computer program that measures road distances and travel times between zip codes or cities. The origin point for visitors in any county was defined as the largest city in the county, determined from census data. The origins and destinations were coded in such a way that several hundred thousand combinations could be input to a PC, with resulting distances for each combination computed.

With counties as the observation unit, there typically were not more than 200 or so for any given site, even in the southeastern US where there are very large numbers of small counties. However, by the time each of the water-based substitute opportunities were calculated, each county having a slightly different price and quantity of substitute opportunities, there were several hundred thousand travel distances calculated. All these combinations or origin-to-destination driving distances took but one evening to calculate, thus cutting down substantially on the hundreds of hours it would have taken less than ten years ago in pre-PC days.

Up to four destination points were chosen for each site, some of which are quite large. Visitors were assumed to travel to the nearest major recreation area on the reservoir. A computer program typically used by trucking companies who look for efficient travel routes was used to calculate the one-way travel distance from the largest city in county i to each potential recreation area at site j.

Since the software calculates distance between cities only, the distance between recreation areas and the closest city needed to be estimated for the calculations. Once travel distance to each potential recreation area was calculated, the smallest travel distance was chosen to represent the one-way travel distance from county i to site j. The associated travel times based on the most practical routes were also computed using the software.

Both travel distance and travel time are important elements in total travel costs. Failure to include travel time understates estimated recreation benefits (Cesario, 1976). Including each as an independent variable typically produces unreliable results, as travel distance and time are highly correlated. Travel costs were defined in this study as the sum of actual travel costs plus travel time costs.

Time was valued at 1/3 the average per-capita county wage rate given in the 1980 census. This value is recommended by the US Water Resource Council (1983). Also, 1/3 the wage rate reflects the median of Cesario's (1976) survey on the revealed value of travel time in the transportation literature and has been widely used in subsequent TCMs (Ward and Loomis, 1986). Because no data were available on the distribution of children and adult visitors from the visitor's survey, no separate opportunity cost of time accounting was made for children. Valuing time in this manner was a compromise, for travel time valuation is a major unresolved issue in travel cost modeling.

Data on the costs of operating motor vehicles were obtained from the US Department of Transportation. Using national averages, variable vehicle operations costs in 1980 dollars per mile were found to range between $0.03 and $0.06 over this study's time period.

While all visitors to a site who travel together in the same vehicle expend the same travel time, vehicle costs can be shared. All visitors in a vehicle were specified to share vehicle costs equally. Data were available from the CE exit surveys on the number of visitors in each vehicle. An average value of it was calculated for each site.

As a final consideration, each trip involves a fixed cost consisting of some amount of planning, preparation and loading and unloading. An additional $1 was added to travel costs for all observations to account for this fixed cost. The added $1 eliminated extremely high prediction from nearby zones of origin that would otherwise result from the log-linear model used for this study. The log-linear form is shown in Table 5.1.

For any applied TCM study, we would expect similar effort expended in specifying the price variables. Many unresolved issues still continue to be dealt with in defining the price variable. One example is the issue of dividing travel costs between exogenous (pre-determined) versus endogenous (determined in part by the visitor). This issue is considered further later in this book.

Substitutes
Potential visitors to the CE reservoirs and most other recreation facilities, typically have many other opportunities that may substitute for their

destination. Substitutes for the CE study were based on a similar water-based recreation opportunities. Although not tested formally with the data, access to free-flowing rivers was not considered a sufficiently close substitute. However, if a national dataset on free flowing rivers were cheaply available, it would be an important hypothesis to test. Data were collected on the location of all lakes and reservoirs within 250 miles of each county in the database as well as the recreational surface acres of each substitute site.

A substitute site is assumed to be more attractive to visitors the closer it is to their origin and the larger it is. A substitute index approach similar in spirit to Knetsch, Brown and Hansen (1976) was adopted. For the ith county of visitor origin, the substitute variable was measured as the surface area of water-based recreation accessible to that county's visitors deflated by distance. It is equal to:

$$Sub_i = (Surface\ area)_k\ /\ Miles_{ik} \qquad (5.6)$$

where k is the kth substitute water body facing visitors from the ith county.

This substitute index is *ad hoc* because its algebraic form showing the interaction between price (miles) and substitute quality (surface acres) in the demand function is not derived from utility maximizing behavior. (Appendix 4A shows a form consistent with utility theory.) Still, it has some attractive properties, because counties with larger, closer or more substitute water are expected to send fewer visits to CE sites. This substitute measure does not account for the proximity of many counties to ocean-based recreation sites. Visitors interested in swimming may consider the ocean or a Great Lake as a valid substitute.

Results

Using the variables and data for the study described above, two regional recreation demand models were estimated for 26 CE sites in three regions. Separate models were estimated for day use recreation and overnight camping.

As expected, both sets of price elasticities were negative. However the camping model was much less price elastic (−1.6) than the day use model (−3.3), suggesting that, for a given number of visits, overnight camping facilities produce a much higher total benefit than do day-use facilities. Substitute surface area of water was a strong negative predictor in both the day use (elasticity = −1.5) and camping models (elasticity = −1.1). On-site surface acres of water entered positively in both models (day use elasticity 0.39 and camping elasticity = 0.43).

Average benefits per recreation visit in 1994 dollars ranged from a high of $6.68 at Lake Isabella in the Sacramento District to a low of $1.87 at Beaver Lake in the Little Rock District for day-use visitors. For overnight visitors, equivalent values range from $30.35 at Lake Barkley in the Nashville District to a low of $7.38 at Lake Kaweah in the Sacramento District.

The recreation economic value of one additional acre foot of water held for one month at a reservoir varied from a high of $110 at Success Lake in the Sacramento District to a low of $0.27 at Laurel River Lake in the Nashville District. Formulas for computing marginal values and also for transferring them to unstudied sites are in Ward, Roach, and Henderson (1996).

As a general principle, recreation values per additional acre foot of water are highest for reservoirs that are closest to population centers and for market areas in which visitors have few water-based recreation substitutes. They are also highest for projects that possess extensive on-site recreational facilities, and reservoir banks that have shallow flat slopes at the water level.

RRDMs can be used to estimate recreation benefits under actual site conditions and potential future management actions. However, we attach higher levels of confidence to some uses of these models for management decisions than to others.

The methods of analysis used for this study were designed to obtain good estimates of the important demand elasticities. We have most confidence in management applications of these models that require only the estimated elasticities. For the algebraic form of the demand model used (log-linear), average benefits per day for a given county depend only on the elasticity on travel cost. Therefore, we have high confidence in our estimate of average benefits per recreation visit.

CONCLUSION

Two essential steps in estimating a TCM are building a model that answers policy questions and getting the right data organized so that model can be estimated. This chapter has discussed several kinds of models, in which it is concluded that regional models and models that are consistent with choice theory can answer large numbers of important policy questions.

First, models should be specified with algebraic functional forms to avoid producing absurd results from extreme management actions implemented outside the range of past observed data. On the surface, it is expected that linear models should cause little trouble. However, linear models can predict negative visits for extreme values of the explanatory variables. For this and other reasons, log-log models are often used. Attempts should be made to formulate models consistent with economic theory. Models should correctly account for substitution relationships, site characteristics and visitor demographics. Models based on poor economic theory cause computed benefits to mean little inside the range of past data and less outside that range.

Practically, functional forms for economic benefit models should account for diminishing incremental visitation and benefits from improvements. That is, management actions that improve facilities should not increase benefits or visits at an increasing rate. Models should also account for effects of substitute opportunities and limited incomes that constrain visitation in the region.

Models that are consistent with visitors' budget constraints are likely to produce the most coherent results over the widest range of management actions. That is, economic benefit models should be consistent with the microeconomic theory of consumer choice. Unfortunately, data needed to estimate such theoretically correct models, utility theoretic demand systems, are typically expensive or simply not available.

REFERENCES

Bockstael, N.E., W.M. Hanemann and I. Strand (1989), 'Measuring the Benefits of Water Quality Improvements Using Recreation Demand Models', Report to the US Environmental Protection Agency.

Burt, O.R. and D. Brewer (1971), 'Estimation of New Social Benefits from Outdoor Recreation', *Econometrica*, **39** (5), 813-27.

Cesario, F.J. (1976), 'Value of Time in Recreation Benefit Studies', *Land Economics*, **51** (2), 32-41.

Cicchetti, C.J., A. Fisher and V.K. Smith (1976), 'An Econometric Evaluation of a Generalized Consumer Surplus Measure: The Mineral King Controversy', *Econometrica*, **44** (6), 55-75.

Cicchetti, C.J. and V.K. Smith (1973), 'Congestion, Quality Deterioration and Optimal Use: Wilderness Recreation in the Spanish Peaks Primitive Area', *Social Science Research*, **2** (1), 15-30.

Deyak, T. and V.K. Smith (1978), 'Congestion and Participation in Outdoor Recreation: A Household Production Function Approach', *Journal of Environmental Economics and Management* , **5** (1), 63-80.

Dorfman, R. (1980), 'On Optimal Congestion', *Journal of Environmental Economics and Management*, **11** (2), 91-106.

Knetsch, J.L., R.E. Brown and W.J. Hansen (1976), 'Estimating Expected Use and Value of Recreation Sites', in C. Gearing, W. Swart and T. Vars (eds) *Planning for Tourism Development*, New York: Praeger Publishing.

Loomis, J.B et al., (1995), 'Testing the Transferability of Recreation Demand Models to Army CE of Engineers Sites', *Water Resources Research*, **31** (3), 721-30.

Rosenthal, D. (1987), 'The Necessity for Substitute Prices in Recreation Demand Analysis', *American Journal of Agricultural Economics*, **69** (4), 828-37.

Steins, D.N. (1992), 'Measuring the Economic Value of Water Quality: The Case of Lakeshore Land', *The Annals of Regional Science*, **26**, 171-6.

US Water Resources Council (1983), 'Economic and Environmental Principles for Water and Related Land Studies', *Federal Register*, March 17.

Smith, V.K. and W.H. Desvouges (1986), 'The Generalized Travel Cost Model and Water Quality Benefits: A Reconsideration', *Southern Economic Journal*, **52** (2), 371-81.

Ward, F.A. and J.B. Loomis (1986), 'The Travel Cost Demand Model as an Environmental Policy Assessment Tool', *Western Journal of Agricultural Economics*, **11** (2), 164-78.

Ward, F.A. (1989), 'Efficiently Managing Spatially Competing Water Uses: Application of A Regional Recreation Demand Model', *Journal of Regional Science*, **29** (2), 229-36.

Ward, F.A., B.A. Roach, J.B. Loomis, R.C. Ready and J. Henderson (1995), *Regional Recreation Demand Models for Large Reservoirs: Database Development, Model Estimation and Management Applications*, US Army Corps of Engineers Waterways Experiment Station, Vicksburg, Mississippi, US.

Ward, F.A., B. A. Roach and J. E. Henderson (1996), 'The Economic Value of Water in Recreation: Evidence for the California Drought', *Water Resources Research*, **32** (4), 1075-81.

Ward, F.A., R.A. Cole, K. Green-Hammond and R. Deitner (1997), 'Limiting Environmental Program Contradictions', *American Journal of Agricultural Economics*, **79** (3), 803-13.

6. Design and Administration of Surveys

In this chapter we discuss the conduct of surveys. Specifically, we examine the definition of the relevant population, the selection of the sample, development and testing of the survey instrument or questionnaire, other survey procedures and response rates. Prior to that, however, we discuss briefly whether a survey is necessary.

IS A SURVEY NECESSARY?

The quick answer to this question is another question or rather a set of questions. What are you trying to measure? For what purpose? What degree of accuracy do you require? How much time do you have? How much funding is available?

A survey may not be necessary or it may be vital. Let's think of a case where is survey may not be necessary. Suppose you were trying to measure cheaply and quickly as baseline data the use by family groups of a certain site for which permits to enter were issued. The permits listed name, address, vehicle type and registration number, use of tent or van, number of adults and number of children, date of entry and expected date of departure. A practical way to generate the baseline data would be to analyze the permit records, and select the groups with 1-4 adults and 1-4 children. The number of children and adults used in the formula would probably vary according to the area and culture of the people. Experienced staff know if the site attracted extended family groups with grandparents or family groups with adult children.

Inaccuracy is inherent with this method, but it is faster and cheaper than conducting a survey. However, where the measurement of the economic worth of potential use, for example, was required and adequate staffing and funding are available, a survey would be very useful.

SURVEY TECHNIQUES

Identification of the Population

Before analysts can investigate characteristics of any group or entity, the boundaries of the entity must be known and understood. Hence, the

156

population, that is, all the cases that conform to a set of specifications, must be defined. What is the population for TCM research? As we have noted before, it is likely to be either only the people who visited the site in a given past period or it may be all the people who live in a defined region or are likely to visit within a stipulated period. The generic population will depend on the nature of the research.

However, within those generic bounds, there are points which must be considered in relation to the definition of populations and the accuracy of results. Data for TCM analyses can be collected by on-site or off-site surveys. Let us consider these two methods in terms of time required, cost and accuracy. While there may be small differences between the two methods in the time required to collect data, these are usually immaterial.

What about differences in cost? Some analysts believe on-site surveys are cheaper than off-site; others believe the opposite. Issues to be considered are the costs of postage and labor in administering the questionnaire. Typically, public sector managers tend to discount the cost of labor when site staff are diverted from their usual duties to hand out questionnaires and talk to visitors about the nature of and need for the survey. There is an opportunity cost, as there is when staff are diverted to conduct an off-site survey. On the other hand, hiring consultants to conduct an off-site survey incurs cash costs. Additionally, there is the question of the size of the sample needed when an off-site sample is likely to include many respondents with no visitation. A larger sample with attendant higher costs will probably be required.

With regard to accuracy, we should introduce some terms, knowledge of which will assist in understanding these design points. Additional detail may be found in Hellerstein (1992). 'Censoring' occurs when values for a dependent variable are bounded. For example, an analyst might assume that no individual in the sample visits a site less than once or more than 25 times a month or both. Visits less than one or more than 25 are thus recorded as one and 25. The visit data are thus censored.

'Truncation' occurs when observations are recorded only when the dependent variable takes values greater than a minimal value or less than a maximal value. Visits, for example, may be thought to have values always greater than zero (equal to or greater than one). 'Endogenous stratification' occurs when the chance of being selected in a sample is a function of the value of the dependent variable. In other words, people who make many visits have a greater chance of being selected in a sample than people who visit only once. Thus, in the case of an on-site survey, people who make no visits would have no chance of selection, and the sample will be truncated.

Off-site surveys can be administered to either known users or total populations. However, a sample of known users will be truncated but will not incur endogenous stratification, when the screen (the mechanism by which users are identified) allows all users equal chance of selection. Off-site surveys of total populations will identify many people with zero visits but no people with less than zero (a negative number of) visits. Hence, as Hellerstein showed, the dependent variable is censored, which produces the following outcomes.

Regression (OLS) coefficients are biased towards zero, where data are censored. An example is visit data from a *total population survey* where many respondents would take less than zero visits, but are constrained to have zero visits. The Q-axis intercept becomes smaller, the slope of the Q-dependent curve is flatter, and the measured choke price is overstated. Measured demand is less price elastic, and the bias will increase as the number of censored observations increases. Consumer surplus is overstated.

Regression coefficients also will be biased, where truncated data are gathered from *known participants in an off-site survey*. The Q-axis intercept becomes smaller, the slope of the Q-dependent curve is even flatter than with censored data, and the apparent choke price is higher again. Consumer surplus is inflated over that of the correct model.

Where truncated and stratified data are gathered from an *on-site survey* with respondents having a greater chance of selection as their numbers of visits rise (e.g. by selecting the first 500 through the gate), the Q-axis intercept becomes smaller, the slope of the Q-dependent curve is flatter than the true model, and the apparent choke price is higher again. Consumer surplus can be many times that of the true model.

With regard to the use of permit data which was alluded to above in the section 'Is a survey necessary?', it is worth noting that when these data are used in ZTCM analyses, truncation and endogenous stratification are avoided, because zones may have zero visitation. However, there may be aggregation bias present. Hellerstein (1992) concludes that statistically more complex models may not outperform relatively simple zonal models, but that count data models may offer a useful alternative.

In summary, the analyst will devise the research plan, select the methodology, use an off-site or on-site survey or neither, depending on the purpose and desired outcome for the work. In addition, available funding and required accuracy will have a bearing on the decisions.

Selection of a Sample

Once the population to be surveyed has been decided upon, the researcher must think about and decide how a sample will be collected. Samples are used in many types of testing because examination of part of a population is faster and more cost effective than examining the total population. If a sample is correctly selected, little information is lost in comparison with testing the whole population.

A well-chosen sample is essential for the resultant analysis and conclusions to have high external validity. If there is external validity, the results can be confidently generalized so that correct conclusions are drawn about the whole population. In addition, analysts require internal validity so that conclusions may be drawn about causal effects between the variables of interest.

Sampling techniques can be divided into two general categories: non-probability sampling and probability sampling. Non-probability sampling is often undertaken by TV and newspaper reporters for a quick appreciation of the views of the 'person in the street'. It is convenient and cheap. Accidental sampling occurs when the researcher selects the first 10 people who walk by the TV studio and are willing to answer questions. Quota sampling means the first five males and the first five females who come by and will answer questions are selected. Finally, purposive sampling involves picking people assumed to be representative, for example, of a community. Obviously, this method is highly subjective and the validity depends on the judgement of the selector. The essential characteristics of these sampling techniques are that there is no guarantee that every member of the population has a chance of being selected, nor is there any way of computing the probability that any individual will be selected.

Probability sampling, on the other hand, ensures that every member of the population has a known probability of being selected. Possibly the most common case is that every member has the same chance of being selected, but this is not strictly necessary. The most common types of probability sampling are simple random samples, systematic samples, stratified random samples and cluster samples. Simple random samples use a list of random numbers to select the sample from a pre-coded population. Systematic samples involve selecting a randomly numbered starting point, then selecting systematically every nth individual to make up the required sample size. Stratified random samples involve initial division into groups or strata according to a characteristic and then randomly selecting individuals, while cluster sampling involves breaking the population into clusters or geographically concentrated groups and randomly selecting from them for the sample.

Simple random samples, although simple in concept, tend to become complex in practice. Initially, the population has to be defined, quantified and probably assigned a number. Then a table of random numbers is used to select the required sample. An off-site sampling of the market of possible site visitors, for example, might use an electoral roll or a telephone directory for the area. Care would have to be taken to ensure that electors or listed telephone users were representative of the required population. The actual selection of the sample can require patience, good secretarial skills and diligence.

Selecting an on-site sample as visitors enter a site by this method can be somewhat easier. However, the random numbers must be pre-sorted into ascending order, because it is impossible to go back to the 16th visitor after the 45th has been selected. Visitors in an on-site sample may continue to be selected until the number required in the research design is chosen. Pre-coding is not required in this case. However, diligence and secretarial skills are still required to keep track of the numbers of people entering, so that the correct (randomly-numbered) individuals are selected. It is best not to attempt selection during rush periods with staff shortages!

Systematic sampling involves systematically selecting every *n*th individual or record, after a randomly selected starting point. If the sample is 500 from a population of 5000, then every tenth record is selected. This method works equally well in the selection of individuals entering a site, of records of permits issued or of entries on an electoral roll or in a phone book. It is easier to keep track of the selection process than with the random number method. When used with permit records, the method also introduces stratification by dates of issue, and thus can be expected to more efficient than simple random sampling. On the other hand, bias may be introduced with this method if the record contains systematic cycles.

One point to be aware of is the case of ineligible selections. Suppose an analysis related only to visitors from within the state, but the permit records contained a few permits issued to interstate and overseas visitors. Passing over these to select the next eligible record is an incorrect procedure, because this method violates the equal chance of selection characteristic of following records. The correct procedure is to draw a larger sample initially to compensate for the ineligible records which will subsequently be discarded.

Stratified random sampling involves initially dividing the population into two or more cross-sectional groups or strata. These might be based on, for example, age, sex, campers with tents or campers with vans/camping trailers. A sample is then drawn randomly from each stratum and combined to form the whole sample. Stratification has the ability to contribute to the efficiency of the sampling if the strata are correctly selected and defined. If we can isolate strata which are internally homogeneous, then we will need a smaller sample overall to achieve efficient results.

Cluster sampling takes account of the cost of research, especially with face-to-face interviews. Rather than send interviewers far and wide to scattered localities, the population is grouped into clusters, which may be geographically or perhaps institutionally-based. The clusters are selected randomly and individuals within the clusters are also selected randomly. Some sampling efficiency may be lost with this method, depending on the size of the selected sample. Cluster sampling could be used with an electoral roll divided into sub-districts.

Sample Size

A major research design question involves the size of the sample to be selected. What sample size is large enough, bearing in mind that the larger the sample, the greater the cost, but the larger the correctly-selected sample, the greater the accuracy of estimations?

Repeated measurement of the mean (average value) of a given variable from numerous samples drawn from a population will yield different results. In addition, those values will normally be different from the true population value. This difference is called the sampling error. Theoretically, the size of a required sample can be computed by taking into account the margin of sampling error we are prepared to tolerate together with the population standard deviation. The larger the population standard deviation, the larger the sample required to achieve acceptable accuracy.

In practice, we usually do not know the variation in the parameters in the population which we are interested in measuring. All we know for sure is that we are faced with a trade-off between cost and accuracy. Another factor to be considered is the expected response rate. What percentage of people who are selected in the sample and receive a questionnaire will fill it in and return it? This question is considered below. Expected response rate has a bearing on the size of the selected sample. Many investigators conducting small to medium-scale (that is, not a national survey) like to have 300-500 useable records. If the response rate is expected to be about 20 per cent, the selected sample to gain 500 records would have to be 2500. If, on the other hand, the response rate is expected to be about 50 per cent, the selected sample would have to be 1000. Non-response in itself is an issue to be considered apart from merely its effect on the required sample size, and this will be examined later.

DEVELOPMENT OF THE QUESTIONNAIRE

While the use of questionnaires is just one of several methods available to elicit information, it is much cheaper than other methods and hence is more commonly used than, for example, personal or telephone interviews. The ability to answer questionnaires in their own environments and time also appears to reassure respondents of their anonymity and allows reflection about questions before offering answers. A further advantage of written questionnaires is the circumvention of possible interview bias, caused by the interviewers' demeanour, speech, dress, or the way in which questions are asked.

Anonymity is important to many people when asked to give personal information. In addition, it is thought that people will give more truthful responses where their identities are not known. Researchers are obliged to protect anonymity unless arrangements are specifically made with respondents. In practice, this means that questionnaires should not be numbered before being administered, nor should there be any secret marks which enable investigators to match completed forms with names. While anonymity creates a problem with double-mailing, as we shall see later, researchers should adhere strictly to ethical practices.

After deciding to use a questionnaire, investigators should think about the information that is really needed for the study. There is a difference between information 'we would like to have' and information we must have to complete the study. Unnecessary questions and asking for unnecessary detail should be avoided. We must assume that respondents are short of time and that they are doing us a favour by answering our questions, not that we are doing them a favor by entertaining them or flattering them that we have bothered to ask their opinions.

Another issue is the matter of open-ended or closed-ended questions. Open-ended in contrast to closed-ended questions allow respondents to answer more freely, but take greater time to answer. Closed-ended questions present respondents with two or more alternative responses, and respondents select the answer or answers which most closely describe their situation. For example, a question asking people what travel costs they considered before they decided to make a journey might list with separate checkboxes: fuel and oil, tire repairs, other repairs such as broken windshield, food, accommodation, entry fees, souvenirs and incidentals.

The advantages of closed-ended questions are that the alternatives can jog people's memories, can help to clarify the question and are easier and cheaper to input and analyze later. To overcome any perception that the investigators know respondents' views better than they do themselves, it is often useful to provide another alternative called 'other' together with a few lines for an explanation. Additionally, it is wise to run a pre-test survey with open-ended questions to get a 'feel' for the sorts of responses which can be expected, then design the response alternatives.

Sometimes we need to ask about attitudes. The most commonly used method of obtaining such information is a ratings scale and, of the various types of scales, the Likert scale is most frequently used. Likert scales allow respondents to indicate their degree of agreement or disagreement with a statement, proposition or reason. The positions available on the scales usually number four (strongly agree, agree, disagree and strongly disagree) or five (the addition of a middle neutral position to the four positions). For example, 'From your experience in camping in national parks, how pleasing or annoying do you find the following sounds? – birds, insects and animals at night' – 'very pleasant', 'fairly pleasant', 'neutral', 'fairly annoying', 'very annoying'. The positions on the scale are usually allocated a numerical code on the questionnaire to assist eventual data input. These codes range from one to five with three as the neutral position.

Questions which relate to a particular topic should be grouped. Sometimes an explanatory note before the series of questions can be useful. Enough questions should be asked to gain a full understanding of the issue. A pretest survey will often be useful in assisting the division of a complex question into a series of smaller issues.

To ensure that a questionnaire works well, the critical paths through the questions should be well marked. Investigators must anticipate the numerous personal situations which will be reported and give adequate directions to go to the next relevant question. Nothing annoys respondents more than reading a direction to go to a question which is not relevant nor consistent with their last answers. Pretesting will help to identify these pathways.

Demographic Characteristics

Most questionnaires contain questions on demographic characteristics. We have seen that these are integral to both ITCM and ZTCM studies. Additionally, it is often useful to test whether the demographic characteristics of people who responded are consistent with the demographic description of the population as a whole. Demographic characteristics of interest to TCM researchers include sex, age, education, income, race, place of residence, occupation, employment and length of vacations. There are others. For example, investigators conducting a study of the users of a small local park might find statistical significance of a variable indicating high-rise residence versus detached ground-level residence. Not all of these demographic factors would usually be investigated in a single survey.

One issue regarding demographic characteristics that is worth examining is their place on the questionnaire. One rule of questionnaire design is to put easy questions first, so that respondents are encouraged to complete the survey. Are demographic questions suitable as the initial easy questions? We think not. Some respondents are sensitive to questions about, for example, income or education levels. It is accepted practice to try to entice and encourage response with the initial questions. Thus, they should be easy, but interesting, and relevant to the study. We suggest the demographic questions should be placed at the end of the form.

'Sex' should present no problem. There are two usual alternatives. 'Age' is best asked for in categories, for example, 'under 15', '16-25', 26-35', ... or as 'year of birth'. Some people are sensitive about their age. 'Year of birth' appears to avoid this problem somewhat, but increases processing costs later. Age categories are best set to be compatible with available census data, so that testing of the sample for representation of the population is possible. 'Education' may be asked for in terms of years completed or highest award gained.

Some people are sensitive about disclosing their income. Hence, it is best to provide categories with quite wide ranges, for example, 'under $20 000, '$20 001 − $30 000'. Again, census data may be available as a guide to categories. Other issues to be made clear on the questionnaire are whether the required income information is gross or net after the deduction of taxes, individual or household, last year or expected this year. Alternative answers regarding race will be dictated by the dominant races living in the market area. It is always a good idea to provide an 'other' box, with the space for an explanation.

The type of investigation will govern how 'place of residence' is asked, whether open-ended or closed-ended. If all that is required is urban versus rural, then those alternative boxes will suffice. If, for example, investigators wish to check stated travel costs or travel time, then actual place of residence and perhaps distance from the site also will be asked.

'Occupation' is usually best asked in terms of categories: professional, managerial, clerical, trades, semi-skilled, etc. Students, housewives and retirees are usually separate categories. Currently employed or unemployed can be asked as a separate question or as a category of occupation. It is probably better to ask it as a separate question, however, because an unemployed professional person, for example, usually retains the preferences of a professional. The advantage of categorization of occupation is that respondents know better than investigators just what sort of duties they carry out in their employment; additionally, the cost of processing is reduced. Length of vacation should be asked for in categories of days, for example, '1-5', 6-10', etc. The categories naturally will be mutually exclusive, and it should be made clear whether the figure for total annual vacation days or this vacation only is required.

PRETESTING THE QUESTIONNAIRE

Pretesting questionnaires has two general purposes. An initial draft of the instrument may be circulated among colleagues and experts for suggestions regarding the flow of questions, aptitude of questions to elicit the required information, wording, critical paths, possible ambiguities and so on. In addition, no matter how much we try to envisage other people's situations, there often will be sets of circumstances that we could not foresee. Similarly, we tend to build our own world view and values into our work. Constructive comments by others can help to neutralize these idiosyncrasies. The initial draft is then amended as necessary.

The second pretest, often called the 'pilot' test, is a dummy run among the same population who will be asked to complete the real survey. This process is vital to sampling by survey. Normally, individuals who take part in the pilot are not selected in the final sample. In addition to mailing the pilot questionnaire, researchers will often conduct some interviews. Pilot testing allows investigators to judge whether respondents have any difficulties with wording, if there are still any ambiguities or if there are any cases where further options should be included in answers. Question sequences are also tested. Topics or questions that don't 'work' can be clarified or dropped. The questionnaire is again amended as necessary. If the changes have been major, another pilot test should be held to ensure the new draft has not incorporated a new problem.

OTHER SAMPLING PROCEDURES

So far, we have considered the selection and size of the sample and the development and testing of the questionnaire. Other factors in the design of research include the method of administration and whether there will be a double-mailing in the case of a mailed survey.

Surveys by written questionnaire may be administered in person in the case where entrants to a site are handed a survey form or by mail where either known users or all people living in a market area are in the selected population. Return of completed questionnaires in an on-site survey may be effected by means of several drop-in boxes set up at strategic points around the site. If the site attracts vandals, it is best to locate these boxes where they are under supervision. In addition, a reply-paid envelope should be handed out with the form so that people who take the form away with them when they leave the site are not discouraged from returning it.

Each mailed questionnaire should be accompanied by an explanatory letter and a reply-paid envelope. The explanatory letter should give an adequate explanation of the reason for the research and should be friendly and persuasive. In addition, it should stipulate a date by which time investigators need the completed questionnaire to be returned. There are differences in view as to the length of time people should be given to respond. If the time is too short, some people who may not be able to complete the form in time due to absence or pressure of work will discard it. On the other hand, if the period is long, many people will put off sitting down to complete it and then forget to do so. In our view, asking people to complete the form within a week or so of its receipt is not unreasonable.

Double-mailing is a survey technique which allows researchers to test whether attributes or views of non-respondents are different from those of respondents (Moser and Kalton, 1971). A second set of survey materials is sent to the same sample of people as in the first mailing. The reason for this is that people who respond to the second mailing, but not to the first, are thought to be more likely to be like those that did not respond at all rather than like those people who responded initially.

The explanatory letter in the second mailing must be carefully worded. People who have already responded are apt to wonder why they (the researchers) are wasting usually public funds. Additionally, the researchers don't want these respondents to respond again, because there is no way with an anonymous survey to know who has responded and who has not. On the other hand, researchers want people who have not responded to be encouraged to respond and not to be offended by the letter. How the letter is worded probably is related to the culture of the area. In Australia, for example, mentioning that the pet galah might have eaten the first set of materials or the dog paw-printed the first questionnaire seems to work well. The second set of materials is mailed shortly after the initial return date.

The time required to collect data may vary between an on-site survey and a mailed survey. While time is saved with an on-site survey in not having to mail material out and wait to receive it back, often many days must pass before sufficient visitors come on site for a representative sample to be selected.

Response Rates

We have already seen that response rates are important to researchers on two fronts: the expected response rate will affect the size of the sample and a high non-response has implications for the ability to generalize the results to the whole sample, let alone the whole population. What response rate can we expect? Mailed surveys usually have the lowest response rate among mailed, telephoned or personal interview surveys. This is probably because people find it easier to refuse a written request than a personal request. The response rate is generally less than 50 per cent when the general public are involved. Response rates of 20-25 per cent are common. (This is a good reason to elect to double-mail, because researchers gain information on late respondents and also increase the response rate.) On the other hand, among a specialized population such as national park enthusiasts, it is not uncommon to achieve a 60 per cent response. From a group of ethical investors, one of us achieved an 87 per cent response rate and responses were still trickling in long after the analysis was completed.

CONCLUSION

In this chapter we have examined survey techniques, after discussing briefly whether a survey is required at all when permit data are available. The steps in devising and administering a survey were considered: identification of the population, selection of a sample, development and testing of a questionnaire and other survey procedures such as the method of administration and the advisability of double-mailings. Finally, the issue of response rates was examined.

REFERENCES

Hellerstein, D. (1992), 'The Treatment of Nonparticipants in Travel Cost Analysis and Other Demand Models', *Water Resources Research*, **28** (8), 1999-2004.
Moser, C. and Kalton, G. (1971), *Survey Methods in Social Investigation,* London: Heinemann.

7. Measurement of the Variables

Survey instruments are designed so that as many respondents as possible are able to provide accurately and easily the information needed by the researcher. The object of a pilot test, as we have seen, is to improve the design in terms of the flow of questions and ease of comprehension by respondents. Even so, responses from some recipients are likely to indicate that they have personal situations and perceptions which had not been anticipated. Analysts must thus develop protocols for managing the data so that the objective of the investigation is not jeopardized. This process involves the establishment of appropriate rules to interpret answers consistently.

The first part of this chapter deals with some technical issues relating to dummy and proxy variables, then goes on to comment on some of the variables that might be included in an analysis. The next part of the chapter examines the protocol development process with examples relating to a few of the variables, and gives a few practical tips to smooth the research path. In addition, it examines some issues relating to zonal methodology and discusses controlling the cost of gathering data.

DUMMY VARIABLES

A variable is an entity which can assume different values. A continuous variable has any numeric value and therefore can have an infinite number of values between any two adjacent units on a scale. Discrete variables, on the other hand, take only specified values such as whole numbers only. Dummy variables are one form of discrete variable, usually a binary or dichotomous variable. That is, dummy variables usually take one of two values: 1 or 0, yes or no, on or off. Dummy variables are used to incorporate qualitative data (for example, sex, race or changes in policy), rather than quantitative data.

The preference of site visitors for certain sorts of recreational activity, for example, might be incorporated into a demand equation by use of a dummy variable. A suitable question could be: 'Do you generally seek active or passive forms of recreation?' The answers to this question may then be coded '1' for 'active' and '0' for passive.

Dummy variables can be used very effectively to improve the reliability of demand estimates, because they increase the amount of observed visitation explained by the model. However, they should not be used indiscriminately nor should they be used when a true underlying variable is easily measured.

A number of dummy variables may be included in an analysis. The general rule is that, if a dummy variable has *n* categories or mutually exclusive classes, then use *n−1* dummy variables. For example, (highest) level of education might be considered to have four mutually exclusive classes – high school or less, college or trade certificate, undergraduate degree or postgraduate degree. Three dummy variables could be used with the fourth possibility being that to which the other three are compared. Thus, every possible level of education is covered. A 'yes' for any one of the three included variables naturally indicates that particular level, while a 'no' response to each dummy indicates a positive response for the final category.

The coefficient of a dummy variable is easily envisaged as a demand curve shifter or shift factor. If all other determinants are held constant, the coefficient of the dummy variable will shift the curve outwards or inwards according to the algebraic sign by the estimated value of the coefficient. This, of course, is no different from the effect of any other determinant, but perhaps is a little easier to interpret.

PROXY VARIABLES

Proxy variables are used to characterize determinants when it is difficult to collect direct values. 'Proxy' here has its ordinary meaning of 'substitute' or 'acting for another'. In recreational research, perhaps 'tastes and preferences' is the classic demand determinant for which it is difficult to assign a value spectrum.

Researchers have used many variables as proxies for tastes and preferences. Level of education has been used, because it has been noted in many countries that outdoor, nature-based recreation is sought by people with higher education. Formal school and university education is an important medium for the transmission of values while exposing students to new concepts. Distinguishing cause and effect is difficult, but a strong positive relationship is often observable between education and seeking active recreational pursuits.

Age and sex have been used as proxies, because there is a relationship between them and outdoor recreation. We do not see, for example, as many middle-aged and elderly women spending their recreation hours rock-climbing in national parks as we see young men! Similarly, household income has a bearing on the type of recreation sought.

In order to try to overcome the proxy problem, Driver and Rosenthal (1982) developed a series of questions elucidating preferences for outdoor recreation. Ratings on a Likert scale on the various factors, when amalgamated, would give descriptions of many personality types and their preferences. The factors included, among others, developing skills for better sense of self-worth, exercising to feel good, resting, social interaction, privacy and solitude, experiencing largely unmodified nature, enjoying family gatherings and teaching children, personal freedom, self-testing, learning about nature, exploring and recuperating. Robust descriptions of personality types would be useful information to recreational planners.

MEASUREMENT OF VARIABLES

Table 7.1 lists many variables of interest to TCM analysts. A classification of their types is given and comments made to assist with their measurement. As noted many times before, the variables incorporated in an analysis depend on its purpose. In the 'Type' column below, 'C' means a continuous variable, 'D' means discrete, 'Q' is qualitative, 'CG' means a grouped continuous variable, and 'QG' means a grouped qualitative variable.

WHO WILL RESPOND FOR WHOM?

One of the issues which should be thoroughly considered as the research plan is being developed is the question of whom the researcher desires to respond to the survey. Is it the driver, the senior male, the senior female ...? In these days of greater equality, researchers have to be careful how they indicate their preference in this matter. We cannot say 'the husband', because there may not be one in each party or there may be several. If there is one and one only, his wife may be there and take offence. We cannot say 'the driver', because there may be several. However, we can settle on 'a responsible adult', without offending too many potential respondents, and we can request that adult to fill in the questionnaire on behalf of the whole party.

One member of each party will be able to respond to the questions of travel cost for the vehicle, food costs for the party and so on. But what about the number of times visited if some members have visited more than others, for example, within a group of single persons? What about household income, when there are members of several households in the party? What do you want done about ages, education levels and occupations for a party of six people? Do you want those details for each person or for only one? If for one, then which one? These are the sorts of questions research designers have to anticipate, settle on the required information, design the appropriate questions and give adequate direction to respondents.

PROTOCOLS FOR THE MEASUREMENT OF VARIABLES

Accurate measurement of the variables to be included in a TCM stems from thorough planning, a detailed view of what is required, anticipation of respondents' difficulties, clear wording of questions, adequate additional instructions and, finally, rules to sort out unanticipated problems.

These rules have to be formulated as responses are received so that decisions are consistent. Appropriate and detailed planning and testing is undertaken to keep uncertainties after the questionnaire is administered to a minimum. A few cases are given here.

Take the case of the cost of food purchased during the trip. In asking for food costs during travel, we are strictly trying to ascertain the cost of any food additional to the cost of food consumed at home. An instruction to that effect should be given on the questionnaire. Even so, there can be differences in interpretation. For example, a family might report buying hamburgers for lunch as extra food cost, when they always buy hamburgers, even when at home. Analysts are constrained to accept what appears to be a likely range of costs, given the individual circumstances.

While not wanting to censor data, analysts have to be careful that unlikely values are not inadvertently included. One problem which can arise involves actual, but not necessary, costs. It would be inappropriate for the researcher to decree that an expensive restaurant meal, for example, was not necessary and thus was not a relevant cost, when the respondents considered it a cost of their trip. One respondent to one of our surveys reported that additional food cost was $1000 for a three-day trip for two people, but that the $1000 was spent on restaurant meals and stocking up his wine cellar while in a wine-producing area. He argued that the fine dining and wine purchases were legitimate and normal extra food cost for his travel, because that is what he always did when he travelled to that area. An analyst would have to concede that the cost of restaurant meals could be incorporated into the TCM, but including the cost of purchases of wine for future consumption certainly raises questions about the incremental cost in visiting the destination site. Researchers try to overcome this sort of difficulty by giving adequate guidance on the questionnaire. Most of the TCM literature concludes that the minimum incremental cost is the correct concept.

Table 7.1   Classification of TCM variables

Variable	Type	Comment
No. of trips per time period	D	Discreteness is exaggerated if visit numbers are grouped into classes. Greater problem with more frequently visited sites where respondents tend to round estimates. Dobbs (1993) recommended specification of visit classes where individual visitation rates high.
Cash costs of travel	C	Additional information may be needed to compute the economic costs of travel, e.g. additional vehicle servicing or repairs.
Cost of time	C	Additional questions are needed to elicit personal circumstances – e.g. wages foregone; opportunity cost of recreation time.
Intrinsic benefit of travel	C	If positive, may deduct from cost of travel. See Walsh, Sanders and McKean (1990).
Value of on-site time	C	Difficult issue; relevance depends on the purpose of the analysis. See discussion elsewhere.
Quality of the site	C, Q	Use quantitative variables which describe recreational quality or Likert scales to gain information on various quality attributes – e.g. physical attractiveness, recreational satisfaction (e.g. fishing success, challenging ski slopes, number of species seen).
Price of substitute sites	C	The problem with this variable is which substitute sites. Additionally, there may be very high correlation with own site price, unless you sample from many zones.
Quality of substitute sites	C, Q	Which sites remains a problem. Measure quality the same way as with the quality of own site.
Price of complement-ary sites	C	Similar problems as with price of substitute sites.
Quality of complement-ary sites	C, Q	Which sites remains a problem. Measure quality as with the quality of own site.

Age	C	May be strictly considered a discrete variable, because respondents will give full year ages.
	CG	Supplying grouped age ranges and tick boxes makes answering easier and usually improves response rates. Ranges best conform to available census data to facilitate testing of samples.
Sex	Q	Two categories only are usual.
Education	C (D)	Ask 'years of formal education'.
	QG	Ask 'highest level of education completed' and give classes – e.g. 'high school or lower', 'technical or trade qualification', 'undergraduate degree', etc.
Income per individual or household	C or CG	Grouped incomes ranges usually improve response rates.
Occupation	Q or QG	Allowing respondents to classify occupation into supplied occupation categories (e.g. professional, managerial, trades) makes answering easier and usually improves response rates.
Ethnicity	Q	Supplying types and tick boxes makes answering easier and usually improves response rates.
Place of residence	QG	Usually rural/urban is the required categorization. Supply tick boxes.
Family size	D	Give direction as to how extended the family unit.
Leisure time	C or CG	Supplying ranges and tick boxes makes answering easier.
Tastes and preferences	Q	Use Likert scales. See the discussion above for proxy variables which could be used.

Some Practical Tips

Whatever the model you have in mind, data on numbers of trips by individuals are a necessary precursor. Questions to elicit information on the number of trips to the site undertaken by respondents in the last 12 months might consist of a simple 'How many times did you visit ...?' or a more complex picture might be built up by a series of questions.

The gathering of data may be made more complex by users sometimes making day visits and sometimes longer overnight visits. Respondents should be given adequate instructions so that they understand what is required. If possible to do so, researchers try to incorporate questions which enable data to be checked to ensure that each response is internally consistent. As an internal check on the accuracy of data, responses should be scrutinized as they are received to ensure that answers appear reasonable.

ZTCM requires the definition of zones of origin of visitors and population statistics. In Australia, for example, the major official statistical region is the statistical division. Within those divisions, data are available by smaller local government administrative (LGA) and postcode areas. Respondents may be asked for the name of their suburb, town or district or, alternatively, their LGA or postcode. Phrasing a question on residence in terms of a zip code, postcode or similar numerical identifier is useful for the researcher, because the number can be input as stated without having to be coded. Additionally, records can be easily manipulated and respondents have greater assurance of anonymity. Counties are the most commonly used zones in the US.

The measurement of the costs of travel is not an elementary task in practice when survey methodology is involved, because individuals have different perceptions of cost. Given that a demand curve is a model of consumer behaviour, consumers base their demand on expected cost. In contradiction to this fundamental premise of consumer demand theory, 59 per cent of respondents to one of our surveys answered 'not at all' to the question whether they estimated the travel cost before they left home.

It is apparent that these consumers do not consider costs in great detail; they nevertheless subconsciously judged that they would still capture some consumer surplus even if costs proved to be at the upper end of the likely range. Moreover, 77 per cent of the respondents who estimated costs either roughly or accurately before leaving home reported they had over-estimated the cost. This apparently hazy view of expected cost may be rational in that respondents have decided to avoid the transaction costs of estimating accurately the cost of the trip.

In order to minimize potential bias from this source, as it is apparent from the evidence that consumers do not perceive costs precisely, it is worthwhile to list the categories of costs that may be incurred. These would include fuel, vehicle repairs, tire replacements, vehicle servicing, accommodation, food and entry fees. Additional instructions should be given on the questionnaire, for example, that the full cost of fuel used for the trip should be given, not just the fuel purchases made while on the road. In order to check fuel use, the analyst needs to know the approximate distance travelled, road conditions and the type of vehicle. Thinking about these checks before administering the survey will suggest further questions to include.

DEFINITION AND IDENTIFICATION OF ZONES

Zonal TCM relies on the definition and use of zones in the analysis so that travel cost from those zones can be related to visitation rates. As the early developers of the methodology were thinking in terms of a regular increase in the distance travelled and consequent increases in travel cost in order to obtain the necessary variation in the data to estimate a demand curve, concentric circles around the site delineating regions were first used. Later developments have changed that methodology.

Concentric Zones

Clawson and Knetsch (1966) illustrated their explanation of TCM as they perceived it with data on visits to Lewis and Clark Lake in South Dakota. The lake, which is a reservoir on the Missouri River, was surrounded by an irregularly distributed population, with few people nearby, more in the next zone, relatively fewer per unit area in the third and rather more in the fourth due to the location of a large city. Five zones were designated according to distance from the lake: less than 50 miles, 50-100 miles, 100-150 miles, 150-200 miles and 200 miles and over within the designated area.

The numbers of visits per standardized party of four were estimated (in thousands) as 333, 363, 50, 161 and 20. Clawson and Knetsch then reduced these estimated numbers of visits to a variable, estimated visits per thousand base population, to take account of the differences in resident populations in the zones. Obviously, the greater the resident populations the greater the likelihood of visits being made, all other factors being equal. Adjusting the raw visits data to a standardized base accounts for the effects of differing population levels.

The adjustment process obviously needs access to accurate population data. While concentric circles are appropriate in theory, incorporating them into the analysis is a problem. Population data typically is not collected and published in smooth concentric circles around outdoor recreation sites!

Census data is collected in many countries by census collectors' districts, local government administrative areas such as shires, counties, towns and cities, statistical divisions and states. Additionally, many countries publish population data by postcode or zipcode. Hence, researchers who design concentric circles into their ZTCM analyses are forced to allocate small statistical area data to their regions. A considerable amount of adjustment of data is then made necessary.

We have seen a number of studies where researchers have tried to conform to the concentric circle approach. They usually are constrained to make heroic assumptions about populations and population densities. In our view, it is usually unnecessary because a better method is available.

Zones based on Administrative Regions

Zones may be based on administrative regions. There is no need to define concentric circles. We can incorporate more accurate and more easily obtained population data by fitting our zones to the population data available. The only remaining issue then is to ensure that the visit data can be appropriately related to the identified zones. Possibly the best way to do that is through the use of postcodes or zipcodes, so long as the zones are not too large or, through some quirk in geography or roads, there is not too much variance in values of the other independent variables.

How Many Zones and How Far Distant?

There are a number of questions to be considered here. Firstly, how many zones? In statistical practice, the rule generally is that data are grouped so that values within groups are as homogeneous as possible, but that the values between groups vary as much as possible. Obviously, for our purposes the answer depends on the type of analysis being undertaken. The smaller the zones are, the more likelihood of internal homogeneity, in relation to many of the demand determinants. Income for a household in a rural area, for example, is more likely to be similar to income of a household on a nearby farm than that of either a tradesperson or a professional in a nearby city.

The statistical reliability of an estimated model is likely to improve as the number of zones increases, because the number of observations increase. What is a reasonable number for statistical purposes? Many researchers like to see at least 25-30 zones, although some well-known analyses have been completed with 15-20 zones.

One additional issue which may arise when a zonal framework such as statistical regions is adopted is what to do about zones with zero visitation rate. In some datasets, some zones have zero visits even though they are equidistant from the site as other zones with positive visitation rates. Omission of these zones will truncate the data set. This will bias the coefficient estimation and result in a more inelastic demand curve (Hellerstein, 1992). Some analysts have combined zero visit zones with nearby zones with positive visitation rates.

How far distant should zones be extended? TCM is based in part on the assumption that trips are made with the sole purpose of visiting the site in question. However, as Smith and Kopp (1980) and others have shown, as distance increases, it becomes less and less likely that each trip is made for a single purpose. Smith and Kopp suggested statistical testing should be used to determine when behavioral parameters change. Remaining distant zones should then be dropped.

CONTROLLING THE COST OF GATHERING DATA

Gathering data can be an extremely expensive exercise, in both cash or opportunity costs. On the other hand, in some circumstances, it can cost nothing. An example of these circumstances is the case where a gate attendant collects places of origin from vehicle license plates and numbers of occupants in vehicles which enter a site. If the attendant otherwise would be 'doing nothing' (for example, reading a novel) and does not have so much traffic that waiting costs are imposed on potential customers whilst details are being recorded, then there are no opportunity costs of collecting the data. Waiting costs of clients may transpose to future lost demand and lost benefits for the site managers. Generally, however, accuracy and cost are positively related, and cheap data may not prove to be as useful in the long run as data which cost more.

Data may be gleaned from records already collected, but often the records are not completely apposite. Hence, additional information must be collected, and this usually means a survey.

Survey expenses may be controlled through proper planning and attention to detail. As noted above, adequate planning will minimize the need for protocols for handling the input of data. Additionally, proper planning will minimize time answering phone calls from concerned respondents and will maximize the number of useful responses. Hence, cost effectiveness of the survey will increase.

One major expense is postage and clerical time for specifically addressed mail. If the survey design will allow, the use of 'householder delivery' is an excellent way to reduce costs. 'Householder delivery' exists under one name or another in many countries, and involves the delivery of mail to all addresses within a specified area. Because all addresses receive an envelope, there is no sorting cost. In many countries, the postal charge is less than 20 per cent of normal postage. With this form of administration of the questionnaire, normally the number of envelopes sent out will increase and the response rate will decrease, but the handling and postage costs will decrease significantly. While we are not advocating the deliberate sacrifice of accuracy for cost-savings, the use of this service is one more option for researchers to consider in the research design.

CONCLUSION

This chapter highlights the importance of adequate planning, having a thorough view of what is required, and being able to anticipate respondents' difficulties. The chapter discusses dummy and proxy variables, and examines the measurement of the variables which may be used in the regression analysis. To minimize difficulties, questions should be worded clearly and incorporate adequate additional instructions. Rules to sort out unanticipated problems must be formulated as soon as the first of those problems are encountered as the responses are received. These steps are important, and none should be omitted. In addition, the chapter incorporates some useful practical tips from the authors' own experiences and examines briefly some issues relating to ZTCM. It concludes with a brief discussion of the cost of data.

REFERENCES

Clawson M. and J.L. Knetsch (1966), *Economics of Outdoor Recreation*, Washington: Resources for the Future.

Dobbs, I.M. (1993), 'Individual Travel Cost Method: Estimation and Benefit Assessment with a Discrete and Possibly Grouped Dependent Variable', *American Journal of Agricultural Economics*, 75, 84-94.

Driver, B.L. and D.H. Rosenthal (1982), 'Measuring and Improving Effectiveness of Public Outdoor Recreation Programs', Washington: George Washington University.

Hellerstein, D. (1992), 'The Treatment of Nonparticipants in Travel Cost Analysis and Other Demand Models', *Water Resources Research*, 28 (8), 1999-2004.

Smith, V.K. and R.J. Kopp (1982), 'The Spatial Limits of the Travel Cost Recreational Demand Model', *Land Economics*, 56, 64-72.

Walsh, R.G., L.D. Sanders and J.R. McKean (1990), 'The Consumption Value of Travel Time on Recreation Trips', *Journal of Travel Research*, Summer, 17-24.

8. Data Management and Analysis

In this chapter, we move from considering the design and flow of questions to elicit data from respondents to the mechanical processes of managing data so that it can be coded and analysed. In addition, we briefly examine OLS regression analysis. Many readers will already be fully conversant with OLS and will have no need to consult this section. Several sections of this manual assume a basic knowledge of OLS regression analysis.

To facilitate the management of data, the questionnaire must be set out so that coding and data input are made as simple and efficient as possible. That issue is discussed in this chapter, and then we proceed to an examination of the processing of responses once they start to be received. The following section discusses the input of data to whatever means of analysis are to be used when researchers are satisfied that few more responses will be received.

DESIGN TO FACILITATE CODING

To facilitate analysis, responses to most questions on a survey instrument are coded in a numeric form. Efficiency and ease of data coding and input are directly related to the layout of the questionnaire. For example, where information is needed about the types of expenses incurred other than those in a given list, a dotted line might be placed to the left of the column and space left at the right for a code to be written in so that it can be easily read by the data input person. Similarly, if tick boxes are more or less vertically aligned, input is easier and faster.

Another useful practice which enhances efficiency of data input is to print codes next to tick boxes. For some variables, the choice of code numbers is arbitrary. Thus, we could use 1 and 2, or 1, 2, 3 ... n or any other set of numbers. These arbitrary numbers are used when the scale is nominal. In other words, we can sort the responses into different groups, but they cannot be ranked. Examples are sex of respondent and activities undertaken while at the site. For responses about variables which contain an ordinal ranking, the rank order should be preserved in the coding scheme.

The point was made in the last chapter that the response rate for the survey will be enhanced if respondents are able to answer the survey quickly and easily without striking problems of definition and without needing to write in a great deal of information. Tick boxes are extremely useful in cutting down the need for long written responses. Additionally, as we have just seen, tick boxes also assist the data input process. One danger is that responses are constrained to fit the boxes available; a researcher can encourage a win:win situation by designing many appropriate tick boxes and having a final 'other' choice with a line or two for explanation. This explanation can then be coded as appropriate.

PROCESSING RESPONSES

When responses are received, either by mail, drop-in box or both, they must be processed. It is best to do this everyday of the receival period to keep up to date and to cut down on the utter boredom of doing the job. In addition, if you keep the work up to date, you stay abreast of the climbing response rate. When it gets over the magic 50 per cent, you can start to sleep more easily at night!

Processing involves many tasks: consecutive numbering of responses, checking for omissions and inconsistencies, coding any uncoded responses and writing up a code book and filing.

A number is placed on the front page of the questionnaire as an identifier. This number might start at 1 or perhaps 101, 201, 301, etc, if there are codes designed into the numbers. Codes could be designed to indicate, for example, a particular site in a multi-site survey or perhaps the time of receipt. Codes can be hand-written or, with a large survey response, stamped with a numbering machine.

Checking for omissions and inconsistencies is tedious but necessary. Sometimes, omissions can be overcome by perhaps adding to the survey questionnaire some information from the envelope before it is discarded. Care must be taken in doing this that unwarranted assumptions are not made. For example, just because a survey form bears a postmark from one state does not necessarily mean that the respondent actually lives in that state.

Sometimes, researchers can clear up apparent inconsistencies when intentions are clear. Researchers' superior knowledge of respondents and the sites in question can be exploited here rather than leaving inconsistencies to the haphazard interpretation of research assistants. A red or other readily identified pen should be used to amend data. In a few cases, the answers received on a response will be patently absurd or wilfully misleading, or only a few questions will be answered. In these cases, researchers must decide whether to discard these responses. Again, it should not be done lightly, nor should this task be left to the least qualified member of the research team.

As mentioned above, having an 'other' category is useful to catch responses where respondents cannot decide which box to tick. A senior member of the research team should consider the 'other' explanation and decide whether it is appropriate to allocate it to one of the boxes or to give it a new code number. It is possible with some well thought out and properly tested surveys still to have to use a number of new codes. A code book or code list should be started and kept, with adequate descriptions of each code, so that consistency of classification can be assured throughout the whole of the data receipt processing.

Missing data is a further issue to be considered at this stage. A missing data code should not be printed on the questionnaire for obvious reasons. Nothing which would allow respondents to assume that some people will not answer or will not answer all questions should be done. The person processing the responses thus should write in a missing data code where data are missing. '99' is often used, except where 99 could be a legitimate response. The use of a missing data code means that data input can be checked for accuracy more easily.

Punching and filing is the last step in data receipt. Here 'punching' does not mean the 1960s punching of computer-readable cards, but merely the punching of the questionnaires with a two-hole punch so that they might be filed in a two-ring binder. With a very large survey, often the questionnaires are punched at the printery after being printed to save having to hand punch later. Filing in a two-ring binder keeps the responses in order and in a neat package for transport to the data input person.

DATA INPUT

Nowadays, most data analysis is conducted by means of personal computers, rather than pen and calculator. While the pen and calculator and personal computer methods both typically occur in the office of the researcher, there was an intervening stage where data were taken away to be analysed at a central processing point on mainframe computers. This outsourcing step often meant that researchers lost control of and contact with their data. The availability of relatively cheap and powerful personal computers has made research markedly easier.

Data may be quickly entered into whatever program is to be used, once the preparation discussed in the section above has been completed. If the research team have better things to do than keying in data, it can easily be input by an assistant and the file made available to the team.

Some software packages allow researchers to pre-enter ranges of acceptable values for each variable, so that the computer continually runs a check on correct data input. If a value outside the range is entered, the computer will flag a warning that the data should be checked. Regardless of this facility, data entry should be checked, either by physical check or by re-entering data and comparing the two files. Once data entry is complete, you are ready to run the analysis and find some exciting answers to your questions.

OLS REGRESSION ANALYSIS

What is Regression Analysis?

Whenever several factors act in common to produce a single result, researchers have a natural interest in trying to disentangle their separate effects. There are two methods to do this. The first is a controlled experiment where all but one of the factors are physically controlled, the experiment performed and the result observed and recorded. In this manner the effect of each factor can be isolated. Unfortunately, the opportunity to conduct controlled experiments is usually unavailable to social scientists, resource managers and policy analysts.

When a controlled experiment is not possible, multiple regression offers a second method for disentangling the effects of the various factors, such as travel cost, income and demographic factors. This statistical method offers an opportunity for setting up what amounts to an indirect, nonphysical control. In multiple regression, variables are permitted to vary under natural conditions. An observation consists of a single value for each variable in the regression model. Each observation provides a small piece of useful information because what occurs at any one time depends on the values taken by the full complement of factors. Determination of the relative impacts of the separate factors comes only from an analysis of a number of observations.

Regression analysis is an approach used to study the relationship between variables, particularly how the values of one variable depend on the values of one or more other independent variables. While here we are suggesting it be used to estimate a demand function, managers who master the use of the technique will find it extremely effective in estimating cost or production functions as well. Having a thorough understanding of how costs behave in a business unit can be uncommonly beneficial for managers who wish to manage costs well.

The aim of regression analysis is to estimate a quantitative relationship between variables. The term 'regression' which etymologically means to 'step backwards' was used by Francis Galton about a century ago to indicate the 'return to the mean or average value'. He published a paper in which he argued the average height of adult sons of tall fathers was less than their fathers' height, and the average height of adult sons of short fathers was greater than their fathers' height, but that there was a positive relationship between the height of fathers and the height of their sons.

In short, we use regression analysis for two purposes: firstly, to understand how the independent variables influence the dependent variable and, secondly, to be able to predict or estimate a value for the dependent variable based on specific values for the independent variable or variables. The value of regression analysis lies not only in the consistency of its predictions but also in the superiority of its predictions. The use of regression gives analysts a systematic way of disentangling the influences of numerous predictor variables. Properly applied, regression analysis can be a very powerful tool indeed among econometric techniques. Two popular and useful econometrics textbooks are Kennedy (1992) and Greene (1993).

Suitable Software

Analysis of the type we are discussing is usually completed by means of spreadsheet or statistics software. Spreadsheets are simplified data bases, which are designed to facilitate manipulation of data. Typical spreadsheets are Excel, JOSS and Lotus 1-2-3, and some statistics packages are SPSS, SAS, Micro TSP and Systat. Data are entered into a matrix, with variable names heading the columns and the numbers of the records (the numbers given to each response as it was received) entered in the first column and thus referencing each row. Commands are then entered to run the regression analysis with stipulated variables.

Estimation and Interpretation of Regression Coefficients

As noted above, the most important variables which have been found to be statistically significant predictors of visitation include travel cost, travel time, tastes and preferences, substitute and complementary sites, site quality and socioeconomic variables such as age, sex, education, income, occupation, residence and family size. These then are the variables which we consider when designing and estimating a TCM model.

The steps in estimating the regression model are these. The first step which was completed long before the data input stage is consideration of the model to be estimated. What variables would we want in the model? Can we collect data for all of them? Are data available for each required variable and what is the cost of collection? How far will our funding stretch?

The second step is to express the model in a linear additive fashion, even though we suspect some variables will be related in a negative direction and we additionally may suspect the relationship is not linear. Thus, the model may be specified, for example:

$$V = a + bTC + cSP + dT + eA + fE \qquad (8.1)$$

where V is the number of visits, TC is the round trip travel cost to the site including travel time, SP is the travel cost to and from a substitute site, T is a measure of tastes and preferences, A is age of visitor and E is the highest education level gained by each visitor. We hypothesize that the estimated coefficients for TC and possibly A would have algebraically negative signs and that the others would be positive. We have to be careful at this stage to note the units in which each variable is measured. Some variables may be measured in dollars or another unit of currency and some in perhaps hundreds or thousands of another unit. A variable like education might be measured in years or as a dummy variable with several categories.

The third step is to run the data with the software of choice, firstly as the linear functional form. There are many issues which are raised at this point and which we must understand before we can move further forward. Since we cannot deal with everything at once, let's assume first that the estimated relationship was judged satisfactory. Suppose the model was:

$$V = a + bTC_1 + cSP_2 + dT_3 \qquad (8.2)$$

and the results of the estimation were:

$$V = 24.2 - 0.01TC_1 + 5.32SP_2 + 0.56T_3 \qquad (8.3)$$

The printout of results would give us the values of the coefficients, a, b, c and d, together with values for the standard errors of the coefficients, adjusted coefficient of determination, the standard error of the V estimate and the F value. On the basis of these values, we would be able to judge whether to accept that functional form and, indeed, whether all the independent variables were statistically significant. We will deal with these statistical tests later in the chapter.

A fourth step which is usually undertaken is to test other functional forms. It is possible that the linear functional form does not provide the best 'fit' for the data. So long as the functional forms that are tried are appropriate under the constraints of the underlying demand theory, it is pertinent to estimate them and test their suitability. Two common functional forms include the log-linear and the semi-log models, discussed in Chapters 4 and 5. These functional forms can be handled using inherently linear statistical techniques by transforming the independent variable, the dependent variables or both. A common variable transformation is to take natural logs.

A final step may or may not be taken, depending on the TCM model being estimated. Where a two-stage TCM is being estimated to derive a demand curve for entry to the site, values for visits demanded, usually designated V, are estimated at various entry prices using the regression equation. The TC, V combinations may then be graphed or, if required, can be expressed as an equation, again using regression analysis. The R^2 value is used as a statistical test to determine the most appropriate functional form this time. The other tests are all inappropriate because the data have been derived by the use of regression analysis.

What Regression Does Revisited

With regression analysis we are estimating the quantitative relationship between independent variables and the dependent variable, now referred to in the general notation for a dependent variable, Y. Although we are content to accept, for example, that $Y = 80$ when $X = 2$, if we have estimated that $Y = 100 - 10X$, no unique value of Y exists when $X = 2$ because Y is a random variable. Still, on average the equation we have estimated using the dataset is appropriate for the possible values of Y. In particular, we assume with linear regression that the conditional mean of Y, given X, follows a straight line.

When we estimate the coefficients describing this line using sample data drawn from the whole population, we are in effect estimating the value of the conditional mean of Y. Thus, for each value of X, the dependent Y has a resultant mean value with the difference between the observed and estimated values being a random variable. These random variables are often called the 'residuals'.

The significance of regression theory lies in our ability to generalize results. Before we can make any inferences about the population from our sample estimates, we must understand some important assumptions about the residuals. These are, for all values of X, that the residuals have a zero mean and constant variance, the residuals are mutually uncorrelated and the residuals are normally distributed. If any of these assumptions are violated, our estimates are biased, so that they will be misleading if used for managerial decision support. It is worthwhile to run some checks on the residuals of an estimated regression to test their behavior against the assumptions above. These tests will give you improved confidence in your results.

Effects of Violation of the Assumptions

Several assumptions may be violated through omitted dependent variables or an incorrectly specified functional form. The parameter estimates tend to be biased if a relevant independent variable is omitted. The size of the bias is related to the nature and extent of the influence of the omitted variable and the degree of correlation between it and the incorporated independent variables.

The specification of an incorrect functional form will also bias estimated coefficients. The extent of the bias depends on the nature of the real relationship and the incorrect function form specified. Unfortunately, inspection of the data is of only limited use to detect this problem. The safest ground for any analyst is to abide by the primary rule of statistical analysis which is that the underlying theory well accepted by practitioners in the discipline must drive the statistical analysis. Good statistics do not substitute for weak theory. However, as has been discussed above, demand theory can accommodate several functional forms and we therefore have the latitude to choose one from among many. This choice will be discussed further below in the section dealing with tests of statistical significance.

Heteroscedasticity
Heteroscedasticity occurs when the assumption that the residuals exhibit constant variance throughout the regression is violated. This may occur when the model is incorrectly specified through omitted variables or the incorrect functional form. It is useful to check for these problems before proceeding to test for constant variance. If the model is correctly specified but the variance of the residuals is not constant, the estimates are unbiased, but the standard error is inflated.

Autocorrelation
Autocorrelation occurs when the residuals exhibit a cyclical or perhaps sequential pattern such as progressively becoming larger or smaller. This pattern in the residuals indicates that a variable not currently included in the regression is influencing the dependent variable. The problem can be removed by adding a new variable which assists to explain the variation. In the absence of correction in a properly specified model, it is likely that the

estimate of the slope coefficient will be unbiased, but the standard error of the coefficient will be biased downwards.

Autocorrelation is also known as serial correlation and is only found in time series data. The Durbin-Watson statistic may be used to indicate the presence of autocorrelation.

Multicollinearity

Multicollinearity refers to the degree of correlation between any two or more of the independent variables. Ironically, in multiple regression analysis we desire some degree of correlation between the variables, but not too much. If, at one extreme, we have no correlation between two independent variables, a simple regression analysis run with either variable will give the same estimated equation. Correlation between two independent variables makes it important that both are included in the specification. On the other hand, if two variables are highly correlated, inclusion of both will inflate the standard errors of each and possibly lead to the rejection of both. The higher the correlation, the more difficult it is to isolate and estimate the separate effects.

One classic sign of multicollinearity is the combination of a high R^2 value together with the individual independent variables appearing as not significant when t-tests are conducted on the estimated coefficients. A simple way to check for multicollinearity is to check for strong correlations between pairs of variables. If the correlation between any two independent variables is higher than the overall model R^2, you likely have a multicollinearity problem.

Multicollinearity is the problem which was referred to earlier in this manual when developers of TCM tried to include travel time in estimates as well as travel cost. If both variables are included in an analysis, it is likely that one or other would appear as not significant by means of the t-test of its estimated coefficient. Comparison of the adjusted R^2 value is likely to show little decrease in explanatory power, when one of the two variables was deleted. However, visitors to a site do incur both monetary and time costs in choosing to visit, and somehow those cash and opportunity costs should be incorporated in many analyses, depending of course on the nature and purpose of the investigation. Solutions to the problem of multicollinearity include excluding independent variables with high standard deviations and low t-ratios, obtaining and including more relevant data and reformulating the model.

Tests of Statistical Significance

Tests of statistical significance that concern us are the coefficient of determination, R^2, which is used to test the overall applicability of the specified model, the F test which is used to test the statistical significance of entire regression equation and t-tests (used to test the statistical significance of estimated regression coefficients). In addition, the standard error of the estimate (SE) will provide a forecast of a range of outcomes with given degrees of confidence.

Let's assume the printout tells us that the estimated regression equation, with standard errors in parenthesis, is:

$$Q = 159.04 - 0.96TC - 5.88SP + 10.89T \qquad (8.4)$$
$$\quad (87.94) \quad\quad (0.41) \quad\quad (4.22) \quad\quad\quad (2.56)$$

the adjusted R^2 is 0.58, the F value is 52.1, and the SE is 20.76.

Coefficient of determination

The coefficient of determination (R^2) is a measure of the goodness of fit of the OLS estimated line to the data. It tells us the proportion of the variation in the dependent variable which has been explained by the independent variables. With multiple regression, it is more usual to use the adjusted R^2, which is adjusted for the degrees of freedom. The adjusted R^2 provides a good estimate of the coefficient of determination in the population.

R^2 or $\overline{R}^2$ takes values between 0 and 1 (0 per cent and 100 per cent). Empirically, we would like to find our estimated equation having an R^2 high in the range, perhaps 0.8 to 0.9, but often we have to be content with lower values. When the underlying theory provides for a number of functional forms, then the value of the R^2 perhaps together with the tests for statistical significance of the coefficients are taken into account in a judgement about relative superiority and which functional form to accept. In relation to the example given above, the R^2 is relatively low. We might well in this case try another functional form. Another factor to note is that we expect lower R^2 values with cross-sectional data than with time series data, where variables tend to move together.

F-test

The F-test is a statistical test which indicates whether the equation as a whole has acceptable predictive ability. It tests a null hypothesis that all of the estimated slope coefficients are no different from zero. Large values of F imply that at least one of the independent variables has an effect on the dependent variable. Tables of the F distribution are used to determine the probability that an observed value of F could have arisen by chance, if none of the independent variables has any effect on the dependent variable. Rejection of the null hypothesis in favor of the alternative hypothesis means that we accept that at least one of the slope parameters is different from zero. It is usual to apply the *F*-test before decisions are made about the statistical significance of individual slope coefficients.

Tests of Slope Coefficients

Individual parameters for variables in the model are evaluated by testing the estimated slope coefficients for statistical significance. The *t*-ratio, the estimated slope coefficient divided by its standard error, is used as a test. If the *t*-ratio is less than a critical value, we could delete that independent variable from the equation, unless there is a strong theoretical reason for keeping it. Modern statistical software give the standard errors, *t*-values and significance levels of each estimated coefficient as a matter of course. It is thus a simple matter to decide whether to accept or reject a variable, based on the required level of significance. In addition, the 'rule of 2' test can be used as a handy rule of thumb. This rule is that we can accept an estimated coefficient as statistically significant at the 0.05 level if it exceeds twice the value of its standard error.

Looking to the standard errors of the coefficients in the example given above, we can see that coefficients for *TC* and *T* are greater than twice their standard errors, but the coefficient for *SP* is not greater than twice its standard error. We have thus established that *SP* is not a statistically significant determinant variable at the 0.05 level, but *TC* and *T* are. Moreover, as is the case here, we often find estimated intercepts are not statistically significant at the 0.05 level. Depending on the purpose of the analysis, this may not matter a great deal, because we are often less interested in the intercept than in the relationship between the independent variables and the dependent variable.

SE

Once we have subjected the model to the statistical testing above, we are interested in its ability to predict. If we assume the residuals are normally distributed, the SE value can give us confidence intervals for predicted values of the dependent variable. Thus, when we substitute values into the estimated demand equation for the independent variables, and estimate a value for *V* (number of visits), the SE value will give us a range of likely outcomes. For example, if $V = 14.2$ and SE = 2.4, the 68 per cent confidence interval is 14.2 $\pm$ SE which is 14.2 $\pm$ 2.4 or 11.8 -16.6, and the 95 per cent confidence interval is $V \pm 2$ (SE), which is 9.4 -19.0.

NON-RESPONSE

Non-response is an issue with empirical research. Although a sample may be selected carefully and in accord with proper statistical method, not all selected people will respond to a survey, as we have seen. The question then is: are the people who respond representative of the whole sample and indeed of the whole population? If the people who respond belong to a specific group, for example, enthusiastic hikers who are willing to spend time in answering questions in the hope that more trails are built, then their responses taken in isolation are likely to lead to incorrect conclusions or predictions about the whole population.

Non-response bias can be tested for in perhaps two ways. Firstly, as noted in Chapter 6, double-mailing is one technique which can be used to try to detect non-response bias. A second set of materials is sent to the same sample of people as in the first mailing, but people are asked to respond only if they did not do so to the first mailing. The rationale for this technique is that people who respond to the second mailing are more likely to be like those who did not respond than like those who responded quickly. Responses from the second mailing may be compared with the first n complete responses that were received. Testing for differences in demographic characteristics or attitudes may be undertaken using Chi-squared methodology.

The second method which may be used to test for non-response bias is to compare the attributes of a group of last received responses with a group of first received responses. This method mimics the double mailing technique, but is cheaper. It may be appropriate where responses are received over a long period.

CONCLUSION

This chapter has dealt with the management of data and regression analysis. Data management starts in the survey planning stage, continues through the receipt of responses processes and culminates in data input and analysis. Data management on the surface may appear mechanical and mundane, but in reality is crucial to the successful outcome of the research.

Data analysis in TCM based research centres on regression analysis, with testing for non-response bias usually conducted with Chi-squared methodology. The use of regression analysis allows us to detect the relationship between the independent and dependent variables. In particular, it permits us to identify the strength of various factors in determining demand and to make predictions on that basis. The steps which should be taken in conducting a regression analysis are discussed in the chapter, as are some of the most important underlying assumptions. Violation of these assumptions can lead to biases in the estimates. Potential problems are examined as well as some of the solutions which may overcome these shortfalls.

REFERENCES

Kennedy, P. (1992), *A Guide to Econometrics*, Cambridge: MIT Press.
Greene, W. (1993), *Econometric Analysis*, New York: Macmillan.

9. Developing and Maintaining Expertise

So far in this manual, we have dealt with TCM as a decision-support tool, given a brief outline of its history and examined necessarily succinctly the economic theory underlying the methodology. We have devoted several chapters to the design and management of various processes necessary for the successful completion of analyses. We have now arrived near to the end of the story.

The frontier of knowledge is continually being expanded. In order to assist you to keep up with new developments and build your expertise, this chapter first discusses criteria for a good model and examines current scholarly debates. It then examines some new approaches and notes the most relevant journals where you will find papers published on new developments.

CRITERIA FOR A GOOD MODEL

Like other econometric models, a good TCM should be based on theories of economic behavior, it should be policy-relevant and it should fit the data on observed behavior. Success in getting closer to at least one of these ideals is the standard we commonly use to evaluate the contribution of new TCM research.

Consistency with Choice Theory

Theory is especially important for TCM since the CV and EV welfare measures are not directly measurable. Thus, it is difficult to identify errors in logic such as incorrect variables or functions by confronting them with the data. The theory of consumer choice lets us derive the CV and EV *from* observed behavior but only if the empirical demand model is produced by the same optimizing behavior that produced the CV and EV welfare measures. To put it negatively, we cannot reject estimates of CV and EV unless the utility maximization theory undergirding the demand function is correct. If an estimated TCM merely predicts behavior well but is inconsistent with utility maximization, then whatever numbers are assigned to CV and EV mean little. Figure 9.1 represents the application of scientific method to the estimation of a TCM.

We could duck the theoretical consistency problem with the time-honored fallback in which we measure the CS from an *ad hoc* demand function specification and simply ignore the CV and EV. A common intellectual justification is to appeal to Willig's famous finding that assures us that our CS

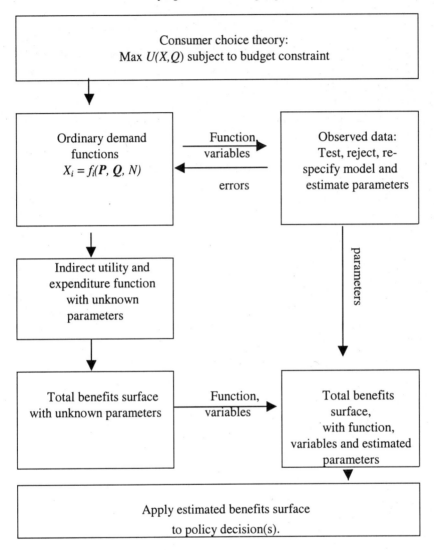

Figure 9.1 Critical path from choice theory to policy support

must be close to the CV and EV. After all, CS is nothing more than the area between two price horizontals behind the ordinary demand function. However, that is a little too convenient. Willig's proof makes no claim that the CS from an *ad hoc* demand function is near anything. It says we can use the CS without apology only if our observed demand is consistent with utility theory (Willig,

1976).

In TCMs we do not directly observe the welfare measures, but instead see only visits responding to various prices, qualities and incomes. Because the CV and EV are one step away from observed behavior, we must be even more careful to specify demand functions consistent with economic theory. Otherwise our measured benefits lie on the wrong side of Popper's (1959) line of demarcation between science and non-science, since their measurement is not known to be correct through the process of rejecting errors.

There is still more to the theory issue. TCM demand models based on choice theory give us even more confidence in predicted visits under historical data and in predicted visits under a wide range of future conditions. Restrictions produced by theory to irrational economic behavior mean the visitor is constrained from responding to policy changes with behavior he cannot afford or would never do. CV and EV estimates have little meaning if they're estimated by methods that do not account for rational economic behavior.

Three common functional forms, linear, semi-log and log-linear, are all consistent with choice theory for a single site model. For the multi-site demand system, on the other hand, the two most common forms, log-linear and linear, are not. For a single site model, consistency with choice theory means there must be price and income variables. In addition, almost any other variable can be put into the model to fit the visitor choice situation being dealt with in the analysis. This includes a wide range of site variables and a large number of visitor characteristics. The correct equations for these three common functional forms are given in Chapter 4.

When one or more site quality variables are incorporated in a single site model, there is less consensus in the current literature on what constitutes a theoretically correct (choice theoretic) model. Until more consensus emerges, Bockstael, Hanemann and Strand (1989) in their Appendix 2.1 show how direct utility functions lead to the single site demand specification along with the various benefit measures. They sometimes refer to the single site model in these pages as a two site model, but their second site is an aggregation of other goods and not strictly a second site.

As a general strategy, we suggest inserting the environmental quality variable of interest into the direct utility function, then watching how quality gets pulled through the utility maximization derivation to end up in the demand equation. Some economists like beginning with the indirect utility function, and some even like starting with the expenditure function. We prefer starting with the direct utility function simply because this method tells you more explicitly what you're assuming about the relation between quantity and quality prior to its optimization. That is, it shows you what confronts the visitor one step before the derivation of his optimized demand function.

For a multi-site demand system model without quality, estimating a choice-theoretic travel cost demand system imposes more restrictions than it does for the single site model. It means the demand equation for each site has its own price and, for most specifications (but not the Cobb-Douglas utility), substitute site prices are included. If some of the substitute price variables come in with weak statistical support, you may wish to delete them unless the culprit behind the poor fit is high collinearity in prices. In that case, you may want to keep all price variables if signs and sizes of the coefficients are reasonable. High collinearity is a major problem in multi-site demand models simply because the top recreation sites often occur in groups, so visitors who live close to one are often close to all.

The multi-site model also needs an income variable. By income we mean total recreational expenditure, since we have never seen a complete travel cost demand system estimated. They are only partial demand systems. To be consistent with theory, the income variable needs to be defined quite carefully, so that the sum of all predicted quantities demanded multiplied by prices equals the constant income. The sum of those prices times quantities must always equal the same income, under all possible values of the independent variables.

This special aggregation property is probably the most important characteristic of a demand system, simply because it guards against absurd visitor behavioral responses to new policies. Responses beyond what visitors can afford produces meaningless numbers. In fact, the easiest way to make this work with regression models may be to exclude the income variable from the model and define income as the sum of prices times observed quantities instead. If the demand system is consistent with theory, the sum of those prices times quantities cannot change under any future policies.

The simplest way to specify a multi-site model to be choice theoretic is to follow the steps using the calculus and LaGrange multiplier technique and derive the demand system using one of the common utility functions. Another easy way is to find a graduate text in microeconomic theory and use one of the demand systems already derived. However, before you use the textbook demand system, multiply each price by the corresponding demand function and be sure they add up to income and that income never changes with changes in the independent variables.

After you write the mathematical demand system, you need to estimate its parameters econometrically, using your data on visitation and prices at your sites. The econometric estimation may require a nonlinear least squares technique or possibly maximum likelihood. These methods sometimes converge slowly or not at all. We've found much more reliability in transforming the equations to become linear in the parameters. This lets you estimate everything with OLS, which is guaranteed to produce parameters in a finite amount of time.

For a multiple site TCM with quality variables, we see little consensus in the published literature on the best way to proceed. In particular we are still looking for a better way to specify quality into the multi-site demand model that is choice theoretic, policy-relevant and fits the data. Like the single site case, we suggest using the same principle of beginning with one of the textbook standard utility functions, then inserting quality variable(s) in appropriate spots. One reliable method is to insert a mathematical function of quality and parameters where the constant parameters normally appear. This method gives you enough room to creatively experiment with mixes of parameters and quality variables without damaging the basic quantity-price structure of familiar and well-understood utility functions. The Bockstael, Hanemann and Strand (1989) report describes other ways for incorporating quality into demand systems along with some excellent behavioral interpretations. But bring your coffee cup along. This report is tightly packed with mathematics and economic theory.

Policy Relevance

Among all equations that predict use consistent with choice theory, the better TCMs help policymakers answer questions, as we illustrate with examples. If the policy question centers on how to reallocate stocked fish for maximum angler benefit, then the TCM should have variable(s) relating the fish catch rates. For biologically simple waters, sites that are fished out quickly or when the catch rate data are expensive or unreliable, the variable could simply be number of fish stocked.

If the policy question deals with what society can afford to pay to avoid the costs of fish kills due to toxic dumps, then the demand model also needs variables measuring fish catch rates. Additionally, it needs observations with enough sites or time periods with zero catch rates and high catch rates. A similar policy question deals with insect infestations of trees in forested recreation areas. At which locations should the pests be fought, with what intensity of effort, and with what combination of resources? For a TCM to support these decisions, it needs to say something about the benefits of reduced tree damage as a function of site location, extent of existing damage and existing density of undamaged trees. Practically, that means the TCM should probably be a multi-site model with one or more indicators of tree density in each site's demand equation.

Finally, consider the example of fitting a TCM to support national policy decisions dealing with proposed regulations governing coal emissions. The TCM should have variables as visit predictors which reflect changes in coal emissions and the impact on visits. Two examples of such variables could be tree density and fishing success rates, if reduced emissions decreased downwind acid rain, which in turn reduced fish kills and damaged fewer trees.

Statistical Fits

TCMs are used to make better decisions by giving information on estimated benefits of proposed policies. The decision made depends on the computed welfare measure (e.g. CV) which depends on the estimated parameters, typically a price coefficient, an income coefficient and sometimes a quality coefficient. It will be a wrong decision if the benefit is measured from a biased estimate of the parameters.

The cost of making a wrong decision, called a loss, depends on the estimated CV in addition to its true value. Because the estimated CV is random, so is the loss from making the wrong decision. There is a greater probability of incurring a loss as the CV estimate has a larger variance or greater bias. However, we might accept a slightly biased CV (one whose average value over many samples is not equal to the true value) only if its variance is smaller. One way to quantify the loss produced by using the wrong CV estimate for decisions is to account for damages produced by both high variance and high bias. The term is mean square error (MSE). The MSE of the estimated CV is:

$$MSE(\hat{C}) = Var(\hat{C}) + \left(Bias(\hat{C})\right)^2$$

(9.1)

where *C* is the CV and the hat means estimated value. Unfortunately there has been little research in the published literature showing how mistakes from wrong functional forms, mis-specified choice sets, excluded variables, theoretically incorrect demand equations and the like contribute to mean square error. Kling has done the best work we are aware of in this area (e.g., Kling 1991; 1992).

A recent paper by Larson, Lew, and Loomis (1999) showed that significant price coefficients can lead to insignificant benefit estimates. McConnell (1992) emphasized the important role of judgement in selecting variables and ways to measure them. In any case, much remains to be done. Benefit cost analysis is expensive (e.g. Arrow et al., 1996), so it should only be done for the really important decisions. Still, it would be valuable information to know more about the net benefits of research resources pressed into efforts to reduce mean square error in TCMs. Randall (1994) called for an agenda of improvements that could help us reduce the number and cost of bad decisions in TCM applications.

While it's obvious that the price and site characteristics variables need good fits to make precise statements about welfare, what's less obvious is that we also need good fits for the income variable, especially in single site models. Table 4.3 shows that the income coefficient appears in the CV and EV formulas for the three common algebraic forms.

Large changes in the income coefficient, due to low *t*-statistics on the income coefficient (wide confidence intervals), have very large impacts on estimated CV and EV. In fact, this problem caused by the income variable has lead some TCM researchers to delete the income variable altogether from single site models unless it enters the equation with t-statistics much better than the 0.95 confidence level. Deleting the income variable occurs because we cannot declare it significantly different from zero. A zero income effect obviates the need to estimate CV and EV and enables us to use the CS, since all three are then equal.

SCHOLARLY DEBATES

Economists have extensively developed the TCM since the early 1960s. It has been used to value the benefits of built environments like museums and historical treasures and human-altered environments like forests and ecosystems. Our confidence in applying TCM varies according to the situation. During these years of application and development, many theoretical and methodological issues have faced TCM workers. Many issues continue to attract lively scholarly debate. We discuss some of those issues and debates.

Price

Ever since Hotelling's original letter, there has been agreement that travel costs based on travel distance should bear most of the burden in defining the price variable. However, there has been a surprisingly amount of debate about how that principle should be applied.

If the price variable is based on good theory, measured with good methods and estimated with correct econometric tools, then the price coefficient is unbiased. This means that, with repeated sampling, its expected value equals the true value of the parameter. If there are no other errors in the analysis, use of TCM for decisions will select programs for which benefits exceed costs and will reject the others. Thus, in many ways, obtaining an unbiased price coefficient is the main goal of a TCM. This puts considerable pressure on the correct measurement of price.

Early travel cost models typically measured travel cost as a proportional function of travel distance from the visitor's home to the site in question, based on the cost per mile of operating a vehicle. Cesario and Knetsch (1970) may have been the first to recognize that recreational trips imposed a cost on both the money income constraint and on the fixed time constraint. Failure to identify the opportunity cost of travel time risked biasing the estimated benefits downward, thus leading to misallocation of resources and decision errors of not building or fixing recreation resources when the benefits exceeded the costs.

Many studies since then have re-examined the question of how price should be defined. The main two unresolved issues are the problem that travel costs are partly determined by the visitor and are not truly a pre-determined variable, especially for the case of on-site time, and developing a defensible method for valuing travel time that correctly accounts for all opportunities (including negative opportunities) displaced by travel. An important issue here occurs when visitors are institutionally constrained in the labor market from making optimal tradeoffs between work and leisure.

In our view the most theoretically complete treatment of the travel time value problem is the work of Bockstael, Strand and Hanemann (1987). The demand model is set up to depend on the visitor's labor market situation. For visitors who are constrained to work more or less than they prefer (corner solutions), utility maximization is subject to two constraints, which leads to a site demand function with travel costs and travel time as independent variables. In this case, travel time is not formally valued, but simply entered as an added constraint. When the visitor can make optimal work/leisure choice (interior solutions in the labor market), time is valued at the wage rate and combined with travel costs to produce a single full cost price. The authors illustrate their methods by estimating benefits based on their model for a sample of sport anglers.

Substitute Prices

One essential requirement to find an unbiased estimate of the price coefficient is to include all important visit predictors in the model and delete all unimportant ones. One especially important set of visit predictors is substitute prices. Because of the importance of properly accounting for substitute sites, a considerable literature has sprung up around this issue since the 1970s. Three studies stand out.

Rosenthal (1987) found that omitting substitute prices from a TCM lead to a significant difference in benefit estimates from their inclusion. Three sets of travel cost models were developed from Army Corps of Engineer reservoirs in Kansas and Missouri. The first set of models omitted substitute prices; the latter two sets included them. Findings from an analysis of variance showed that benefit estimates from the first set of models were significantly higher than those from the other two.

Kling (1989) wanted to find the extent of error in welfare estimates from omitting substitute prices or qualities in TCMs. She found that the presence of error (bias) depended on whether single or multiple site changes are examined. It also depends on the degree of correlation between omitted and included prices. For price or quality changes at multiple sites, even when omitted price is uncorrelated with included price, welfare estimates could be biased. Overall, the amount of the error depends on both the degree of correlation and whether single or multiple changes occur.

Wilman and Perras (1989) found that the price of both substitutes and complementary sites should be included as a visit predictor in the travel cost demand equation for a recreation site. Omitting either can cause bias in the estimated coefficients and in the resultant CS estimates. Not only is it important to include the correct substitute price variables, but more importantly the included variable(s) should also be an accurate measurement of the way in which recreationists view substitute or complementary recreation alternatives.

The consensus on the substitute price (and quality) issue seems to issue a clear warning to ensure the TCM correctly accounts for all the substitute opportunities facing the visitor or the estimated price coefficient will ascribe changes in visits from price alone that in fact are caused by differences in substitute opportunities. This problem becomes less severe the more nearly unique a recreation area is.

Quality

Several issues regarding site quality have been debated for years, with little clear consensus in sight. The first is the endogenous quality problem. The second is the issue of how to value quality characteristics that are rationed through some non-price mechanism because of limited carrying capacity. A third issue, how to specify quality correctly in the utility and demand function, has been discussed elsewhere. Other issues involve changes in facilities at sites, congestion and collinear and interacting quality effects.

Endogenous versus exogenous quality
Proposed policies commonly affect site characteristics but, when the observed site characteristic is partly determined by the visitor, quality can be endogenous. A good example is the case of a policy that would restock fish or reduce pollutants in water bodies, which in turn would increase catch rates per unit of fishing effort. However, at the level of the individual angler, catch rates are determined partly by fishing skill in addition to the fish density. Presumably the policy analyst wants to know the benefits due to that part of the policy that is external to the angler. So the demand and benefits estimation method must somehow separate the exogenous from the endogenous site quality.

A widely cited study that deals with this issue is Samples and Bishop (1985). A theoretical model is presented to show how variations in prevailing catch rates influence an angler's valuation of recreational fishing. A two-stage estimation procedure capitalizes on the principle that angler benefits are sensitive to changes in success rates. The first stage compares benefits at qualitatively different sites using a multi-site TCM. For the second stage, the sensitivity of estimated values to different success rates is measured using a separate regression procedure.

Valuing rationed quality

Many policy decisions proposed measures for increasing a site's carrying capacity. One interesting application of TCMs is the case where lottery-rationed permit systems are used to allocate hunting opportunities where demand for permits exceeds the ability of the animal populations to sustain hunting harvest levels. In an innovative study, Boxall (1995) estimated the values of lottery-rationed hunting use a zonal TCM, in which applications per capita by zone of origin formed the dependent variable and expected travel costs were the price variable. His paper estimated a discrete choice TCM that incorporated the expectation of receiving a permit. The model was estimated for lottery-rationed antelope hunting in Alberta in Canada. The hunter's choice for this lottery-rational context involved selecting one site from a set defined by management regulations. Boxall concluded that the discrete choice TCM is superior to the more conventional continuous choice models because it better represents this behavioral process.

Quality changes

Despite years of research, TCMs are still weak at providing support for policies proposing incremental supplies of natural resources through increased demand and benefits. Scientists who work in biology, hydrology and other technical areas still have considerable difficulty in understanding the economic value of their research, which still mostly remains resource-focused. Examples include restoring ecosystems, developing fisheries, improving water quality, reclaiming damaged forests and cleaning polluted beaches.

An early UK study by Mansfield (1971) which dealt with a policy issue regarding the incremental benefits of added facilities concluded that the TCM has considerable limits. Several more recent studies have come to similar conclusions. Still policymakers keep posing questions dealing with the benefits of on-site quality change, so TCM workers continue improving its methods.

The greatest successes with TCMs have been the estimation of money values of changing natural resources by large new constructions. An example is damming a river for both flood control and recreation. TCMs continue to have limited success in quantifying benefit tradeoffs between competing resources, such as changing the character of recreation at a site. For example, funds might be spent on building a boat dock or improving a hiking trail around a lake, but not both.

Congestion

Most outdoor recreation facilities are capable of being congested, especially in high demand periods such as summer holidays. The treatment of congestion in TCM demand models for recreational sites is a problem of considerable importance for the development, preservation, allocation and management of public lands and waters. Some economists have argued that the use of TCM will always lead to underestimates of the true benefits provided by a site because of the role of congestion. Smith (1981) believes these arguments are misleading and states that it is not possible to unambiguously derive the direction of the bias in the total demand for a recreational site's services due to congestion in a given season.

The consensus to date seems to be that the most appropriate treatment of congestion requires that TCMs be adjusted to reflect the effects of congestion on the modeling of individual behavior, on the estimation of an individual's demand for a site's service and on the description of how a site's services are optimally allocated over individual users. Dorfman (1984) provides an insightful view of optimal congestion at a private recreation facility from the view of a profit-maximizer, and his results should be adjustable to conditions of public management.

Collinear site characteristics

One classic issue is how to isolate the individual effects on visits and benefits of each of many site characteristics that are nearly perfectly correlated when compared among sites. This problem occurs commonly when building a TCM for an organization that has historically constructed facilities in nearly fixed proportions under a blueprint plan.

More extensive experimental design and sampling may help. Still, when existing facilities are built in approximately fixed proportions or built according to regional or national design standards, it's hard to use existing observed data to evaluate proposed changes in design. This problem and potential solutions are described by Adamowicz, Louviere and Williams (1994).

Interactions

Another problem is agreeing on the methods for incorporating many interacting site characteristics into a single TCM demand function. This problem and the collinear facilities problem interact when the sites at which the policy would be implemented have never undergone the kind of changes in characteristics proposed by the policy.

One way to deal with the collinearity problem may be to estimate demand function(s) for a carefully chosen series of sites whose characteristics are different enough to permit statistical estimation of the proposed quality effects.

Vaughan and Russell (1982) used this method in a well known national TCM study of the benefits of improved water quality. This solution along with some of its limits is discussed extensively in Bockstael, McConnell and Strand (1991).

The Quantity Variable

By quantity, we refer to anything having to do with how we specify, measure, interpret or estimate the dependent variable, which is typically some measure of visitor use.

Corner solutions

Individually sampled visitors rarely visit only one site and virtually never visit all possible sites within their available choices. This means that most sampled visitors take zero trips to many sites. This is called a 'corner solution' to the visitor's optimization problem. Once visitors are observed taking zero trips, further price increases rotate their budget line inward, but they are already boxed into a corner of their choice area and cannot take fewer than zero trips.

The corner solution may not seem to cause much of a problem until we realize that most of our theoretically correct demand functions are based on optimizing behavior. Therefore, the visitor takes a number of trips, usually larger than zero, to one or more sites under most conditions. For utility functions that are best understood, visitor's optimization almost always produces interior (tangency) points between the utility function and the budget constraint, which leads to finite numbers of non-zero trips under all possible conditions. These models predict smooth and continuous adjustments. For small changes in any possible site price or quality, there is a small but non-zero change in visits. Smooth continuous models that always predict positive visits pose a credibility problem where actual visitors take zero trips to a large number of sites under a wide range of conditions.

One problem produced by corner solutions is the econometric one of simply trying to estimate the price coefficient when many visitors' measured trips are lined up on the price axis at zero trips. The simple linear single site demand curve illustrates the problem well. At any price higher than the choke price, predicted trips are negative. All negative predictions are reset to zero. A regression model estimated with all the zero resets included will produce a price coefficient that is too low, for there is too small a response to a price increase. Deleting the zeros may produce an unbiased estimate of the price coefficient, but it throws out valuable information. In the view of some economists, this is a problem.

Another challenge posed by corner solutions is in finding welfare estimates. CV and EV benefit measures are typically based on optimizing behavior in

which visitors are assumed to operate at some internal point on their budget line
where an equi-marginal condition occurs.

The debate centers on what to do about corner solutions, both in estimating
demands without bias and in correctly measuring welfare from proposed
policies. The ideal solution will likely come when somebody figures out how to
develop a consistent, utility theoretic model of a multiple site recreation demand
incorporating site quality while also allowing for the discrete/continuous nature
of the decision problem. Additionally, estimation methods to account for this
process are needed. A good start has been developed by Bockstael, Strand and
Hanemann (1987), and Bockstael, Hanemann and Strand (1989), but much work
remains.

Length of visit
A very old debate centers on the question of how we should measure the
dependent variable when visits are of different lengths. We think of most
commodities as being fairly homogenous, and their units of measurement for
quantity are clear when it comes to estimating their demand elasticities. But what
are the right units for recreation: visitor trips, visitor days or hours? And what
about on-site time and time traveling to the site? The consensus seems to be that
trips are the best measure, since visitors typically make a decision to take a trip,
then worry later about how long it will be. In addition, total expenses per season
are typically viewed as varying more with the number of trips than with days or
hours per trip. However, all these are testable hypotheses and the debate is far
from being settled. Wilman (1987) developed a method for establishing a
constant trip length, so that trips of varying length could be reduced to a
common denominator, so all trips in the dataset could be treated as equal.

We could say that the right way to measure visits depends on the problem
being analyzed, but that partly ducks the issue. We still need general principles
to guide us towards computing the visitor's benefits from policies that would
alter a site's price. Also, we need to estimate an ordinary demand, which means
we need some measure of site use that has historically varied according to an
externally imposed change in price per unit of use. All our theories of demand
and benefits come from a utility function limited by a budget constraint. The
budget constraint we understand best is the one for which income and prices are
externally imposed. The best solution may come from defining the length or unit
of visits so that its price per unit is external to the visitor. Another approach may
come from observation of visit behavior that has been most influenced by
external price differences.

Aggregation
Hotelling's original idea suggested that the unit of observation should be average
participation rates per capita of zone-of-origin population. That is, he suggested

summing all observed visits from a given zone, then dividing that total by the zone's population. However, the use of simple zone of origin participation rates as the dependent variable made it hard to isolate the separate impacts of time versus out-of-pocket costs. People who lived at great money distance from a site also tended to live at a great time distance. So getting both a money cost variable and a time cost variable to enter a regression equation proved to be difficult, because the two variables were highly collinear.

Brown and Nawas (1973) suggested using individual observations rather than zone-of-origin averages to overcome the problem. A later paper (Brown et al., 1983) raised doubts about the earlier proposal. They realized that the use of individual observations ignores that fact that both individual trips and per capita participation rates from farther distance zones are lower because a larger percentage of visitors choose not to visit at all. In the intervening years both individual and zone averages have been used many times.

To our knowledge the issue remains unresolved because there are two forces at work affecting the individual visitor. First, the decision whether to take any trips at all to a site is a zero-one decision: to visit or not. Second, given that a decision has been made to make a trip, the visitor then decides how many trips per season to make. Many papers have proposed methods for capturing this two stage decision process, but to date there seems to be no consensus.

Hellerstein (1995) observed that both the individual and zonal models have problems. The problem with individual observation models is sample selection that can require using distribution-sensitive limited dependent variables estimators. Hellerstein used Monte Carlo simulation methods to find whether bias from aggregation is worse than bias from the distribution-sensitive estimators. He found the rather surprising result that zonal models often outperform the individual-observation models, especially when using an aggregate model that incorporates variance of the explanatory variables across travel distance zones.

Multiple Destination Trips

A TCM normally assumes that the sampled trip is for the sole purpose of visiting a site. However, when the site in question is merely a stop-off point for a trip including many other sites, we could mistakenly assign all the trip costs to the site. Again we have a problem of defining price. In principle, the solution lies in turning to the opportunity cost question again. What is the incremental cost imposed on the visitor as a consequence of the trip to the site? In benefit-cost analysis, this is sometimes called the *with* and *without* principle; that is, what are the incremental trip costs to the visitor with the site versus without the site?

This question has been asked many times, but what may be the most visible study was done by Haspel and Johnson (1982) regarding a policy question facing the US Interior Secretary, who needed to make a decision on whether or not to declare a proposed coal mine on federal lands near Bryce Canyon National Park. It was a classic tradeoff between development versus preservation.

A TCM was commissioned in the summer of 1980, and the National Park Service found a large percentage of the very expensive trips sampled at Bryce Canyon were multi-destination trips. Without a formal visitor travel optimization model in which marginal cost due to the presence of Bryce Canyon could be empirically determined, the average cost per destination was determined. Results showed that this method reduced benefits per visit from about $2000 without the cost allocation to about $80 with it.

In an innovative more recent paper by Mendelsohn et al. (1992), an attempt was made to come up with a behaviorally-based method to uncover the marginal cost of travelling to a site on a multiple destination trip. Again the application was the Bryce Canyon National Park visitor dataset. Combinations of multiple destinations were treated as unique sites and incorporated into a demand system. Empirical demand functions for multiple destination trips that included Bryce National Park were estimated and benefit calculations for single destination and multiple destination trips were compared.

Choice Sets

A very important factor influencing benefits measured from a TCM is what choices we assume visitors have when deciding on their visit patterns. A major issue here is how we should define choice set used in TCMs, especially in random utility models (RUMs). Parsons and Hauber (1998) developed a model of day trip fishing in Maine and examined the sensitivity of parameter and welfare estimates to changes in the spatial boundary. Preliminary evidence suggests that there is some threshold distance beyond which adding more sites to the choice set has negligible effects on the estimation results. This is good news for, if estimated benefits uniformly changed with greater sites in the choice set, we would be left not knowing at what point to stop adding sites.

A related study (Parsons and Kealy, 1992) presented an analysis for dealing with large numbers of sites. They estimated a model using randomly drawn opportunity sets. They used each visitor's chosen site plus a random draw of as few as eleven other sites (when hundreds are available) to estimate a plausible behavioral model in which benefits showed little variation across the random choice sets.

Spatial Limits

A very important question centers around the spatial limits of the TCM being estimated. Here we ask what is the relevant market area. No matter what the estimated price coefficient predicts, if the maximum distance that consistently pulls in observed visitors is 150 miles, there isn't much justification for pretending that the choke price occurs at 500 miles travel distance simply because the price coefficient predicts this to be the case.

One of the more innovative and widely-cited papers dealing with this problem is Smith and Kopp (1980), who suggested looking at the regression residuals from different maximum market areas. This means running TCMs with different upper bounds on travel distance zones. The travel distance at which the residual pattern changes significantly from the lower distances is the upper limit of the market. Depending on the draw of the site in question, the spatial limit of the TCM could be one mile (for a local city park) to several thousand (for the Grand Canyon, Yosemite, or the Great Barrier Reef). Of course for policy questions dealing with the value of quality improvements, the entire aim may be to increase the spatial limits of the site.

A more recent study by Parsons and Hauber (1998) reach similar conclusions, using different methods. The authors were concerned with the spatial boundaries used to define choice sets, not simply travel distance zones. Using a model of day trip fishing in Maine, the authors tested the sensitivity of parameter and welfare estimates to changes in the spatial boundary. They found that there is some threshold distance beyond which adding more sites to the choice set has little effect on the estimation results.

Supply Side v. Demand Issues

Much of this book emphasizes the importance of estimating benefits of quality improvements. However, to apply principles of cost-benefit analysis comprehensively, costs are just as important. It is the rule rather than the exception that all the physical impacts of a decision on an ecosystem cannot be measured. Precise estimates of the benefits of a decision that improves one dimension of environmental quality are not much help in formulating decisions unless there is equivalent knowledge on the physical impact (cost) on the environment.

Even if all the relevant dimensions of an environmental production possibilities surface could be estimated, it is not clear how it should be combined with a multi-site benefits surface with quality. In principle, one solution could be based on estimating multi-site TCMs with quality to deal with the demand (benefits) side while building a production possibilities frontier model containing natural and financial resource limits to deal with the supply side. A programming model could then be built in which the multi-site CV and EV from the TCM is the objective and the production frontier the constraint. This kind of analysis is becoming more feasible in a day when very powerful computers are comparatively inexpensive. However, obtaining credible estimates of the supply and demand side coefficients is still typically expensive.

Regulatory Reform

TCM has had limited success in providing decision support for formulating revisions to major regulatory programs, such as those under the US *Endangered Species Act, National Environmental Policy Act,* and *Clean Water Act.* Implementation of proposed revisions of these Acts can have major economic consequences.

Sampling Bias

Designing a sample is important for a TCM as is knowing how to manage secondary data if it was collected by an on-site survey. When the statistical assumptions underlying the chosen demand model are inconsistent with the sample design, price coefficients and benefit estimates will be biased. Maximum likelihood econometric methods appear to be the best way to account for these problems (Cramer, 1986).

Validation

Surprisingly, after a TCM is estimated and applied to the policy question at hand, then published, it is often forgotten. Like other benefit-cost analyses, we see very few *ex poste* validations of TCMs, either by getting new data to test the stability of the estimated elasticities statistically or on-the-ground management experiments in which the site quality characteristics are varied to see if the quality coefficients are correct.

In an ongoing study being conducted in cooperation with the New Mexico Department of Game and Fish, a recreation demand model was estimated in the summer of 1998, based on a sample of trout anglers who fished at 35 sites at which only catchable-sized trout were stocked. A trout stocking elasticity of about 0.55 was computed for these waters. An optimization model was then built using that stocking elasticity, and it showed that total angler days could be increased by about 15 per cent by reallocating trout among the waters so that incremental angler days from added fish were equal at all sites. Now we are left with a difficult question. For how long do we continue testing the model by resampling anglers at these sites? At what point do managers implement policies that use the optimization model based on the elasticities by reallocating the fish according to the optimization model? And at what point do we want to test the elasticities with experimental stocking programs but not with a complete optimized allocation?

External validation of TCMs raises difficult questions and we have seen few answers in the published research. One way to increase the faith held by managers and policymakers in TCMs is to conduct *ex poste* testing of the models, whether or not policies were actually based on the models.

NEW APPROACHES

A TCM study is approached like any other scientific effort. Formulate a theory that lets you draw out its logical consequences for observed behavior. Then test the theory by comparing its implications for the behavior against the observed behavior. Reject and reformulate those parts of the theory that don't square with observed behavior, and repeat the process until the implications of the theory match the behavior.

The ideal TCM applies this scientific method to support better policy decisions. For TCM, this means formulating a visitor behavioral model unique to the policy situation at hand. The behavioral model reflects the goals, opportunities and constraints facing the visitor. The model also identifies how various proposed implementation of the program objectives alter the visitor's opportunities and constraints. The visitor behavioral model is tested on observed data over a suitably large range of proposed policy space so that the test results are used to accurately measure the total recreation benefits surface defined over that policy space.

This rather grand view of the TCM process can mean something as simple as valuing recreation benefits displaced by a policy that would remove a forest recreation site for a proposed residential development. It can mean something as big as a national TCM with a total benefits surface defined over a large enough policy space to help policymakers formulate amendments to the *Clean Water Act*. There have been many developments since the 1960s that have attempted to overcome some of the classic limitations of TCM and bring us closer to the ideal of better science-based natural resource policy analyses.

Discrete Choice Models

TCM workers from the very earliest days have struggled with the zeros problem. Most visitors only visit a small number of sites among the many choices they face, which means that they choose to take zero trips to most sites. This problem does not disappear when zonal models are estimated. Unless the sample is very large or the counties have large populations, we usually see zero total visits from many counties with increased distance from the site.

One way to deal with this problem using the continuous TCM is to delete the observed zero visits from the dataset and estimate the model for only those visitors or zones that registered some trips. Then after the equation is estimated, apply the estimated coefficients to all the observations. For all visit predictions that are less than zero, reset them to zero. This approximately replicates the observed data by stacking all high cost visitors on the price axis at a level of zero visits. All observations located on the price axis receive zero benefits from the site under current policies. However these current zero visits may accrue benefits if site quality increases by enough to produce positive predicted visits. This method poses difficulties for multiple site models, for the entire dataset may be deleted if there are no visitors or zones that have positive visits for all sites.

Another way to deal with this problem is to think of the decision of whether or not to visit a site as discrete rather than continuous. By discrete choices, we mean that the decision to visit a site is a yes/no discrete choice while the number of trips taken, given that the site will be visited, will be larger than zero. Discrete choice models are a special case of what's called limited dependent variables, whose estimation is described more fully in Madalla (1983).

One way the discrete choice problem has been modeled is through a random utility model (RUM), which focuses attention on the choice among substitute sites for any given recreational trip. The RUM is particularly suitable when substitution among sites differentiated by their quality accurately represents the problem. The RUM has mostly been used to value changes in site characteristics, such as fish catch rate per unit of effort. Variability in site characteristics is essential to explain how visitors allocate their trips.

The RUM is set up to predict the probability of choosing a given site among many possible choices. It predicts a probability between zero and one for all sites in the system. Whichever site produces the highest probability of a trip larger than zero is presumed to be the one selected. The functional form of the demand model generated by the basic RUM model is the multinomial logit, which is typically estimated with maximum likelihood methods. For details of the theory underlying the RUM and for applications, see Smith (1989).

Unfortunately the RUM has several shortcomings. One problem is that it only predicts which site is chosen on a given trip. It explains neither the total number of trips in the season nor the allocation of those trips across sites, both of which are done by the continuous model. It also does not explain benefits per visitor day, which is something many managers want to defend or allocate their budgets.

Despite the difficulties of the RUM, it is able to model trip choices among very large numbers of quality-differentiated sites, which the continuous TCMs only accomplish either with great difficulty or not at all. For this reason developing improvements in RUM models continues to attract the attention of many resource economists. A short list of TCMs estimated as RUMs include Rowe et al. (1985), Kaoru and Smith (1990), Kaoru (1991), Morey, Rowe and Watson (1993), McConnell and Strand (1994) and Feather, Hellerstein and Hansen (1999). What may be the most impressive in terms of the complex structuring of decisions is Wegge, Carson, and Hanemann's (1988) application to Alaska sport fishing.

Hedonic TCMs

Site characteristics have been an important policy issue for a very long time. So a very old question involves how a TCM can be estimated for systems of site characteristics. Brown and Mendelsohn (1984) estimated a special kind of TCM they named a hedonic TCM. In it travel cost distances are regressed on the least cost way for visitors to access given site characteristics. In one application the method was used to value steelhead density in Washington State streams.

The hedonic TCM has been controversial because the prices of these characteristics are set by nature, based on their location rather than by market equilibrium forces. So the prices may bear little relationship to marginal benefits to the visitor, being instead simply irrelevant marginal costs. For example, when a visitor is unwilling to spend an extra $100 in travel distance to visit a site with 10 per cent greater tree density, this means his marginal benefit of the greater density is less than $100. It could be zero. The only thing the $100 indicates is that added costs are guaranteed greater than added benefits if $100 is spent on increasing tree density by 10 per cent.

We might naturally ask under what condition will the hedonic TCM give unbiased estimates of the marginal value of a quality change at a given site. Englin and Mendelsohn (1991) found the condition to be when the marginal cost of a site attribute is equal to its marginal value.

As a general principle, one should be able to observe visitors' willingness to incur greater costs to travel from site A to B to access higher quality as a lower bound on the marginal value of the increased quality. Furthermore, at the point where visitors are observed not incurring the greater travel costs, then marginal costs exceed the marginal value of the added quality, and marginal cost becomes irrelevant for valuing policies that would increase site A's quality. This simple analysis obviously raises many complicated empirical questions. We expect to see much continued work in this area.

Benefits Transfer

In the realm of recreation demand, benefits transfer refers to an organized process in which information about recreation benefits and their predictors at one or more sites is transferred to a target site where there is information about the same benefit predictors but for which information on benefits is missing. Boyle and Bergstrom (1992) observed that the process of gathering information from existing past studies has been an ongoing, practical activity for years in legal proceedings and government policy analyses where timely benefit estimates are critically dependent on the use of existing data. However, there have been few studies that have statistically tested the results of a benefits transfer. Several examples of a method for transferring benefits from studied to unstudied regions, meta analysis, are described later in this chapter.

One such study done by Loomis et al. (1995) tested the interchangeability of two travel cost demand models for recreation at US Army Corps of Engineer reservoirs in Arkansas and Tennessee/Kentucky. Statistical tests of equality of price coefficients suggested close estimates of average benefit per visitor day between Arkansas and Tennessee/Kentucky. Thus, a more limited form of transferability which focuses on average benefit per day, rather than predicting total use and total benefits, looks promising.

Flexible Forms

We never know the visitor's true demand function, nor do we know the true set of indifference maps that generated it. All we ever see is the data. The idea of using equations that can adapt to various true forms, called flexible forms, has been popular for a number of years.

Typically these are algebraic functions of a polynomial form of suitably high degree, and are based on Taylor Series approximations. For a given range of the independent variable, if you're patient enough to write down enough polynomial terms of that variable, you can get a prediction that is as close as you would like to the true underlying function. That is, over the relevant range, the difference between the true function's dependent variable and the polynomial approximation to it can be made arbitrarily close to zero.

A recent paper by Shaikh and Larson (1998) examined application of flexible form estimation techniques to travel cost data for California whale watching trips. They found that their globally flexible form approximates the true underlying demand function with as much precision as needed. Their results look encouraging and we expect to see more work along these lines.

Household Production

The household production function is an intuitively appealing way to model visitor's interaction with nature. Its appeal lies in viewing the consumption of outdoor recreation as requiring so much time, planning and expense that the generation of visitor days by the household can be treated as a production process. Two papers by Bockstael and McConnell (1981; 1983) modeled the interaction between the household's behavior and publicly provided inputs into outdoor recreation. These papers showed how to compute benefits, based on estimating the household production function. A very important finding was that the household production function collapses to the simple TCM approach when households are unable to substitute their own inputs for publicly provided inputs. Thus, it appears that the household production model has considerable potential to improve the way we think about, specify and test TCMs.

RELEVANT JOURNALS

To collect the material for this book's annotated bibliography, we searched the electronic databases, specific review articles and other reports to find articles relevant to the topic. Naturally we also had our own favorite articles which have assisted us in our own research. Our final database has about 270 studies that deal in some form or another with TCMs. This database, shown in the annotated bibliography, includes about 200 journal articles, together with books, reports and Masters and PhD theses.

Based on total number of TCM articles published, the following journals are rich lodes of TCM material and any reader wanting to keep abreast of TCM developments will find these of interest. In descending order of interest to TCM enthusiasts, based on numbers of citations, they are: *Land Economics, American Journal of Agricultural Economics, Journal of Environmental Economics and Management, Water Resources Research, Journal of Agricultural and Resource Economics*, formerly the *Western Journal of Agricultural Economics, Canadian Journal of Agricultural Economics, Marine Resource Economics, Journal of Agricultural Economics, Journal of Agricultural and Applied Economics*, formerly the *Southern Journal of Agricultural Economics*, and *Applied Economics*.

For those of you who want to publish your TCM work in a journal, these seem to be the places where you will find the friendliest reception. Most of them require that your paper make a contribution, that is, do something beyond apply standard theories using standard methods. For TCMs, a contribution to theory typically means new insights into predicting visitor behavior or behavioral response to proposed policy changes. A contribution to methodology means finding a new way to test existing theories on visitor behavior.

REFERENCES

Adamowicz, W.L., J. Louviere and M. Williams (1994), 'Combining Revealed and Stated Preference Methods for Valuing Environmental Amenities', *Journal of Environmental Economics and Management*, **26**, 271-92.

Arrow, K.J, M.L Cropper, G.C Eads, R.W. Hahn, L.B. Lave, R.G. Noll, P.R. Portney, M. Russell, R. Schmalensee, V.K. Smith and R.N. Stavins (1996), 'Is there a Role for Benefit-Cost Analysis in Environmental, Health, and Safety Regulation', *Science*, **272**, 221-2.

Bockstael, N.E. and K.E. McConnell (1981), 'Theory and Estimation of the Household Production Function for Wildlife Recreation', *Journal of Environmental Economics and Management*, **8**, 199-214.

Bockstael, N.E. and K.E. McConnell (1983), 'Welfare Measurement in the Household Production Framework', *American Economic Review*, **73**, 806-14.

Bockstael, N.E., K.E. McConnell and I.E. Strand (1991), 'Recreation', in J.B. Braden and C.D. Kolstad (eds), *Measuring the Demand for Environmental Quality*, Amsterdam: Elsevier, pp. 227-270.

Bockstael, N.E., I.E. Strand and W.M. Hanemann (1987), 'Time and the Recreational Demand Model', *American Journal of Agricultural Economics*, **69** (2), 293-302.

Bockstael, N.E., W.M. Hanemann and I. Strand (1989), 'Measuring the Benefits of Water Quality Improvements Using Recreation Demand Models', Report to the U.S. Environmental Protection Agency.

Boxall, P. C. (1995), 'The Economic Value of Lottery-Rationed Recreational Hunting', *Canadian Journal of Agricultural Economics*, **43** (1), 119-31.

Boyle K.J. and J. C. Bergstrom (1992), 'Benefit Transfer Studies: Myths, Pragmatism, and Idealism', *Water Resources Research*, **28** (3), 657-63.

Brown, G.M., Jr. and R. Mendelsohn (1984), 'The Hedonic Travel Cost Method', *Review of Economics and Statistics,* **66** (3), 427-33.

Brown, W.G. and F. Nawas (1973), 'Impact of Aggregation on the Estimation of Outdoor Recreation Demand Functions', *American Journal of Agricultural Economics*, **55** (2), 246-9.

Brown, W.G. et al. (1983), 'Using Individual Observations to Estimate Recreation Demand Functions: A Caution', *American Journal of Agricultural Economics*, **65** (1), 154-7.

Cesario, F.J. and J.L. Knetsch (1970), 'Time Bias in Recreation Benefit Estimates', *Water Resources Research*, **6** (3), 700-4.

Cramer, J.S. (1986), *Econometric Applications of Maximum Likelihood Methods*, Cambridge: Cambridge University Press.

Dorfman, R. (1984), 'On Optimal Congestion', *Journal of Environmental Economics and Management*, **11** (2), 91-106.

Englin, J. and R. Mendelsohn (1991), 'A Hedonic Travel Cost Analysis for Valuation of Multiple Components of Site Quality: The Recreation Value of Forest Management', *Journal of Environmental Economics and Management*, **21** (3), 275-90.

Feather, P., D. Hellerstein and L. Hansen (1999), *Economic Valuation of Environmental*

Benefits and the Targeting of Conservation Programs: The Case of the CRP, Agricultural Economic Report No. 778, Washington: US Department of Agriculture.

Haspel, A.E. and F.R. Johnson (1982), 'Multiple Destination Trip Bias in Recreation Benefit Estimation', *Land Economics*, **58** (3), 364-72.

Hellerstein, D. (1995), 'Welfare Estimation Using Aggregate and Individual-Observation Models: A Comparison Using Monte Carlo Techniques', *American Journal of Agricultural Economics*, **77** (3), 620-30.

Kaoru, Y. (1991), Valuing Marine Recreation be the Nested Random Utility Model: Functional Structure, Party Composition and Heterogeneity. Unpublished, Woods Hole Oceanographic Institution.

Kaoru, Y. and V.K. Smith (1990), 'Black Mayonnaise and Marine Recreation: Methodological Issues in Valuing a Cleanup', Discussion Paper Q91-02, Washington: Resources for the Future.

Kling, C.L. (1989), 'A Note on the Welfare Effects of Omitting Substitute Prices and Qualities from Travel Cost Models', *Land Economics*, **65** (3), 290-6.

Kling, C.L. (1991), 'Estimating the Precision of Welfare Measures', *Journal of Environmental Economics and Management*, **21** (3), 244-59.

Kling, C.L. (1992), 'Some Results on the Variance of Welfare Estimates from Recreation Demand Models', *Land Economics*, **68** (3), 318-28.

Larson, D. M., D. K. Lew and J. B. Loomis (1999), 'Are Revealed Preference Measures of Quality Change Benefits Statistically Significant?', *Western Regional Research Publication,* W-133, 12th Interim Report.

Loomis, J.B. et al. (1995), 'Testing Transferability of Recreation Demand Models across Regions: A Study of Corps of Engineer Reservoirs', *Water Resources Research*, **31** (3), 721-30.

Maddala, G.S. (1983), *Limited Dependent and Qualitative Variables in Econometrics*, New York: Cambridge University Press.

McConnell, K.E. (1992), 'Model Building and Judgment: Implications for Benefit Transfers with Travel Cost Models', *Water Resources Research*, **28** (3), 695-700.

McConnell, K.E. and I.E. Strand (1994). 'The Economic Value of Mid and South Atlantic Sportfishing', University of Maryland.

Mansfield, N.W. (1971), 'The Estimation of Benefits From Recreation Sites and the Provision of a New Recreation Facility', *Regional Studies,* **5**, 55-69.

Mendelsohn, R. et al. (1992), 'Measuring Recreation Values with Multiple Destination Trips', *American Journal of Agricultural Economics*, **74** (4), 923-33.

Morey, E.R., R.D. Rowe and M. Watson (1993), 'A Repeated Nested Logit Model of Atlantic Salmon Fishing', *American Journal of Agricultural Economics*, **75** (3), 578-92.

Parsons, G.R. and A.B. Hauber (1998), 'Spatial Boundaries and Choice Set Definition in a Random Utility Model of Recreation Demand', *Land Economics*, **74** (1), 32-48.

Parsons, G.R. and M.J. Kealy (1992), 'Randomly Drawn Opportunity Sets in a Random Utility Model of Lake Recreation', *Land Economics*, **68** (1), 93-106.

Popper, K.R. (1959), *The Logic of Scientific Discovery,* New York: Basic Books.

Randall, A. (1994), 'A Difficulty with the Travel Cost Method', *Land Economics*, **70** (1), 88-96.

Randall, A. and J. Stoll (1982), 'Existence Value in a Total Valuation Framework,' in R. Rowe and L. Chestnut (eds), *Managing Air Quality and Scenic Resources at National Parks and Wilderness Areas*, Boulder: Westview Press.

Rosenthal, D.H. (1987), 'The Necessity for Substitute Prices in Recreation Demand Analyses', *American Journal of Agricultural Economics*, **69** (4), 828-37.

Rowe, R.D., E.R. Morey, A.D. Ross and W.D. Shaw (1985), 'Valuing Marine Recreation Fishing on the Pacific Coast', Boulder: Energy and Resource Consultants.

Samples, K.C. and R.C. Bishop (1985), 'Estimating the Value of Variations in Anglers' Success Rates: An Application of the Multiple-Site Travel Cost Method', *Marine Resource Economics*, **2** (1), 55-74.

Shaikh, S.L. and D. M. Larson (1998), 'Towards Globally Flexible Estimation of Recreation Demand', *Western Regional Research Publication* W-133, 11th Interim Report.

Smith, V.K. (1981), 'Congestion, Travel Cost Recreational Demand Models, and Benefit Evaluation', *Journal of Environmental Economics and Management*, **8** (1), 92-6.

Smith, V.K. (1989), 'Taking Stock of Progress with Travel Cost Recreation Demand Methods: Theory and Implementation', *Marine Resource Economics*, **6** (4), 279-310.

Smith, V.K. and R.J. Kopp (1980), 'The Spatial Limits of the Travel Cost Recreational Demand Model', *Land Economics*, **56** (1), 64-72.

Vaughan, W.J. and C.S. Russell. (1982), *Freshwater Recreational Fishing: The National Benefits of Water Pollution Control*, Baltimore: Johns Hopkins University Press.

Wegge, T.C., R.T. Carson, and W.M. Hanemann (1988), 'Site Quality and the Demand for Sportfishing for Different Species in Alaska', in D.S. Liao (ed.), *Proceedings of the Symposium Demand and Supply of Sportfishing*, South Carolina Wildlife and Marine Resources Department.

Willig, R.D. (1976), 'Consumers' Surplus Without Apology', *American Economic Review*, **66** (4), 589-597

Wilman, E.A. (1987), 'A Simple Repackaging Model of Recreational Choices', *American Journal of Agricultural Economics*, **69**, 603-12.

Wilman, E.A. and J. Perras (1989), 'The Substitute Price Variable in the Travel Cost Equation', *Canadian Journal of Agricultural Economics*, **37** (2), 249-61.

Conclusion

TCM is a method for valuing the environmental and built resources that complement outdoor recreational activities. It is based on an idea originally proposed by Harold Hotelling in 1947, an idea which has shown remarkable insight and staying power. We reproduce Hotelling's letter to the National Park Service in full, in view of its historical interest and the fact that we have not seen it reproduced in full elsewhere (Prewitt, 1949).

THE UNIVERSITY OF NORTH CAROLINA
INSTITUTE OF STATISTICS
CHAPEL HILL
DEPARTMENT OF MATHEMATICAL STATISTICS

June 18, 1947

Mr. Newton B. Drury, Director
National Park Service
Department of the Interior
Washington 25, D.C.

Dear Mr. Drury:

After a letter from Mr. A. E. Demaray, and a conference with Dr. Roy A. Pruitt of the National Park Service, I am convinced that it is possible to set up appropriate measures for evaluating, with a reasonable degree of accuracy, the service of national parks to the public.

The development of criteria for evaluating benefits to the public has been a long-term interest of mine. Following the example set a hundred years ago by the French engineer, Jules Dupuit, who wrote formulae for the benefits of roads, bridges, and canals, I have worked out more general formulae for benefits from wider and more complicated classes of public services.

These formulae, of course, involve coefficients which must, in each case, be determined by factual statistical studies. The development of such studies I believe to be possible through several modes of attack which Dr. Pruitt and I discussed. One of these, of whose feasibility I am confident, and which might be pursued further, is as follows:

Let concentric zones be defined around each park so that the cost of travel to the park from all points in one of these zones is approximately constant. The persons entering the park in a year, or a suitably chosen sample of them, are to be listed according to the zone from which they come. The fact that they come means that they presume the service of the park is at least worth the cost, and this cost can probably be estimated with fair accuracy. If we assume that the benefits are the same no matter what the distance, we have, for those living near the park, a consumers' surplus consisting of the differences in transportation costs. The comparison of the cost of coming from a zone with the number of people who do come from it, together with a count of the population of the zone, enables us to plot one point for each zone on a demand curve for the service of the park. By a judicious process of fitting it should be possible to get a good enough approximation to this demand curve to provide, through integration, a measure of the consumers' surplus resulting from the availability of the park. It Is this consumers' surplus cost (calculated by the above process with deduction for the cost of operating the park) which measures the benefits to the public in the particular year. This, of course, might be compared directly with the estimated annual benefits on the hypothesis that the park area was used for some alternate purpose.

The problem of relations between different parks can be treated along the same lines, though in a slightly more complicated manner, provided people entering the park will be asked which other national parks they have visited that year. In place of a demand curve, we have as a result of such an inquiry, a set of demand functions. The consumer surplus still has a defining meaning, as I have shown in various published articles, and may be used to evaluate the benefits from the park system.

This approach through travel costs is one of several possible modes of attack on this problem. There are also others, which should be examined, though I think the method outlined above looks the most promising.

Very sincerely,

Harold Hotelling

TCM is now widely accepted by resource economists, as well as in US Federal guidelines, both for water project evaluation (US Water Resources Council, 1983) and for natural resource damage assessments. TCM is used to measure the value of benefits associated with the natural or man-made resources that complement outdoor recreation. Two major reasons for needing to know those values are to justify budget or other requests for resources or to design policies that increase public benefits more than the costs. There may be a need to demonstrate that an existing activity has benefits exceeding costs or a desire to design such a plan. It's been our personal experience that the first reason motivates something like 70 percent of commissioned TCMs and the second the other 30 percent.

The basic idea is to measure in terms of money the benefit gained by visitors by using the resource. By relating differences in travel cost to visit rates, a demand for the resource is derived and benefits estimated. We expect to see an inverse relationship between the travel cost incurred and the frequency of visits per year to a site. For example, people who live in Flagstaff, Arizona, 60 miles from the Grand Canyon, face a lower cost of visiting it and thus are expected to visit more often than do people from Tucson who live 320 miles away. A plot of travel cost and frequency of visits can provide an estimate of the demand for the area. TCM is different from contingent valuation in that the behavior of visitors is observed in real markets rather than in hypothetical circumstances.

Evaluating the reliability of a TCM amounts to determining how good a job the analysts have done in isolating all the non-price factors that affect recreation demand. Several factors influence demand other than price, so it's essential that the most important of these are included in the analysis, otherwise the price coefficient will be over- or understated, producing under- or overestimated benefits.

Several meta-analyses have been completed for TCM studies in which regression methods are used as an efficient way to summarize results from many independent studies. For example, Walsh, Johnson and McKean (1992) summarized results of 169 travel cost studies using a meta-analysis, updating an earlier study by Sorg and Loomis (1984). Their results indicated that median benefits per activity day in 1987 dollars were about $34. Big game hunting increased that value by $23, while salt water or anadromous fishing increased it by $43.

Smith and Kaoru (1990a) published a meta-analysis summarizing price elasticities from 200 TCMs. Their results showed that lakes, rivers and forests had more negative price elasticities indicating lower benefits, while price elasticities at state parks were higher and provided greater benefits. Presence of substitutes made the elasticity more negative and reduced benefits. Linear estimates of demand had less negative elasticities and higher benefits. Smith and Kaoru (1990b) reporting in another study that these elasticities translated into a mean CS per unit of use of $24.

Freeman (1995), who reviewed several studies of the benefits of water quality improvements for marine recreational fishing, found similar results. Studies that had used TCMs showed average values per trip to range from $10 to $100 for marine recreational fishing, $25 to $90 for beaches and swimming and from $8 to $80 for increasing fish catch rates by one fish per trip, depending on species. Smith, Desvouges and Fisher (1986) used several TCMs to estimate impacts of increasing water quality from boatable to fishable, using a water quality ladder developed by Mitchell and Carson (1981). Results showed that, in 1977 dollars, values of the water quality improvements ranged from $1 per trip at Hords Creek Lake in Texas to about $10 per trip at Millwood Lake Arkansas.

TCMs are based on many assumptions. These include: individuals perceive and respond to changes in travel costs in the same way they would to changes in a site admission fee; the only purpose of the trip taken is to visit the site in question; all visits are homogenous and require the same amount of time; there is no utility or disutility to the visitor involved in travel to the site; and the visitor's wage rate or some fraction of it is the correct opportunity cost of time. These assumptions add up to the larger assumption that what we estimate from on-site visit patterns amounts to a true demand curve based on rational economic behavior (Bockstael, Hanemann and Strand, 1989) Much of the current literature on TCM continues to examine these assumptions and look for ways of correctly estimating demand curves if any of these assumptions are violated.

A fundamental limit of TCM is that it computes values only for people who visit the site. Non-users are not sampled. The benefits estimated from TCM do not include any option values to future users (Bishop, 1982) nor existence values (Randall and Stoll, 1982) nor bequest values (Krutilla, 1967). For designated wilderness areas, wild and scenic rivers, unique wildlife species such as bighorn sheep or whooping cranes, these off-site benefits may equal or exceed the on-site benefits (Walsh, Loomis and Gillman, 1984). Practically, the method is limited to sites that are visited frequently enough to allow estimation of the demand curve. Necessarily, the value of benefits derived therefrom must be viewed as strict minima.

Future research work will move, we believe, on several fronts. While much will be driven by policy questions needing immediate answers, other work will focus on areas seen currently as problems in theory or methodology. This kind of work is best thought of as investment, for which success leads to better future natural resource policy decisions. These areas include the following. Better information on households' recreation decisions is needed as well as more complete descriptions of recreation site characteristics that affect those decisions. In addition, we need a more complete understanding of the relation of site characteristics to visitors' perceptions of those characteristics. In the matter of environmental degradation, for example, particularly 'green' visitors may view an area as extremely degraded, while others see no signs of deterioration and indeed may welcome change as an example of familiar human activity.

More rigorous testing of TCMs is needed. This means tests of structural estimates (elasticities) and comparisons of TCM visitation forecasts to actual visitation patterns that emerge. It also means comparing results of policy decisions that have influenced use by altering a site or its characteristics with policy simulations previously produced by a TCM.

The value of travel time continues to be a problem as do the definition of visits, substitute sites and utility theoretic behavioral models that account for zero consumption (corner solutions). Policymakers continue to ask for benefits transfer studies; that is, the adjustment of past studies to estimate recreation benefits for proposed policies. Benefits transfer involves developing an understanding of the variables that explain the observed differences in past benefit estimates. More research is needed to fully understand this process. Having better methods of controlling for effects of sources of variation in benefits estimates from previous studies is important and promises more efficient use of research funding.

A better theoretical understanding of the general household production model, from which many variations of the travel cost model come, is necessary. The continuous TCM, RUM and hedonic TCM are all special cases of a more general household production function approach. Learning more about the household production model will improve our knowledge on the kind of TCM to be matched to an individual policy analysis. This improved understanding is likely to produce major breakthroughs in how we handle exogenous versus endogenous site quality and price, definition of visits, travel time valuation and many other issues that now appear to be isolated problems.

A more comprehensive understanding of the principles governing the behavioral relation between visitors, natural environments and benefits produced by environmental change will drive and focus future TCM research. Inevitably, changes in public policy produces winners and losers. The development of TCM to greater refinement, through research, will assist in the quest to measure consistently and accurately net benefits from policy-driven change.

REFERENCES

Bishop, R.C. (1982), 'Option Value: An Exposition and Extension', *Land Economics*, **58**, 1-15.

Bockstael, N.E., W.M. Hanemann and I. Strand (1989), 'Measuring the Benefits of Water Quality Improvements Using Recreation Demand Models', Report to the U.S. Environmental Protection Agency.

Freeman, A.M. (1995), 'The Benefits of Water Quality Improvements for Marine Recreation: A Review of the Empirical Evidence', *Marine Resource Economics*, **10**, 385-406.

Krutilla, J.V. (1967), 'Conservation Reconsidered', *American Economic Review*, **57**, 787-96.

Mitchell, R.C and R.T. Carson (1981), 'An Experiment in Determining Willingness to Pay for National Water Quality Improvements', Draft Report to U.S. Environmental Protection Agency. Washington: Resources for the Future.

Prewitt, R. (1949), *The Economics of Public Recreation,* Washington: National Parks Service.

Randall, A. and J. Stoll (1982), 'Existence Value in a Total Valuation Framework', in R. Rowe and L. Chestnut (eds.), *Managing Air Quality and Scenic Resources at National Parks and Wilderness Areas*, Boulder: Westview Press.

Smith, V.K. and Y. Kaoru (1990a), 'What Have We Learned since Hotelling's Letter? A Meta-analysis', *Economics Letters*, **32** (3), 267-72.

Smith, V.K. and Y. Kaoru (1990b), 'Signals or Noise? Explaining the Variation in Recreation Benefit Estimates', *American Journal of Agricultural Economics*, **72** (2), 419-33.

Smith, V.K., W.H. Desvousges and A. Fisher (1986), 'A Comparison of Direct and Indirect Methods for Estimating Environmental Benefits', *American Journal of Agricultural Economics,* **68** (2), 280-90.

Sorg, C.F. and J.B. Loomis (1984), 'Empirical Estimates of Amenity Forest Values: a Comparative Review', General Technical Report RM-107, Rocky Mountain Forest and Range Experiment Station, Fort Collins: USDA Forest Service.

U.S. Water Resources Council (1983), *Economic and Environmental Principles and Guidelines for Water and Related Land Resources Implementation Studies*, Section VIII, Appendix I. Washington: US Government Printing Office.

Walsh, R.G., D.M. Johnson and J. McKean (1992), 'Benefit Transfer of Outdoor Recreation Demand Studies, 1968-1988', *Water Resources Research*, **28** (3), 707-13.

Walsh, R.G., J.B. Loomis and R.A. Gillman (1984), 'Valuing Option, Existence and Bequest Demands for Wilderness', *Land Economics*, **60** (1), 14-29.

Annotated Bibliography

This bibliography lists many of the TCM papers which have been published in the last several decades. In order to be more useful to readers, it is annotated concisely. Annotation follows the last line of each entry, with codes used for the resource types and policy issues involved.

The key for the resource type is: land (1), water (2), forest (3), wildlife (4), wilderness (5), parks (6) and developed recreation and all other (7). The codes for policy issues are: reservoir management (RE), water supply (WS), hydro dam relicensing (HD), natural resource damage assessments (NR), water quality (WQ), outdoor recreation and environment (OR), rangelands management (MG), forest management (FS), river basin management (RV) and wildlife management (WL). Where the classification is not applicable, * is used. Some entries where the subject is obvious from the title are not annotated.

Adamowicz, W.L., J.J. Fletcher and T. Graham Tomasi (1989), 'Functional Form and the Statistical Properties of Welfare Measures', *American Journal of Agricultural Economics,* **71** (2), 414-21. Discusses variation of welfare estimates across functional forms; 4; OR.

Adamowicz, W.L., S. Jennings and A. Coyne (1990), 'A Sequential Choice Model of Recreation Behavior', *Western Journal of Agricultural Economics,* **15** (1), 91-9. Uses previous trips to predict future trips; 4; OR.

Adamowicz, W.L. and T. Graham Tomasi, (1991), 'Revealed Preference Tests of Nonmarket Goods Valuation Methods', *Journal of Environmental Economics and Management,* **20** (1), 29-45. Compares values derived from TCM and CV studies; 4; OR.

Adamowicz, W.L. (1991), 'Valuation of Environmental Amenities', *Canadian Journal of Agricultural Economics,* **39** (4), 609-18. Reviews methods of valuing non-market goods; *;*.

Adamowicz, W.L. (1994), 'Habit Formation and Variety Seeking in a Discrete Choice Model of Recreation Demand', *Journal of Agricultural and Resource Economics,* **19** (1), 19-31. Develops a site choice model based on previous experience; 2,4; OR.

Adamowicz, W.L., J. Louviere and M. Williams (1994), 'Combining Revealed and Stated Preference Methods for Valuing Environmental Amenities', *Journal of Environmental Economics and Management,* **26**,

271-92. Compares results from a TCM and a CV study to determine if underlying preferences are equal; 2,4; OR.

Adger, N. and M. Whitby (1991), 'Accounting for the Impact of Agriculture and Forestry on Environmental Quality', *European Economic Review,* **35** (2-3), 629-41. Values environmental impacts of agriculture and forestry in the UK using TCM and CVM; 1,2,3; FS, WQ, NR.

Agnello, R.J. and Y. Han (1990), 'Some Findings on the Valuation of Fishing Success in a Multiple Site Travel Cost Model', *Operations Research and Management in Fishing,* NATO Advanced Science Institute Series E: Applied Sciences, **189**, 239-54. Measures the marginal value of fishing success in a multiple site framework; 2,4; OR.

Agnello, R.J. and Y. Han (1993), 'Substitute Site Measures in a Varying Parameter Model with Application to Recreational Fishing', *Marine Resource Economics,* **8** (1), 65-77. Values recreational saltwater fishing, based on site uniqueness; 2,4; OR.

Allen, P.G., T.H. Stevens and S. Barrett (1981), 'The Effects of Variable Omission in the Travel Cost Technique', *Land Economics,* **57** (2), 173-80. Describes specification error due from deleting travel time and congestion variables; 1,2,3; OR.

Anderson, C.L. et al. (1988), 'The Economic Value of Derby Fishing: An Application of Travel Cost Methodology in Lake Superior', *Regional Science Perspectives,* **18** (1), 3-18. Values travel time using respondent reported expenditures and time costs; 2,4; RE.

Anderson, L.G. (1983), 'The Demand Curve for Recreational Fishing with an Application to Stock Enhancement Activities', *Land Economics,* **59** (3), 279-86. 2,4;WL.

Balkan, E. and J. Kahn (1988), 'The Value of Changes in Deer Hunting Quality: A Travel Cost Approach', *Applied Economics,* **20** (4), 533-9. Illustrates welfare changes when deer hunting quality increases; 4; WL.

Bateman, I.J. et al. (1996), 'Measurement Issues in the Travel Cost Method: A Geographical Information Systems Approach', *Journal of Agricultural Economics,* **47** (2), 191-205. Estimates value of a recreation site using geographical information system software to measure travel costs; 3; FS, OR.

Batie, S.S., R. B. Jensen and L. Hogue (1976), 'A Lancasterian Approach for Specifying Derived Demands for Recreational Activities', *Southern Journal of Agricultural Economics,* **8** (1), 101-7. Investigates use of household behavior theory in estimating demand for recreation.; 2; RE.

Beal, D.J. (1995), 'A Travel Cost Analysis of the Value of Carnarvon Gorge National Park for Recreational Use', *Review of Marketing and Agricultural Economics,* **63** (2), 292-303. Measures the value of a national park and tests TCM for rapid valuation appraisal; 6; OR.

Beal, D.J. (1995), 'The Cost of Time in Travel Cost Analyses of Demand for Recreational Use of Natural Areas', *Australian Journal of Leisure and Recreation,* **5** (1), 9-13. Reports survey respondents' views of the cost of their time; 1; OR.

Beal, D.J. (1995), 'Sources of Variation in Estimates of Cost reported by Respondents in Travel Cost Surveys', *Australian Journal of Leisure and Recreation,* **5** (1), 3-8. Reports survey respondents' views of the costs of travel; 1;OR.

Beal, D.J. (1996), 'Estimation of the Elasticity of Demand for Camping Visits to a National Park in South-East Queensland by the Travel Cost Method', *Australian Journal of Leisure and Recreation,* **7**, 21-6. Estimates a single site ZTCM model with survey data;1;OR.

Beardsley, W. (1971), 'Bias and Noncomparability in Recreation Evaluation Models', *Land Economics,* **47** (2), 175-80. Describes sources of bias in travel cost models and proposes corrections; 1,2,3,4; OR.

Beggs, J.J. (1984), 'The Value of Travel to Recreational Facilities: The Uncertainty Issue', *International Journal of Transport Economics,* **11**, 53-9. Incorporates use of subjective analysis by local traffic engineers in estimating demand curves for recreational travel; 2; OR.

Bell, F.W. and V.R. Leeworthy (1990), 'Recreational Demand by Tourists for Saltwater Beach Days', *Journal of Environmental Economics and Management,* **18** (3), 189-205. Estimates value of Florida saltwater beach days, isolating tourists and local demand; 1, 2, 4; OR.

Bishop, R.C. and T. A. Heberlein (1979), 'Measuring Values of Extramarket Goods: Are Indirect Measures Biased?', *American Journal of Agricultural Economics,* **6**, 926-30. Compares TCM and CVM values to actual cash transactions; OR; WL.

Bockstael, N.E. and K.E. McConnell (1980), 'Calculating Equivalent and Compensating Variation for Natural Resource Facilities', *Land Economics,* **56** (1), 56-63. Discusses the difference between compensating variation and equivalent variation; *; *.

Bockstael, N.E. and K.E. McConnell (1981), 'Theory and Estimation of the Household Production Function for Wildlife Recreation', *Journal of Environmental Economics and Management,* **8**, 199-214. Discusses methods for measuring benefits of policy changes with household production function; 4; WL.

Bockstael, N.E. and K.E. McConnell (1983), 'Welfare Measurement in the Household Production Framework', *American Economic Review,* **73**, 806-14. Measures welfare in a household production function framework; *;*.

Bockstael, N.E., W.M. Hanemann and I. Strand (1986), 'Measuring the

Benefits of Water Quality Improvements Using Recreation Demand Models', *Report to the U.S. Environmental Protection Agency,* College Park, Md.: University of Maryland. Measure benefits of water quality improvements; 2; WQ.

Bockstael, N.E. and I.E. Strand (1987), 'The Effect of Common Sources of Regression Error on Benefit Estimates', *Land Economics,* **63** (1), 11-20. Describes impacts of error on benefit measurement; *; *.

Bockstael, N.E., I.E. Strand and W.M. Hanemann (1987), 'Time and the Recreational Demand Model', *American Journal of Agricultural Economics,* **69** (2), 293-302. Develops a model with time cost determined by labor market constraints; 4; WL.

Bockstael, N.E., W.M. Hanemann and C. Kling (1987), 'Estimating the Value of Water Quality Improvements in a Recreational Demand Framework', *Water Resources Research,* **23** (5), 951-60. Compares three methods of valuing water quality improvements; 2; WQ.

Bockstael, N.E. and C.L. Kling (1988), 'Valuing Environmental Quality: Weak Complementarity with Sets of Goods', *American Journal of Agricultural Economics,* **70**, 654-62. Explains rules for measuring welfare effects of environmental quality changes with weak complementarity; 2; WQ, OR.

Bockstael, N.E., K.E. McConnell and I.E. Strand (1989), 'A Random Utility Model of Sport Fishing: Some Preliminary Results from Florida', *Marine Resource Economics,* **6**, pp. 245-60. Develops a RUM; 4; OR.

Bockstael, N.E., I.E. Strand, K.E McConnell and F. Arsanjani, (1990), 'Sample Selection Bias in the Estimation of Recreation Demand Functions: An Application to Sportfishing', *Land Economics*, **66**: 40-9. Explores three methods for correcting sample selection bias; 4; OR, WL.

Bockstael, N.E., K.E. McConnell and I.E. Strand (1991), 'Recreation', in J.B. Braden and C.D. Kolstad (eds.), *Measuring the Demand for Environmental Quality*, Amsterdam: Elsevier Science, 227-70. Describes recreation valuation methods and problems; *; *.

Bouwes, N. W. Snr. and R. Schneider (1979), 'Procedures in Estimating Benefits of Water Quality Change', *American Journal of Agricultural Economics,* **61**, 535-9. Introduces a method to quantify water quality perceptions; 2; WQ.

Bowes, M.D. and J.B. Loomis (1980), 'A Note on the Use of Travel Cost Models with Unequal Zonal Populations', *Land Economics,* **56**, 465-70. Illustrates demand estimation procedures to deal with heteroskedasticity; 2; OR.

Bowes, M.D. and J.B. Loomis (1982), 'A Note on the Use of Travel Cost Models with Unequal Zonal Populations: Reply', *Land Economics,* **58** (3),

408-10. Estimates a TCM with unequal zonal populations; *; *.

Bowker, J.M., D.B.K. English and J. Donovan (1996), 'Toward a Value for Guided Rafting on Southern Rivers', *Journal of Agricultural and Applied Economics,* **28** (2), 423-32. Employs an individual TCM to estimate recreational values for whitewater rafting; 2; OR.

Boxall, P.C. (1995), 'The Economic Value of Lottery Rationed Recreational Hunting', *Canadian Journal of Agricultural Economics,* **43** (1), 119-31. Incorporates expectation of a permit into a discrete choice TCM; 4; WL.

Boxall, P.C., W.L. Adamowicz and T. Graham Tomasi (1996), 'A Nonparametric Test of the Traditional Travel Cost Model', *Canadian Journal of Agricultural Economics,* **44** (2), 183-93. Tests assumptions about consumer behavior in travel cost models as they apply to hunters; 4; WL.

Boyle, K.J. and J.C. Bergstrom (1992), 'Benefit Transfer Studies: Myths, Pragmatism, and Idealism', *Water Resources Research,* **28** (3), 657-63. Discusses methods and issues in benefit transfer studies; *; *.

Breffle, W.S. and E.R. Morey (1999), 'Investigating Heterogeneity of Preferences in a Repeated Logit Recreation Demand Model Using RP Data', *Western Regional Research Publication,* 12th Interim Report. Tests TCM model to account for heterogeneous preferences; 4; WL.

Brown, G.M., Jr. and R. Mendelsohn (1984), 'The Hedonic Travel Cost Method', *Review of Economics and Statistics,* **66** (3), 427-33. Values quality changes for Atlantic Salmon fishing; 4; WL.

Brown, W. G., A. Singh and E. N. Castle (1965), 'Net Economic Value of the Oregon Salmon-Steelhead Sport Fishery', *Journal of Wildlife Management,* **29** (2), 266-79. Estimates a net value for an Oregon sport fishery using a TCM; 4; WL.

Brown, W.G. and F. Nawas (1973), 'Impact of Aggregation on the Estimation of Outdoor Recreation Demand Functions', *American Journal of Agricultural Economics,* **55** (2), 246-9. Shows that use of individual observations increases TCM efficiency; 4; WL.

Brown, W.G. et al. (1983), 'Using Individual Observations to Estimate Recreation Demand Functions: A Caution', *American Journal of Agricultural Economics,* **65** (1), 154-7. Examines costs of failure to use individual observations on biased consumer surplus estimates; 4; WL.

Burt, O.R. and D. Brewer (1971), 'Estimation of Net Social Benefits From Outdoor Recreation', *Econometrica,* **39** (5), 813-27. Uses demand system to measure benefits of new site development in light of existing sites; 2; OR.

Cameron, T.A., W.D. Shaw and S. Ragland (1996), 'Using Actual and Contingent Behavior Data with Differing Levels of Time Aggregation to

Model Recreation Demand', *Journal of Agricultural and Resource Economics,* **21** (1), 130-49. Combines contingent with actual behavior data to test affects of water level fluctuations on recreation demand; 2,4; RE, WL.

Casey, J.F., T. Vukina and L. Danielson (1995), 'The Economic Value of Hiking: Further Considerations of Opportunity Cost of Time in Recreational Demand Models', *Journal of Agricultural and Applied Economics,* **27** (2), 658-68. Tests two approaches to valuing the opportunity cost of time; 5; OR.

Caulkins, P.P., R.C. Bishop, and N.W. Bouwes, Snr. (1985), 'Omitted Cross Price Variable Biases in the Linear Travel Cost Model: Correcting Common Misperceptions', *Land Economics,* **61** (2), 182-7. Explains relationship of price proxy variables to actual price; *; *.

Caulkins, P.P., R.C. Bishop, and N.W. Bouwes, Snr. (1986), 'The Travel Cost Model for Lake Recreation: A Comparison of Two Methods for Incorporating Site Quality and Substitution Effects', *American Journal of Agricultural Economics,* **68** (2), 291-7. Researches the effects of behaviorial assumptions on predicted changes in recreational activity; 2; RE.

Cesario, F.J. (1976), 'Value of Time in Recreation Benefit Studies', *Land Economics,* **51** (2), 32-41. Estimates travel time values under three different assumptions; 6; OR.

Cesario, F.J. and J.L. Knetsch. (1970), 'Time Bias in Recreation Benefits Estimates', *Water Resources Research,* **6** (3), 700-4. Examines effect of time bias on benefit estimates and proposes correction; *; *.

Cesario, F.J. and J.L. Knetsch. (1976), 'A Recreation Site Demand and Benefit Estimation Model', *Regional Studies,* **10** (1), 97-104. Captures substitution effects and includes time cost surrogate; 6; OR.

Champ, P.A. and R.C. Bishop (1996), 'Evidence on the Accuracy of Expenditures Reported in Recreational Surveys', *Journal of Agricultural and Resource Economics,* **21** (1), 150-9. Compares survey and diary reported recreation expenditures; 4; WL.

Chavas, J.P., J. Stoll and C. Sellar (1989), 'On the Commodity Value of Travel Time in Recreational Activities', *Applied Economics,* **21** (6), 711-2. Explains why the value of travel time is usually less than the wage rate; 2; RE.

Christensen, J.B. and C. Price (1982), 'A Note on the Use of Travel Cost Models with Unequal Zonal Populations: Comment', *Land Economics,* **58** (3), 395-9. Desribes effects of unequal populations on demand estimates; *; *.

Christopherson, D.A. (1978), 'A Status Group Dynamics Approach to

Predicting Participation Rates in Regional Recreation Demand Studies: Comment', *Land Economics,* **54** (4), 520-1.. Describes a method to predict participation rates as a function of group characteristics; *; *.

Cicchetti, C.J. et al. (1972), 'Recreation Benefit Estimation and Forecasting: Implications of the Identification Problem', *Water Resources Research,* **8** (4), 840-50. Distinguishes between demand and participation in recreation studies; *; *.

Cichetti, C.J., A.C. Fisher and V.K. Smith (1973), 'Economic Models and Planning Outdoor Recreation', *Operations Research,* **21**, 1104-13. Reviews approaches for forecasting use and benefit estimation for recreation; *; *.

Cicchetti, C.J. and V.K. Smith. (1973), 'Congestion, Quality Deterioration and Optimal Use: Wilderness Recreation in the Spanish Peaks Primitive Area', *Social Science Research,* **2** (1), 15-30. Investigates effects of congestion and quality deterioration on revealed willingness to pay for a wilderness experience; 2;OR.

Cichetti, C.J., A.C. Fisher and V.K. Smith (1976), 'An Econometric Evaluation of a Generalized Consumer Surplus Measure: The Mineral King Controversy', *Econometrica,* **44** (6), 1259-75. Multisite demand model evaluates benefits of proposed ski facility in the face of strong stubstitutes; 5; OR.

Clawson, M. (1959), *Methods of Measuring the Demand for and Value of Outdoor Recreation,* Reprint No. 10, Washington: Resources for the Future. A classic: one of the first to estimate a TCM based on economic theory; *; *.

Cocheba, D. J. and W.A. Langford (1978), 'Wildlife Valuation: The Collective Good Aspect of Hunting', *Land Economics,* **54** (4), 490-504. Separates collective and private goods benefits; 4; WL.

Creel, M. and J. Loomis (1990), 'Theoretical and Empirical Advantages of Truncated Count Data Estimators for Analysis of Deer Hunting in California', *American Journal of Agricultural Economics,* **72** (2), 434- 41. Describes truncated count data models, and a method to eliminate specification bias in large samples; 4; WL.

Creel, M. and J. Loomis (1992), 'Recreation Value of Water to Wetlands in the San Joaquin Valley: Linked Multinomial Logit and Count Data Trip Frequency Models', *Water Resources Research,* **28** (10), 2597-606.

Crooker, J. and C.L. Kling (1999), 'Nonparametric Bounds on Welfare Measures: A New Tool for Nonmarket Valuation', *Western Regional Research Publication,* 12th Interim Report. Uses nonparametric techniques to bound welfare measures; *; *.

David, E.J.L. (1969), 'Effects of Nonprice Variables upon Participation in

Water Oriented Outdoor Recreation: Comment', *American Journal of Agricultural Economics,* **51** (4), 942-5. Illustrates creative use of dummy variables to handle non price factors on recreation demand; *; *.

Deyak, T. and V.K. Smith (1978), 'Congestion and Participation in Outdoor Recreation: A Household Production Function Approach', *Journal of Environmental Economics and Management,* **5**,   63-80. Employs a household production function model to evaluate the effects of congestion on an indivuals recreation decisions; 5; OR.

Dobbs, I.M. (1993), 'Individual Travel Cost Method: Estimation and Benefit Assessment with a Discrete and Possibly Grouped Dependent Variable', *American Journal of Agricultural Economics,* **75** (1), 84-94. Indicates presence of bias if discreteness or grouping is not taken into account in demand and benefit estimation; 3; FS, OR.

Dobbs, I.M. (1993), 'Adjusting for Sample Selection Bias in the Individual Travel Cost Method', *Journal of Agricultural Economics,* **44** (2), 335-42. Adjusts TCM to account for endogenous sample selection bias, e.g. sampling avid users more often; 3; FS.

Dorfman, R. (1984), 'On Optimal Congestion', *Journal of Environmental Economics and Management,* **11** (2), 91-106. Describes theory for setting socially optimal level of use for congestible facilities; *; *.

Duffield, J.W., C.J. Neher and T. Brown (1992), 'Recreation Benefits of Instream Flow: Application to Montana's Big Hole and Bitterroot Rivers', *Water Resources Research,* **28** (9), 2169.

Durden, G. and J.F. Shogren (1988), 'Valuing Nonmarket Recreation Goods: An Evaluative Survey of the Literature on the Travel Cost and Contingent Valuation Methods', *Review of Regional Studies,* **18** (3), 1-15.

Eberle, W.D. and F.G. Hayden (1991), 'Critique of Contingent Valuation and Travel Cost Methods for Valuing natural Resources and Ecosystems', *Journal of Economic Issues,* **25** (3), 649-87. Explains strengths and weaknesses of CVM and TCM to support natural resource value assessment; *; *.

Englin, J. and R. Mendelsohn (1991), 'A Hedonic Travel Cost Analysis for Valuation of Multiple Components of Site Quality: The Recreation Value of Forest Management', *Journal of Environmental Economics and Management,* **21** (3), 275-90. Illustrates a hedonic TCM that measures the value of multiple site quality changes; 3,5; FS, OR.

Englin, J. and J.S. Shonkwiler (1995), 'Modelling Recreation Demand in the Presence of Unobservable Travel Costs: Toward a Travel Price Model', *Journal of Environmental Economics and Management,* **29** (3), 368-77. Develops a model that allows use of qualitative variables in the calculation of travel cost; 2; OR.

Englin, J. and T.A. Cameron (1996), 'Augmenting Travel Cost Models with Contingent Behavior Data: Poisson Regression Analyses with Individual Panel Data', *Environmental and Resource Economics,* **7** (2), 133-47. Incorporates CVM data into TCM model to reduce omitted variable bias; 2,4; WL.

Englin, J., D. Lambert and W.D. Shaw (1997), 'A Structural Equations Approach to Modelling Consumptive Recreation Demand', *Journal of Environmental Economics and Management,* **33** (1), 33-43. Outlines a two equation model that allows changes in biological factors to link fish catch to recreation demand; 2,4; WL.

English, D.B.K.and J.C. Bergstrom (1994), 'The Conceptual Links between Recreation Site Development and Regional Economic Impacts', *Journal of Regional Science,* **34** (4), 599-611. Provides a framework for measuring regional economic impacts of a recreation site; *; OR.

English, D.B.K. and J.M. Bowker (1994), 'Measuring Use Value from Recreation Participation: Comment', *Journal of Agricultural and Applied Economics,* **26** (1), 311-3. Describes theoretical and empirical problems in a study measuring use values; *; *.

Findlater, P.A., and J.A. Sinden (1982), 'Estimation of Recreation Benefits from Measured Utility Functions', *American Journal of Agricultural Economics,* **64**, 102-9. Estimates recreation demand based on ordinal utility; 6; OR.

Fix, P. and J. Loomis (1998), 'Comparing the Economic Value of Mountain Biking Estimated Using Revealed and Stated Preference', *Journal of Environmental Planning and Management,* **41** (2), 227-36. Applies TCM and CVM to mountain biking, and compares results; 7; OR.

Freeman, A.M., III (1995), 'The Benefits of Water Quality Improvements for Marine Recreation: A Review of the Empirical Evidence', *Marine Resources Economics,* **10**, 385-406. Reviews literature on marine recreation, addressing questions on pollution control policy; 2; WQ, OR.

Fujii, E.T., M. Khaled and J. Mak (1985), 'An Almost Ideal Demand System for Visitor Expenditures', *Journal of Transport Economics and Policy,* **19** (2), 161-71. Estimates a system of demand equations for selected components of vacation travel; *; *.

Gillespie, G.A. and D. Brewer (1968), 'Effects of Non Price Variables upon Participation in Water Oriented Outdoor Recreation', *Journal of Farm Economics,* **50** (1), 820-90. Estimates and forecasts water based recreation demand; 2; RE, OR.

Graham Tomasi, T. and W.L. Adamowicz (1990), 'Errors of Truncation in Approximations to Expected Consumer Surplus', *Land Economics,* **66** (1), 50-5. Illustrates size of potential errors made by truncating and approximation to expected consumer surplus; 4; *.

Green, T.G. (1986), 'Specification Considerations for the Price Variable in Travel Cost Demand Models: Comment', *Land Economics,* **62** (4), 416-8. Examines adjustment factors to account for endogenous price in TCM; *; *.

Greene, G., C.B. Moss and T. Spreen (1997), 'Demand for Recreational Fishing in Tampa Bay, Florida: A Random Utility Approach', *Marine Resource Economics,* **12** (4), 293-305. Estimates Random Utility Model to measure access values for both participants and non-participants; 2,4; WL, OR.

Gum, R.L. and W.E. Martin (1975), 'Problems and Solutions in Estimating Demand for and Value of Recreation', *American Journal of Agricultural Economics,* **57** (1), 558-66. Models demand for multiple recreation activities for entire state of Arizona; 1-7; OR.

Hanemann, W.M. (1980), 'Measuring the Worth of natural Resource Facilities: Comment', *Land Economics,* **56** (4), 482-6. Describes demand function approach to evaluate benefits of natural resource facilities; *; *.

Hanemann, W. M. (1984), 'Discrete/Continuous Models of Consumer Demand', *Econometrica,* **52**, 541-61.

Hanley, N.D. (1989), 'Valuing Rural Recreation Benefits: An Empirical Comparison of Two Approaches', *Journal of Agricultural Economics,* **40** (3), 361-74. Derives and compares benefit estimates from CV and TCM models; 3; OR.

Hanley, N., R.E. Wright and W.L. Adamowicz (1998), 'Using Choice Experiments to Value the Environment: Design Issues, Current Experience and Future Prospects', *Environmental and Resource Economics,* **11** (34), 413-28. Explains the choice experiment method of valuation, and applies it to TCM and CVM; 3; OR.

Haspel, A. E. and F.R. Johnson (1982), 'Multiple Destination Trip Bias in Recreation Benefit Estimation', *Land Economics,* **58** (3), 364-72. Corrects for multiple destination bias by using average distance between major destinations; 6; OR.

Hauber, A. B. and G. R. Parsons (1998), 'The Effect of Nesting Structure Specification on Welfare Estimation in Random Utility Models: An Application to the Demand for Recreational Fishing', *Western Regional Research Publication,* 11th Interim Report. Examines effects of changing scale parameter estimates in logit models on welfare estimates across nesting structures; 2, 4; WL, RE.

Hellerstein, D. (1991), 'Using Count Data Models in Travel Cost Analysis with Aggregate Data', *American Journal of Agricultural Economics,* **73** (3), 860-7. Demonstrates effects choice of estimator has on welfare estimates; 5; OR.

Hellerstein, D. (1992), 'The Treatment of Nonparticipants in Travel Cost Analysis and Other Demand Models', *Water Resources Research,* **28** (8), 1999-2004. Explores consequences of various sample designs and discusses methods of reducing bias; *; *.

Hellerstein, D. (1993), 'Intertemporal Data and Travel Cost Analysis', *Environmental and Resource Economics,* **3** (2), 193-207. Conducts a travel cost analysis using multi year data; 5; OR.

Hellerstein, D. and R. Mendelsohn (1993), 'A Theoretical Foundation for Count Data Models', *American Journal of Agricultural Economics,* **75** (3), 604-11. Corrects for biased trip demand estimation in TCMs by using count data estimators; *; *.

Hellerstein, D. (1995), 'Welfare Estimation Using Aggregate and Individual Observation Models: A Comparison Using Monte Carlo Techniques', *American Journal of Agricultural Economics,* **77** (3), 620-30. Investigates aggregation bias in ZTCMs; shows that they may outperform individual TCMs with narrowly specified variables; *; *.

Hellerstein, D. (1998), 'An Analysis of Wildlife Recreation Using the FHWAR', *Western Regional Research Publication,* 11th Interim Report. Studies impact of Conservation Reserve Program on demand for non-consumptive wildlife recreation; 4; WL.

Hilger, J.R.II (1998), 'A Bivariate Compound Poisson Application: The Welfare Effects of Forest Fire on Wilderness Day Hikers', Reno: University of Nevada, Masters Thesis. Illustrates effects of forest fire on demand for wilderness trails; 5; OR.

Hof, J.G. and D.A. King (1982), 'On the Necessity of Simultaneous Recreation Demand Equation Estimation', *Land Economics,* **58** (4), 547-52. Demonstrates that single site model captures effects of substitute sites; *; *.

Hof, J.G. and D.A. King (1983), 'On the Necessity of Simultaneous Recreation Demand Equation Estimation: Reply', *Land Economics,* **59** (4), 459-60. Elaborates on a previous article dealing with single site models to value recreation in the presence of substitutes; *; *.

Hof, J.G. and D.H. Rosenthal (1987), 'Valuing the Opportunity Cost of Travel Time in Recreation Demand Models: An Application to Aggregate Data', *Journal of Leisure Research,* **19** (3), 174-88. Tests a technique to determine opportunity cost of time in recreation demand models; 2; RE.

Hof, J.G. (1988), 'Some Thoughts on The Multiple Destination Trip Problem in Travel Cost Models', *Western Regional Research Publication,* Interim Report, 145-56. Presents a cost allocation scheme to correct for multiple destination bias; *; *.

Hof, J.G. and D.A. King, (1992), 'Recreational Demand by Tourists for Saltwater Beach Days: Comment', *Journal of Environmental Economics and Management,* **22** (3), 281-91. Describes strengths and limits to an on-site cost approach for valuing saltwater beach days; 1,2; OR.

Hotelling , H. (1947), 'The Economics of Public Recreation', The Prewitt Report, Washington: National Parks Service. Original proposal for TCM; 6; OR.

Hushak, L.J., J.M. Winslow and N. Dutta (1988), 'Economic Value of Great Lakes Sportfishing: The Case of Private Boat Fishing in Ohio's Lake Erie', *Transactions of the American Fisheries Society,* **117**, 363-73. Derives a per day value of fishing in Lake Erie and suggest a public investment rate to maintain the fishery; 2,4; WL.

Jakus, P. M. (1999), 'The Effect of Fluctuating Water Levels on Reservoir Fishing', *Western Regional Research Publication W-133,* 12th Interim Report, in press. Evaluates effect of water levels on fishing demand; 2,4; WS, WL.

Johansson, P.O, K. Bengt and K.G. Maler (1989), 'Welfare Evaluations in Contingent Valuation Experiments with Discrete Response Data: Comment', *American Journal of Agricultural Economics,* **71**, 1054-6. Discusses issue of negative bids in CVM studies; *; *.

Johnson, M.B. (1966), 'Travel Time and the Price of Leisure', *Western Economics Journal,* **4** (1), 135-45. Argues against using wage rate to value travel time; *; *.

Johnson, T.G. (1983), 'Measuring the Cost of Time in Recreation Demand Analysis: Comment', *American Journal of Agricultural Economics,* **65** (1), 169-71. Describes conditions where opportunity cost of time is underestimated; *; *.

Kealy, M.J. and R.C. Bishop (1986), 'Theoretical and Empirical Specifications Issues and Travel Cost Demand Studies', *American Journal of Agricultural Economics,* **68** (3), 660-7. Corrects limits in TCM for trip length; 2, 4; WL.

Keane, M.J. (1996), 'Sustaining Quality in Tourism Destinations: An Economic Model with an Application', *Applied Economics,* **28** (12), 1545-53.

Kling, C.L. (1987), 'A Simulation Approach to Comparing Multiple Site Recreation Demand Models Using Chesapeake Bay Survey Data', *Marine Resource Economics,* **4** (2), 95-109. Shows method of evaluating and comparing recreation demand models; *; *.

Kling, C.L. (1988), 'Comparing Welfare Estimates of Environmental Quality Changes from Recreation Demand Models', *Journal of Environmental Economics and Management,* **15**, 331-40. Presents a method testing reliability of welfare estimates derived from multiple site demand models; *; *.

Kling, C.L. (1988), 'The Reliability of Estimates of Environmental Benefits from Recreation Demand Models', *American Journal of Agricultural Economics,* **70** (4), 892-901. Compares reliability of welfare estimates from several functional forms; *; *.

Kling, C.L. (1989), 'A Note on the Welfare Effects of Omitting Substitute Prices and Qualities from Travel Cost Models', *Land Economics,* **65** (3), 290-6. Specifies conditions under which omitting substitute price and quality data causes bias; * ; *.

Kling, C.L. (1991), 'Estimating the Precision of Welfare Measures', *Journal of Environmental Economics and Management,* **21** (3), 244-59. Examines the accuracy of statistical tests for welfare estimates; *; *.

Kling, C.L. (1991), 'The Welfare Effects of Omitting Substitute Prices and Qualities from Travel Cost Models: Reply', *Land Economics,* **67** (1), 132 - 3. Reply to a comment on a previous article dealing with substitute prices; *; *.

Kling, C.L. (1992), 'Some Results on the Variance of Welfare Estimates from Recreation Demand Models', *Land Economics,* **68** (3), 318-28. Discusses size of variance of welfare estimates; *; *.

Kling, C.L. (1997), 'The Gains from Combining Travel Cost and Contingent Valuation Data to Value Nonmarket Goods', *Land Economics,* **73,** 428-39. Illustrates that combining CV and TCM may produce more precise welfare estimates; *; *.

Knapman, B. and O. Stanley (1991), *A Travel Cost Analysis of the Recreation Use Value of Kakadu National Park*, Resource Assessment Commission, Kakadu Conservation Zone Inquiry Consultancy Series, Canberra: AGPS. Estimates a simple single site model; 5; OR.

Knetsch, J.L. (1963), 'Outdoor Recreation Demands and Values', *Land Economics*, **39**, 387-96.

Knetsch, J.L. and Cheung Hym Kwai (1976), 'Economic Value of Recreation Areas: The Case of Saskatchewan Parks', *Canadian Journal of Agricultural Economics,* **24** (1), 67-71. Estimates value for a park, taking time bias into account; 6; OR.

Kopp, R.J. and V.K. Smith (1989), 'Benefit Estimation Goes to Court: The Case of natural Resource Damage Assessments', *Journal of Policy Analysis and Management,* **8**, 593-612. Investigates differences in resource damage estimates by competing litigants; *; *.

Krutilla, J.V. and J.L. Knetsch (1970), 'Outdoor Recreation Economics', *Annals of the American Academy of Political and Social Science,* **389**, 63-70. Studies the difference beween resource-oriented and population-oriented outdoor recreation; *; *.

Kula, E. (1986), 'The Developing Framework for the Economic Evaluation of Forestry in the United Kingdom', *Journal of Agricultural Economics,* **37** (3), 365-76.

Kulshreshtha, S.N. (1991), 'Research Contributions/Recherches en cours Estimation of Value of Water for Water Related Recreation in Saskatchewan', *Canadian Water Resources Journal, Revue canadienne des ressources en eau,* **16** (3), 207-22. Compares water value estimates from CVM and TCM studies; 2; OR.

Kyeong Ae Choe., D. Whittington and D.T. Lauria (1996), 'The Economic Benefits of Surface Water Quality Improvements in Developing Countries: A Case Study of Davao, Philippines', *Land Economics,* **72** (4), 519-37. Combines CV and TCM studies to estimate value of water quality improvements; 2;WQ.

Lansford, N.H. Jr. and L.L. Jones (1995), 'Marginal Price of Lake Recreation and Aesthetics: An Hedonic Approach', *Journal of Agricultural and Applied Economics,* **27** (1), 212-23. Estimates recreational and aesthetic value of water, and examines their effect on housing prices; 2; OR.

Larson, D.M. (1993), 'Joint Recreation Choices and Implied Values of Time', *Land Economics,* **69** (3), 279-86. Introduces a model that does not assume on-site time is fixed; 4; OR, WL.

Larson, D.M. (1993), 'Separability and the Shadow Value of Leisure Time', *American Journal of Agricultural Economics,* **75** (3), 572-7. Explores the value of time from a utility standpoint; *; *.

Larson, D.M., D.K. Lew and J.B. Loomis (1999), 'Are Revealed Preference Measures of Quality Change Benefits Statistically Significant?', *Western Regional Research Publication,* 12th Interim Report. Examines whether point estimates of welfare change for quality changes are statistically significant; *; *.

Layman, R.C., J.R. Boyce and K.R. Criddle (1996), 'Economic Valuation of the Chinook Salmon Sport Fishery of the Gulkana River, Alaska, under Current and Alternate Management Plans', *Land Economics,* **72** (1), 113-28. Develops methodology for assessing effects of hypothetical policy changes within a TCM framework; 4; WL.

Livengood, K.R. (1983), 'Value of Big Game from Markets for Hunting Leases: The Hedonic Approach', *Land Economics,* **59** (3), 287-91. Derives value of white-tailed deer harvested by lease hunters; 4; WL.

Lohr, L. et al. (1998), 'Integrated Contingent Valuation Travel Cost Models For Expenditure Allocation Decisions', *Western Regional Research Publication*, 11th Interim Report, 128-48. Demonstrates benefits of discrete-continuous choice method of resource valuation; 2; RE.

Loomis, J.B. (1980), 'Monetizing Benefits under Alternative River Recreation Use Allocation Systems', *Water Resources Research,* **16** (1), 28-32. Develops a model to assess efficiency of resource allocation systems; 2; OR.

Loomis, J.B., C. Sorg and D. Donnelly (1986), 'Economic Losses to Recreational Fisheries due to Small Head Hydro Power Development: A Case Study of the Henry's Fork in Idaho', *Journal of Environmental Management,* **22**, 85-94. Estimates effects of fishing quality changes due to hydropower development; 2,4; HD, WL.

Loomis, J.B., C.F. Sorg and D. Donnell, (1986), 'Evaluating Regional Demand Models for Estimating Recreation Use and Economic Benefits: A Case Study', *Water Resources Research,* **22** (4), 431-8. Evaluates U.S. Water Resource Council recommendation that regional or multi site TCMs be relied on over single site models; 2,4; WL.

Loomis, J.B. (1988), 'Travel Cost Demand Models With Linkages to Fishing Quality: Computerized Models for the Pacific Northwest', *Western Regional Research Publication,* Interim Report, 199-216. Describes bio-economic demand models linking changes in fish populations to net economic benefits; 2,4; WQ, WL.

Loomis, J.B., D. Donnelly and C. Sorg (1988), 'Estimation of Marginal Values of Wildlife and Forage Using the Travel Cost Method', *Western Regional Research Publication, Benefits and Costs in Natural Resources Planning,* Interim Report, 157-74. Improves methods to identify efficient forage allocations between cattle and wildlife; 3,4; WL, MG.

Loomis, J.B. and J. Cooper (1990), 'Comparison of Environmental Quality Induced Demand Shifts Using Time Series and Cross Section Data', *Western Journal of Agricultural Economics,* **15** (1), 83-90. Concludes that multi-site demand equation for analysis of single site quality change produces poor results; 4; OR, WL.

Loomis, J.B., W. Provencher and W. Brown (1990), 'Evaluating the Transferability of Regional Recreation Demand Equations', in R.L. Johnson and G.V. Johnson (eds.), *Economic Valuation of Natural Resources: Issues, Theory, and Applications,* Social Behavior and Natural Resources Series, Boulder and Oxford: Westview Press, pp. 205-17.

Loomis, J.B., M. Creel and T.A. Park (1991), 'Comparing Benefit Estimates from Travel Cost and Contingent Valuation Using Confidence Intervals for Hicksian Welfare Measures', *Applied Economics,* **23** (11), 1725-31. Describes techniques to compare CV and TCM values; 4; WL, OR.

Loomis, J.B. et al. (1995), 'Testing Transferability of Recreation Demand Models across Regions: A Study of Corps of Engineer Reservoirs', *Water Resources Research,* **31** (3), 721-30. Tests similarity of reservoir

Valuing Nature with Travel Cost Models

recreation demand across geogaphic regions; 2; RE.

Lupi, F. and J.P. Hoehn (1998), 'The Effect of Trip Lengths on Travel Cost Parameters in Recreation Demand', *Western Regional Research Publication,* 11th Interim Report, 33-52. Illustrates that deleting multiple day trips from analysis biases findings; 4; WL.

Lupi, F. and J.P. Hoehn (1999), 'A Partial Benefit Cost Analysis of Sea Lamprey Treatment Options on the St. Marys River', *Western Regional Research Publication,* 12th Interim Report. Estimates benefits of lake trout recovery from sea lamprey control; 4; WL.

Mansfield, N.W. (1971), 'The Estimation of Benefits from Recreation Sites and the Provision of a New Recreation Facility', *Regional Studies,* **5**, 55-69. Identifies shortcomings in TCMs in predicting demand for a new site in the presence of a perfect substitute; 2; OR.

Martin, W.E., F.H. Bollman and R.L. Gum (1982), 'Economic Value of Lake Mead Fishery', *Fisheries,* **7** (6), 20-4. Estimates value the Lake Mead fishery; 4; WL, RE.

Matulich, S.C., W.G. Workman and A. Jubenville (1987), 'Recreation Economics: Taking Stock [Problems and Solutions in Estimating the Demand for and Value of Rural Outdoor Recreation]', *Land Economics,* **63** (3), 310-6. Calls for more empirical application of valuation techniques, and research to better support policy decisions; *; *.

McClellan, K. and E.A. Medrich (1969), 'Outdoor Recreation: Economic Consideration for Optimal Site Selection and Development', *Land Economics,* **45**(2), 174-82. Examines recreation demand estimation methods and describes a site selection technique; *; *.

McConnell, K.E. (1976), 'Some Problems in Estimating the Demand for Outdoor Recreation: Reply', *American Journal of Agricultural Economics,* **58** (3), 598-9. Discusses the problems from ignoring opportunity cost of time; *; *.

McConnell, K.E. (1979), 'Values of Marine Recreational Fishing: Measurement and Impact of Measurement', *American Journal of Agricultural Economics,* **61** (5), 921-5. Values recreational fishing benefits to evaluate competition with commercial fishing; 4; WL.

McConnell, K.E. (1980), 'Valuing Congested Recreation Sites', *Journal of Environmental Economics and Management,* 7, 389-94.

McConnell, K.E. (1985), 'The Economics of Outdoor Recreation', in A.V Kneese and J.L. Sweeney (eds.), *Handbook of Natural Resource and Energy Economics,* Vol. 1, Amsterdam, The Netherlands: North Holland. Explains theory, methods and applications in recreation economics; *; *.

McConnell, K.E. (1990), 'Double Counting in Hedonic and Travel Cost Models', *Land Economics,* **66** (2), 121-7. Illustrates the difference between pollution damage measured by TCMs and that measured by a Hedonic model; 2; WQ.

McConnell, K.E. (1992), 'On Site Time in the Demand for Recreation', *American Journal of Agricultural Economics,* **74** (4), 918-25. Presents a method of dealing with on-site time; *; *.

McConnell, K.E. (1992), 'Model Building and Judgment: Implications for Benefit Transfers with Travel Cost Models', *Water Resources Research,* **28** (3), 695-700. Discusses role of the researcher's judgement in the benefit transfer process; *; *.

McConnell, K.E., and V.A. Duff. (1976), 'Estimating Net Benefits of Outdoor Recreation Under Conditions of Excess Demand', *Journal of Environmental Economics and Management,* **2** (1), 24-30. Demonstrates that TCM underestimates benefits under conditions of excess demand; *; *.

McConnell, K.E. and I. Strand (1981), 'Measuring the Cost of Time in Recreation Demand Analysis, An Application to Sportfishing', *American Journal of Agricultural Economics,* **63** (1), 153-6. Describes a method of estimating the opportunity cost of time; 4; WL.

McConnell, K. E. and I. Strand (1983), 'Measuring the Cost of Time in Recreation Demand Analysis: Reply', *American Journal of Agricultural Economics,* **65** (1), 172-74. Replies to comments on a previous article on the opportunity cost of time; *; *.

McKean, J.R. and C.F. Revier (1990), 'Omitted Cross Price Variable Biases in the Linear Travel Cost Model: Correcting Common Misperceptions: An Extension', *Land Economics,* **66** (4), 430-6. Elaborates on a previous work dealing with alternate sites; *; *.

McKean, J.R., D.M. Johnson and R. Walsh (1995), 'Valuing Time in Travel Cost Demand Analysis: An Empirical Investigation', *Land Economics,* **71** (1), 96-105. Tests a TCM using income to value opportunity time costs against an alternative model; 4; WL, RE.

McKean, J.R., R.G. Walsh and D. Johnson (1996), 'Closely Related Good Prices in the Travel Cost Model', *American Journal of Agricultural Economics,* **78** (3), 640-6. Tests effects of including on-site time and on-site purchases; 4; WL, RE.

Mendelsohn, R. and G.M. Brown, Jnr. (1983), 'Revealed Preference Approaches to Valuing Outdoor Recreation', *Natural Resources Journal,* **23**, 607-618. Explains simple travel cost models, household production functions and advanced travel cost methods; *; *.

Mendelsohn, R. (1983), 'An Application of the Hedonic Travel Cost Framework for Recreation Modeling to the Valuation of Deer', in V.K. Smith and A.D. Witte (eds.), *Advances in Applied Microeconomics,* Greenwich, Conn: JAI Press.

Mendelsohn, R. (1987), 'Modeling the Demand for Outdoor Recreation', *Water Resources Research,* **23** (5), 961-7. Reviews new methods and research in recreation demand modeling; *; *.

Mendelsohn, R. et al. (1992), 'Measuring Recreation Values with Multiple Destination Trips', *American Journal of Agricultural Economics,* **74**, 923-33.Develops an alternative method of analyzing multiple destination trips; 6; OR.

Menz, F.C. and D.P. Wilton (1983), 'Alternative Ways to Measure Recreation Values by the Travel Cost Method', *American Journal of Agricultural Economics,* **65** (2), 332-6. Illustrates effect of participation equations on study results; 4; WL.

Messonier, M.L. and E.J. Luzar (1990), 'A Hedonic Analysis of Private Hunting Land Attributes Using an Alternative Functional Form', *Southern Journal of Agricultural Economics,* **22** (2), 129-35. Determines significance of certain attributes to private deer hunting lease values; 4; WL.

Miller, J.R. and M.J. Hay (1981), 'Determinants of Hunter Participation: Duck Hunting in the Mississippi Flyway', *American Journal of Agricultural Economics,* **63** (4), 677-84. Predicts participation rates for duck hunters in the Mississippi Flyway; 4; WL.

Milon, J.W. (1988), 'Travel Cost Methods for Estimating the Recreational Use Benefits of Artificial Marine Habitat', *Southern Journal of Agricultural Economics,* **20** (1), 87-101. Compares several TCMs for use in new site planning; 4; WL.

Morey, E.R. (1981), 'The Demand for Site Specific Recreational Activities: A Characteristics Approach', *Journal of Environmental Economics and Management,* **8** (4), 345-71. Explains an individual's allocation of skiing days among alternative sites; 7; OR.

Morey, E.R. (1984), 'The Choice of Ski Areas: Estimation of a Generalized CES Preference Ordering with Characteristics', *Review of Economics and Statistics,* **66** (4), 590-4. Estimates a generalized model of skier behavior when close substitutes exist; 7; OR.

Morey, E.R. (1985), 'Characteristics, Consumer Surplus, and New Activities: A Proposed Ski Area', *Journal of Public Economics,* **26** (2), 221-36. Estimates the demand for ski area development using activity and individual characteristics to define an expenditure function; 7; OR.

Morey, E.R., R.D. Rowe and M. Watson (1993), 'A Repeated Nested Logit Model of Atlantic Salmon Fishing', *American Journal of Agricultural Economics,* **75** (3), 578-92. Compares a nested logit model with six other TCMs; 4; WL.

Morey, E.R. (1994), 'What Is Consumer's Surplus Per Day of Use, When Is

It a Constant Independent of the Number of Days of Use, and What Does It Tell Us about Consumer's Surplus?', *Journal of Environmental Economics and Management,* **26** (3), 257-70.

Morey, E.R. and W.S. Breffle (1999), 'Two Nested CES Models of Recreational Participation and Site Choice: An "Alternatives" Model and an "Expenditures" Model', *Western Regional Research Publication,* 12th Interim Report. Contrasts three alternative models for explaining participation and site choice; 4; WL.

Offenbach, L.A. and B.K. Goodwin (1994), 'A Travel Cost Analysis of the Demand for Hunting Trips in Kansas', *Review of Agricultural Economics,* **16** (1), 55-61. Tests significance of on-site time spent on other activities in modeling hunting demand; 4; WL.

O'Neill, C.E. and J. Davis (1991), 'Alternative Definitions of Demand For Recreational Angling in Northern Ireland', *Journal of Agricultural Economics,* **42** (2), 174-9. Investigates effects of alternative definitions of demand on estimated parameters in a TC study; 4; WL.

Palmquist, R. B. (1986), 'Hedonic Methods', *Measuring Water Quality Benefits,* International Series in Economic Modelling, Dordrecht: Kluwer. Details hedonic methods of resource valuation; *; *.

Parsons, G.R. and M.J. Kealy (1992), 'Randomly Drawn Opportunity Sets in a Random Utility Model of Lake Recreation', *Land Economics,* **68**, 93-106. Presents a method of estimating demand when a large number of alternative sites exist; 2,4; WL, OR.

Parsons, G.R. and M.S. Needelman (1992), 'Site Aggregation in a Random Utility Model of Recreation', *Land Economics,* **68** (4), 418-33. Illustrates effects of bias due to aggregation of alternative sites; 2,4; WL, OR.

Parsons, G.R. and M.J. Kealy (1993), 'Benefits Transfer in a Random Utility Model of Recreation', *Western Regional Research Publication,* 6th Interim Report, 440-58. Describes several methods for benefit transfer; 2, 4; WL, OR.

Parsons, G.R. and M.J. Kealy (1995), 'A Demand Theory for Number of Trips in a Random Utility Model of Recreation', *Journal of Environmental Economics and Management,* **29** (3), 357-67. Models both site choice per trip and demand for trips per season; *; *.

Parsons, G.R. and A.B. Hauber (1998), 'Spatial Boundaries and Choice Set Definition in a Random Utility Model of Recreation Demand', *Land Economics,* **74** (1), 32-48. Examines the effects of spatial boundaries on parameter and welfare estimation; 4; WL.

Peters, T., W.L. Adamowicz and P.C. Boxall (1995), 'Influence of Choice Set Considerations in Modelling the Benefits from Improved Water Quality', *Water Resources Research,* **31** (7), 1781-7.

Phillips, R.A. and J.I. Silberman (1985), 'Forecasting Recreation Demand: An Application of the Travel Cost Model', *Review of Regional Studies,* **15** (1), 20-5. Develops method of predicting recreation demand using cross sectional data; 2; OR

Poor, P.J. (1999), 'Water Contamination From Agricultural Chemicals: Welfare Measures for Chemigation Producers', *Western Regional Research Publication,* in press.

Randall, A. and J. Hoehn (1989), 'Benefit Estimation for Complex Policies', in H. Folmer and E. Van Ireland (eds.), *Valuation Methods and Policy Making in Environmental Economics,* Studies in Environmental Science, No. 36, Amsterdam: Elsevier. Illustrates alternative benefits measuring procedures for evaluating complex policy; *; *.

Randall, A. (1994), 'A Difficulty with the Travel Cost Method', *Land Economics,* **70** (1), 88-96. Outlines shortcomings of TCM welfare measures; proposes solutions; *; *.

Ray, R. (1996), 'Demographic Variables in Demand Systems: The Case for Generality', *Empirical Economics,* **21** (2), 307-15.

Ribaudo, M.O. and D.J. Epp (1984), 'The Importance of Sample Discrimination in Using the Travel Cost Method to Estimate the Benefits of Improved Water Quality', *Land Economics,* **60** (4), 397-403. Tests separate benefit estimation of current and former site users; 2; WQ.

Roach, B.A. and F.A. Ward (1994), 'A Comparison of Methods for Estimating Recreation Demand Models With Collinear Facilities', *Western Regional Research Publication*, 7th Interim Report, 105-116. Tests common approaches to parameter estimation for reliability in the presence of multicollinearity; *; *.

Rosenburger, R., J. Loomis and R. Shrestha (1999), 'Meta Analysis of Outdoor Recreation Use Value Estimates: Panel Data Issues and Convergent Validity Tests', *Western Regional Research Publication,* 12th Interim Report. Reviews literature with meta-analysis for a benefit transfer; 1-7; All.

Rosenthal, D.H. (1987), 'The Necessity for Substitute Prices in Recreation Demand Analyses', *American Journal of Agricultural Economics,* **69** (4), 828-37. Analyzes three TCMs to show effects of substitute price omission on benefit estimates; 2; RE, OR.

Russell, C.S. and W.J. Vaughan (1982), 'The National Recreational Fishing Benefits of Water Pollution Control', *Journal of Environmental Economics and Management,* **9** (4), 328-54. Estimates national benefits of improving water quality; 2,4; WQ.

Samples, K.C. and R.C. Bishop (1985), 'Estimating the Value of Variations in Anglers' Success Rates: An Application of the Multiple Site Travel Cost

Method', *Marine Resource Economics,* **2** (1), 55-74. Examines effets of changes in recreation resource quality; 4; WL, RE.

Sandefur, R.A., F.R. Johnson and R.B. Fowler, 'An Introduction To The Random Utility Model', *Western Regional Research Publication W-133,* 12th Interim report, in press. Explains theory and methodology behind the random utility model; *;*.

Scott, A.D. (1965), 'The Valuation of Game Resources: Some Theoretical Aspects', *Canadian Fisheries Reports,* No. 4, 27-47. Values opportunity cost of time individually according to income and occupation; 4; WL.

Scrogin, D., R.P. Berrens and A.K. Bohara (1999), 'Policy Changes and the Demand for Lottery Rationed Big Game Hunting Licenses', *Western Regional Research Publication,* 12th Interim Report. Examines effects of policy changes on resident welfare and lottery revenues; 4; WL.

Sellar, C., J.R. Stoll and J.P. Chavas (1985), 'Validation of Empirical Measures of Welfare Change: A Comparison of Nonmarket Techniques', *Land Economics,* **61** (2), 156-75. Compares TCM and CV estimates of recreational boating values; 2; RE.

Shaikh, S.L. and D.M. Larson (1998), 'Towards Globally Flexible Estimation of Recreation Demand', *Western Regional Research Publication,* 11th Interim Report, pp. 3-20. Seeks to reduce bias in recreation demand estimation; 4; WL.

Shaw, D. (1988), 'On Site Samples Regression: Problems of Non negative Integers, Truncation, and Endogenous Stratification', *Journal of Econometrics,* **37**, 211-23. Describes regression errors from using on-site samples; *; *.

Shaw, W.D. (1992), 'Searching for the Opportunity Cost of an Individual's Time', *Land Economics,* **68**, 107-15.

Shaw, W.D. and P. Jakus (1996), 'Travel Cost Models of the Demand for Rock Climbing', *Agricultural and Resource Economics Review,* **25** (2), 133-42.Develops a model which explains both the participation and site choice decisions; 1; OR.

Shonkwiler, J.S. (1994), 'Double Hurdle Count Data Models for Travel Cost Analysis', *Western Regional Research Publication,* 7th Interim Report, 89-96. Presents alternative methods for modeling visitor consumer behavior; 4; WL, RE.

Shonkwiler, J.S. and J. Englin (1999), 'Welfare Losses Due to Livestock Grazing on Public Lands: Some Evidence from the Hoover Wilderness', *Western Regional Research Publication,* in press. Examines effect of grazing on backcountry hikers, and compares visitor welfare changes to agency revenues and producer surplus; 5; OR, MG, FS.

Sinden, J.A. (1990), *Valuation of the Recreational Benefits of River*

Management: A Case Study in the Ovens and King Basin, Victoria, Australia: Department of Water Resources. Estimates benefits of river recreation; 1, 2; RV, OR.

Smith, R.J. (1971), 'The Evaluation of Recreation Benefits: The Clawson Method in Practice', *Urban Studies,* **8** (2), 89-102. Estimates trout fishing benefit in the UK using a TCM; 2,4; RE, WL.

Smith, V.K. (1975), 'The Estimation and Use of Models of the Demand for Outdoor Recreation', in Committee on Assessment of Demand for Outdoor Recreation, *Assessing Demand for Outdoor Recreation,* National Academy of Sciences, pp. 91-123. Explains recreation demand modelling methods; *; *.

Smith, V.K. (1975), 'Travel Cost Demand Models for Wilderness Recreation: A Problem of Non Nested Hypotheses', *Land Economics,* **51** (2), 103-11. Estimates the demand for wilderness using a travel cost model; 5; OR.

Smith, V. K. (1981), 'Congestion, Travel Cost Recreational Demand Models, and Benefit Evaluation', *Journal of Environmental Economics and Management,* **8** (1), 92-6. Illustrates methods of treating congestion effects in TCMs; *; *.

Smith, V.K. (1983), 'The Role of Site and Job Characteristics in Hedonic Wage Models', *Journal of Urban Economics,* **13**, 296-321.

Smith, V.K. (1988), 'Selection and Recreation Demand', *American Journal of Agricultural Economics,* **70**, 29-36.

Smith, V.K. (1989), 'Taking Stock of Progress with Travel Cost Recreation Demand Methods: Theory and Implementation', *Marine Resource Economics,* **6** (4), 279-310. Reviews travel cost literature; *; *.

Smith, V.K. (1990), 'Estimating Recreation Demand Using the Properties of the Implied Consumer Surplus', *Land Economics,* **66** (2), 111-20. Proposes method of demand estimation, based on implied consumer surplus; *; *

Smith, V. K. (1990), 'Household Production Functions and Environmental Benefit Estimation', *Measuring Water Quality Benefits,* Lancaster and Dordrecht: Kluwer Academic, pp. 41-76. Describes methods and issues in using the household production function; *;*.

Smith, V.K. (1993), 'Welfare Effects, Omitted Variables, and the Extent of the Market', *Land Economics,* **69** (2), 121-31. Explains theoretical relationships between omitted substitute prices and welfare effects of price or quality changes; *; *.

Smith, V. K. (1993), *Estimating Economic Values for Nature: Methods for Non-Market Valuation,* Cheltenham, UK: Edward Elgar. Looks at past and current research in resource evaluation, policy issues, and ideas for future research; *;*.

Smith, V.K. (1993), 'Nonmarket Valuation of Environmental Resources: An Interpretive Appraisal, *Land Economics,* **69** (1), 1-26. Reviews nonmarket valuation research and discusses performance of valuation methods; *; *.

Smith, V.K., (1996), *Estimating Economic Values for Nature: Methods for Non Market Valuation,* Cheltenham, UK: Edward Elgar. Book length treatment with several papers dealing with non-market valuation methods; *; *.

Smith, V.K. (1998), 'Selection and Recreation Demand, *American Journal of Agricultural Economics,* **70** (1), 29-36. Compares five estimation methods for treatment of selection effects; 2; WQ, OR.

Smith, V.K. and R.J. Kopp (1980), 'The Spatial Limits of the Travel Cost Recreational Demand Model', *Land Economics,* **56** (1), 64-72. Illustrates that spatial limits can impact consumer surplus estimates; 5; OR.

Smith, V.K., W.H. Desvousges and M.P. McGivney (1983), 'Estimating Water Quality Benefits: An Econometric Analysis', *Southern Economic Journal,* **50** (2), 422-37. Measures benefits associated with alternative use designations; 2; OR.

Smith, V.K., W.H. Desvousges and M.P. McGivney (1983), 'The Opportunity Cost of Travel Time in Recreation Demand Models', *Land Economics,* **59** (3), 259-78. Demonstrates that on-site costs are important in opportunity cost estimation; 2,4; OR.

Smith, V.K. and W. H. Desvousges. (1985), 'The Generalized Travel Cost Model and Water Quality Benefits: A Reconsideration', *Southern Economics Journal,* **52** (2), 371-81.Values water quality benefits; 2; WQ.

Smith, V.K., and Y. Kaoru (1986), 'Modelling Recreation Demand Within A Random Utility Framework', *Economic Letters,* **22**, 395-9. Compares simple RUM to conventional TCM; 2; OR.

Smith, V.K. and W.H. Desvousges (1986), *Measuring Water Quality Benefits,* International Series in Economic Modelling, Dordrecht: Kluwer. Values water quality benefits; 2; WQ.

Smith, V.K., W. H. Desvousges, and A. Fisher (1986), 'A Comparison of Direct and Indirect Methods for Estimating Environmental Benefits, *American Journal of Agricultural Economics,* **68** (2), 280-90. Compares benefit estimates of TCM and CVM studies; 2; WQ.

Smith, V.K. and Y. Kaoru (1987), 'The Hedonic Travel Cost Model: A View from the Trenches', *Land Economics,* **63** (2), 179-92. Values waterbased recreation sites using a hedonic TCM; 2; RE.

Smith, V.K. and Y. Kaoru (1990), 'Signals or Noise? Explaining the Variation in Recreation Benefit Estimates', *American Journal of Agricultural Economics,* **72** (2), 419-33. Uses meta-analysis of 200 studies to evaluate influences on benefit estimates; *; *.

Smith, V.K. and Y. Kaoru (1990), 'What Have We Learned since Hotelling's Letter?   A Meta Analysis', *Economics Letters,* **32** (3), 267-72. Meta analysis; *; *.

Smith, V.K., R.B. Palmquist and P. Jakus (1991), 'Combining Farrell Frontier and Hedonic Travel Cost Models for Valuing Estuarine Quality', *Review of Economics and Statistics,* **73** (4), 694-9.

Sohngen, B., R. Mendelsohn and R. Sedjo (1999), 'Forest Management, Conservation, and Global Timber Markets', *American Journal of Agricultural Economics,* **81**, 1-13.

Sorg, C.F. and J.B. Loomis (1986), 'Economic Value of Idaho Sport Fisheries with an Update on Valuation Techniques', *North American Journal of Fisheries Management,* **6**, 494-503. Compares values derived from TCM and CVM studies; 4; WL.

Stephens, R. J. (1984), 'Forestry or a National Park: A New Zealand Case Study', *International Journal of Social Economics,* **11** (3-4), 29-44. Shows that estimates are biased if majority of site visitors are 'transit' tourists; 3; FS.

Stevens, J.B. (1966), 'Recreation Benefits from Water Pollution Control', *Water Resources Research,* **2** (2), 167-82. Develops a methodology for estimating recreational benefits from water pollution control; 2,4; WQ.

Stevens, J.B. (1969), 'Effects of Nonprice Variables upon Participation in Water Oriented Outdoor Recreation: Comment', *American Journal of Agricultural Economics,* **51** (1) 192-3. Discusses the effects of non-price variables; *; *.

Stoeckl, N. (1993), 'A Travel Cost Analysis of Hinchinbrook Island National Park', unpublished M. Econ. thesis, Townsville: James Cook University.

Stoll, J.R., L.S. Freeman and J.C. Bergstrom (1991), *Annotated Bibliography for Regional Recreation Demand Models*, Miscellaneous Paper R-91-1, Vicksburg, MS: US Army Engineer Waterways Experiment Station.

Stynes, D.J., G.L. Peterson and D.H. Rosenthal, (1986), 'Log Transformation Bias in Estimating Travel Cost Models', *Land Economics,* **62**(1), 94-103. Examines bias resulting from log transformation of variables in a TCM; 2; OR.

Sutherland, R.J. (1982), 'A Regional Approach to Estimating Recreation Benefits of Improved Water Quality', *Journal of Environmental Economics and Management,* **9** (3), 229-47. Presents generalized regional model to estimates estimate benefits for one or many sites. Results have been controversial; 2; WQ.

Tadros, M.E. and R.J. Kalter (1971), 'Spatial Allocation Model for Projected Water Based Recreation Demand', *Water Resources Research,* **7** (4), 798-811. Develops an allocation model to spatially distribute market demand;

2; OR.

Tay, R. S. and P. S. McCarthy (1994), 'Benefits of Improved Water Quality: A Discrete Choice Analysis of Freshwater Recreational Demands', *Environment and Planning,* **26**, 1625-38. Estimates a multinomial logit model of destination choice to assess benefits of water quality improvements; 2; WQ.

Train, K.E. (1998), 'Recreation Demand Models with Taste Differences Over People', *Land Economics,* **74** (2), 230-9. Develops a random parameters logit model that allows variation in coefficients over people; 4; WL.

Train, K., D. McFadden and R. Johnson (1999), 'Discussion of Morey and Waldman's "Measurement Error in Recreation Demand Models"', *Western Regional Research Publication,* 12th Interim Report. Compares two methods of reducing measurement error; 4; WL.

Trice, A.H. and S.E. Wood (1958), 'Measurement of Recreation Benefits', *Land Economics,* **34** (3), 195-207. A very early TCM applied to California river recreation; 2; RV.

Truong, T.P. and D. Hensher (1985), 'Measurement of Travel Time Values and Opportunity Cost From a Discrete Choice Model', *The Economic Journal,* **95**, 438-51.

US Water Resources Council (1983), *Economic and Environmental Principles and Guidelines for Water and Related Agencies*, US Government Printing Office, Washington, DC. Describes US federal procedures for use of TCM to value water-based recreation. Originated with the Flood Control Act of 1936; 2; WQ.

Vartia, Y.0. (1983), 'Efficient Methods of Measuring Welfare Change and Compensated Income in Terms of Ordinary Demand Functions', *Econometrica,* **51** (1), 79-98.

Vaughan, W.J. and C.S. Russell. (1982), 'Freshwater Recreational Fishing: The National Benefits of Water Pollution Control', *Freshwater Recreational Fishing: Resources for the Future,* Baltimore, Johns Hopkins University Press. Evaluates costs and benefits of compliance with national water pollution standards; 2,4; WQ.

Vaughan, W.J. and C.S. Russell (1982), 'Valuing a Fishing Day: An Application of a Systematic Varying Parameter Model', *Land Economics,* **58** (4), 450-63. Accounts for characteristics in valuing a freshwater fishing day; 2,4; WL, RE.

Vaughan, W.J., C.S. Russell and M. Hazilla (1982), 'A Note on the Use of Travel Cost Models with Unequal Zonal Populations: Comment', *Land Economics,* **58** (3), 400-7. Examines misspecification of functional form as a source of bias; 2; OR.

Vickerman, R.W. (1974), 'The Evaluation of Benefits from Recreational

Projects', *Urban Studies,* **11** (3), 277-88. Suggests a general equilibrium approach to modelling demand; *; *.

Walsh, R.G., F.A. Ward and J.P. Olie (1989), 'Recreational Demand for Trees in National Forests', *Journal of Environmental Management,* **28**, 255-68. Compares CVM responses to TCM estimates of recreation benefits of forest management of insect infestations; 3; FS.

Walsh, R.G., L.D. Sanders and J.R. McKean (1990), 'The Consumption Value of Travel Time on Recreation Trips', *Journal of Travel Research,* Summer, 17-24.

Walsh, R.G., D.M. Johnson and J. McKean (1992), 'Benefit Transfer of Outdoor Recreation Demand Studies (1968-1988)', *Water Resources Research,* **28** (3), 707-13. Meta analysis: summarizes results of 156 TCM and 129 CVM studies; *;*.

Walsh, R.G., D.M. Johnson and J. McKean (1989), 'Issues in Nonmarket Valuation and Policy Application: A Retrospective Glance', *Western Journal of Agricultural Economics,* **14** (1), 178-88. Updates a previous literature review for a benefits transfer; *; *.

Ward, F.A. (1983), 'Measuring the Cost of Time in Recreation Demand Analysis: Comment', *American Journal of Agricultural Economics,* **65** (1), 167-8. Comments on an article dealing with valuing opportunity cost of time; *; *.

Ward, F.A. (1983), 'On the Necessity of Simultaneous Recreation Demand Equation Estimation: Comment', *Land Economics,* **59** (4), 455-8. Comment on earlier paper by Hof and King; *; *.

Ward, F.A (1984), 'Specification Considerations for the Price Variable in Travel Cost Demand Models', *Land Economics,* **60** (3), 301-5. Replies to comments on a previous article; *; *.

Ward, F.A. (1986), 'Specification Considerations for the Price Variable in Travel Cost Demand Models: Reply', *Land Economics,* **62** (4), 419-21. Presents a framework for isolating exogenous and endogenous costs; *; *.

Ward, F.A. and Loomis, J.B. (1986), 'The Travel Cost Demand Model as an Environmental Policy Assessment Tool: A Review of Literature', *Western Journal of Agricultural Economics,* **11** (2), 164-78. Reviews travel cost literature; *; *.

Ward, F.A. (1988), 'Exact Welfare Values of Natural Resource Quality: A Regional Approach', *Western Regional Research Publication,* Interim Report, pp. 175-97. Describes method for valuing quality changes in multisite models; *; *.

Ward, F.A. (1989), 'Efficiently Managing Spatially Competing Water Uses: New Evidence from a Regional Recreation Demand Model', *Journal of Regional Science,* **29** (2), 229-46. Compares value of water in agriculture and recreation in New Mexico; 2; WS.

Ward, F.A., B.A. Roach and J.E. Henderson (1996), 'The Economic Value of Water in Recreation: Evidence for the California Drought', *Water Resources Research,* **32** (4), 1075-81. Estimates value of water in reservoir recreation with a TCM; 2; RE, RV.

Ward, F.A., R.A. Cole and R.A. Deitner (1997), 'Limiting Environmental Program Contradictions: A Demand Systems Application to Fishery Management', *American Journal of Agricultural Economics,* **79**, 803-13. Shows use of multisite TCM with quality can reduce contradictory environmental programs; 2,4; WL.

Wetzel, J.N. (1991), 'The Welfare Effects of Omitting Substitute Prices and Qualities from Travel Cost Models: Comment', *Land Economics,* **67**, 130-1. Explores effects of deleting substitute prices and quanities when valuing recreational sites; *; *.

Wetzstein, M.E. and J.G. McNeely, Jr. (1980), 'Specification Errors and Inference in Recreation Demand Models', *American Journal of Agricultural Economics,* **62** (4), 798-800. Aggregates data over cost rather than distance; 7; OR.

Wetzstein, M.E. (1982), 'An Economic Evaluation of a Multi Area Recreation System', *Southern Journal of Agricultural Economics,* **14** (2), 51-5. Illustrates method of evaluating welfare changes when a new site is added to an existing system of sites; 5; OR.

Whitehead, J.C. (1992), 'Measuring Use Value from Recreation Participation', *Southern Journal of Agricultural Economics,* **24**, 113-9. Describes a one step method of demand estimation; *; *.

Whitehead, J.C. (1994), 'Measuring Use Value from Recreation Participation', *Journal of Agricultural and Applied Economics,* **26** (1), 314-5. Extends previous article presenting a one step method of recreation demand estimation; *; *.

Willig, R.D. (1976), 'Consumers' Surplus Without Apology', *American Economic Review,* **66** (4), 589-97. Proves that CS of a price change at one site is usually close enough enough to CV and EV to be a good approximation. Very influential paper; *; *.

Willis, K.G. (1991), 'The Recreational Value of the Forestry Commission Estate in Great Britain: A Clawson Knetsch Travel Cost Analysis', *Scottish Journal of Political Economy,* **38** (1), 58-75. Values forest recreation with a zonal TCM; 3; FS.

Willis, K. G. and G.D. Garrod (1991), 'An Individual Travel Cost Method of Evaluating Forest Recreation', *Journal of Agricultural Economics,* **42** (1), 33-42. Assesses the difference in benefit estimates derived from zonal and individual TCMs; 3; FS.

Willis, K.G. and G. Garrod (1991), 'Valuing Open Access Recreation on Inland Waterways: On Site Recreation Surveys and Selection Effects', *Regional Studies,* **25** (6), 511-24. Shows that correcting bias in individual TCMs yields good benefit estimate; 2; OR.

Wilman, E.A. (1980), 'The Value of Time in Recreation Benefit Studies', *Journal of Environmental Economics and Management,* **7** (3), 272-86. Examines the effects of time costs in recreational behavior models; *; *.

Wilman, E.A. (1987), 'A Simple Repackaging Model of Recreational Choices', *American Journal of Agricultural Economics,* **69** (3), 603-12. Describes repackaging model to derive marginal values of use; 4; WL, OR.

Wilman, E.A. and R.J. Pauls (1987), 'Sensitivity of Consumers' Surplus Estimates to Variation in the Parameters of the Travel Cost Model', *Canadian Journal of Agricultural Economics,* **35** (1), 197-212. Shows that treatment of time cost and substitute sites can affect consumer surplus estimates; 5; OR.

Wilman, E.A. and J. Perras (1989), 'The Substitute Price Variable in the Travel Cost', *Canadian Journal of Agricultural Economics,* **37**, 249-61. Explains the importance of including substitute price variables in TCM equations; 5; OR.

Yen, S.T. and W.L. Adamowicz (1993), 'Statistical Properties of Welfare Measures from Count Data Models of Recreation Demand', *Review of Agricultural Economics,* **15** (2), 203-15. Compares benefit estimates from truncated and untruncated models; 4; WL.

Yen, S.T. and W.L. Adamowicz (1994), 'Participation, Trip Frequency and Site Choice: A Multinomial Poisson Hurdle Model of Recreation Demand, *Canadian Journal of Agricultural Economics,* **42** (1), 65-76. Estimates a multivariate demand model that accounts for site choice and trip frequency; 4; WL.

Ziemer, R. and W. N. Musser (1979), 'Population Specific Recreation Demand Models and The Consequences of Polling Sample Data', *Western Journal of Agricultural Economics,* **4** (1), 121-8. Defines several problems in estimation of population specific models; 4; WL.

Ziemer, R.F., W.N. Musser and R.C. Hi (1980), 'Recreation Demand Equations: Functional Form and Consumer Surplus', *American Journal of Agricultural Economics,* **62**, 136-41. Demonstrates effects of functional form on consumer's surplus estimates; 4; WL.

Index